SPEED SAILING

SPEED SAILING

GARY JOBSON AND MIKE TOPPA

Illustrations by Marti Betz

HEARST MARINE BOOKS/NEW YORK

Other books by Gary Jobson

USYRU Sailing Instructor's Manual
Gary Jobson's How to Sail
The Racing Edge (with Ted Turner)
The Yachtsman's Pocket Almanac
Storm Sailing

Library of Congress Cataloging in Publication Data

Jobson, Gary.
  Speed sailing.

  Includes index.
  1. Sailboat racing.   2. Yacht racing.   I. Toppa,
Mike.   II. Title.
GV826.5.J54   1985   797.1'4   84-10947
ISBN: 0-688-03974-X

Printed in the United States of America

First Edition

  2 3 4 5 6 7 8 9 10

BOOK DESIGN BY STANLEY S. DRATE / FOLIO GRAPHICS CO., INC.

Dedication
to Kristi Lynn Jobson
and
to Sheree Toppa

FOREWORD

The title of the book says it all: *Speed Sailing.* There are so many types of boats and the people who sail them, but I've never seen a boat that was designed to go slow or anyone who didn't want to go fast. Everybody who sails wants more speed. The oystermen who sail their Skipjacks on Chesapeake Bay want more speed so they can get their catch into the dock before the other guys. The cruiser doesn't want to sail an old clunker. Even though he's just cruising, he wants a good boat that handles well and has speed. And of course the racing sailor is always in search of more speed while sailing. This book is for every sailor.

There are countless theories and ideas of how to get more speed when sailing. Generally, sailors are a smart bunch who are always experimenting and tinkering with new ways to make their boats faster or more efficient. Because of this, our sport is under constant change and upgrading. Sailing techniques are refined. New materials are discovered so we can make our sails, masts, and hulls lighter and stronger then ever before. And every once in a while the big light bulb appears and someone gets an idea— like putting wings on a keel—that throws everyone for a loop. And because of this even now there are wings on the bottoms of cruising boats. The search for speed continues. And that is what this book is all about.

Mike and Gary spend a lot of time sailing boats. Between the two of them, one of them is probably out on the water every day. And their experience is deep. One-design dingies, M.O.R.C. boats, P.H.R.F. boats, One Ton and Two Ton level racing, I.O.R. regattas, and Twelve Meter America's Cup sailing are all areas where they have excelled. *Speed Sailing* is based on all this experience. All the techniques and sailing smarts that are used by the people who win races are put down in this book. All aspects are covered. Hull construction and design, deck layouts, crew coordination, masts, sails, trimming, and instruments are all detailed. I'm sure anyone who reads this book will have a better understanding of boats and how to make them go faster.

—Lowell North

ACKNOWLEDGMENTS

There are many people who participated in the development of this book. For their efforts we are greatly appreciative. These include:

Jim Allsopp	Bob Horst	Marty Luray
Jonathon Bartlett	Peter Isler	Diane Muhlfeld
Marti Betz	Jack James	Mike Perry
Tom Blackaller	Paul Larsen	Norman Olsen
John Danley	Jim Marshall	Kathy Thompson
Bruce Farr	Tim Cole	Ted Turner
Graham Hall	Rob Nye	Roger Vaughan
Ann Hayes	Karina Paape	Jud Smith
George Hazen	Robby Robinson	Sally Martin

Over the past ten years, numerous articles have appeared by Gary Jobson in *Yacht Racing/Cruising* magazine, *Yachting* and *Sail*. I have borrowed some of the ideas and techniques from these articles in this book. To the editors of these fine publications, I am most grateful.

CONTENTS

INTRODUCTION

When sailing, there are two ways to gain an edge over your competitors. One is to sail better with superior boat handling and tactics. The second is to have greater speed. Over the years, the quest for greater speed has intrigued and tempted sailors, as well as always having been a mystery. Designers have persistently sought the major breakthrough that will give their boat a distinct advantage. Some sailors actually fantasize that with super boat speed they will simply sail away from the fleet. Others care little about boat speed and worry more about sailing technique. The truth is that a combination of better sailing technique, more smarts, and superior boat speed gives the best sailors their edge.

It is rare for a boat such as *Australia II* to come along. Even with *Australia II*'s unique advantage, *Liberty* came within one wind shift of successfully defending the America's Cup in 1983. Thus, if you sail a maxiyacht off the starting line and roll over your competition sailing smaller boats, your ego might feel good momentarily, but deep down inside, you know it is really not a fair contest. The best sailing is when all boats have either the same speed, or they are handicapped fairly. But some sailors go to great lengths to gain a speed advantage. The escalation of the 12-Meter wars is the ultimate case. Just two decades ago 12-Meter sailors couldn't possibly imagine hauling yachts out of the water every day, let alone installing wings on keels, or making sails with the same fabric used in bulletproof vests.

At times the simplest things will give one boat an edge over another. In 1972 at the North American Interclass Solo Championships, Gary was racing against nine other top sailors from North America, and on the second day he was sailing a 15-foot catboat. Because all the mains were reefed, each boat had one spare batten. Gary rigged the batten on his tiller to use as a hiking stick and was able to get his weight out farther than his competitors. Thanks to his hiking stick, Gary gained an edge and won four of four races.

But that extra edge never lasts long in any competition. Other sailors catch on quickly to new ideas. Many fleets go through fads. Some sailors have won major championships by borrowing the go-fast ideas of one class and using them in another. What makes a Snipe go fast can also help a grand prix ocean racer. The principles in sailing are the same no matter what the size of the boat.

For this reason we have written *Speed Sailing* on a broad spectrum, hoping the cross-pollination of ideas in this book will help sailors in all types of boats. The fundamentals of boat speed include sailing techniques and practice, and it is a combination of the factors treated in this book that we hope will make you sail fast. Often major advantages in boat speed or sailing technique come by accident. One idea will lead to another, which will mean success.

It is important to push your boat and equipment hard but not so hard that you have a breakdown, forcing you out of the race. If you baby your equipment while your competitors are loading up more tension, you run the risk of sailing slower. It is important to have strong, reliable equipment you can count on. But you do not want to put too much stress on any piece of gear and run the risk of breaking down. It is a tricky balance that experience will help. *Speed Sailing* will give you these guidelines.

The quest for more speed is in sync with life. After all, everyone wants just a little more. What if we just sailed a little faster? What if we had just a little more money? What if the car was just a little bigger?

The quest for speed takes many forms, ranging from new-wave materials such as carbon fiber, winged masts, winged keels, ultralight catamarans, and Australian 18-footers built out of honeycomb cardboard covered by carbon fiber and S-glass. These 18-foot-long boats are 7½ feet wide and yet weigh less than 100 pounds, excluding the rig, and are capable of speeds over 25 knots. The crew extends over the side from a rack 5½ feet away from the side of the boat. Your head hits every other wave, and the sensation is five times your actual speed.

The fact is that most sailboats are slow. Twelve-Meter boats, which people marvel at, sail only eight knots on the wind. Star boats sail at four knots on the wind. The next time you are driving your car, try to motor along at four knots and you will get a feel of just how slowly boats sail. But how slow boats are is not the key. The key is how fast you are relative to your competition, and this is the essence of speed sailing. The goal of this book is to show you how to sail better with more speed.

Gary Jobson
Mike Toppa

Annapolis, 1984

PART ONE

Designed for Speed

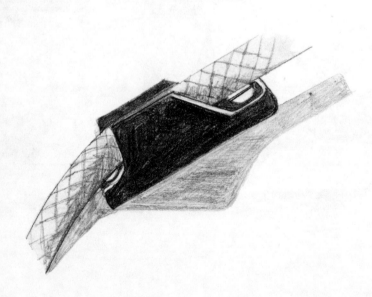

1

THE CONCEPT OF SPEED

No one searching for a way to achieve flat-out, break-the-sound-barrier speed would spend time designing a sailboat. However, this fact has not deterred sailors from a centuries-long quest for ever-increasing wind-powered boat speed.

Speed under sail, having shown itself to be even more elusive than seaworthiness, therefore becomes even more interesting. And though the prime seekers nowadays are equipped for the search with college degrees, computer programs, and many new, exotic materials, no one is brash enough to predict that the ultimate speed under sail, whatever that is, is within reach—yet.

Speed, resulting as it does from a combination of and compromise among many factors, has through the years led one designer down one path and the next down another. Some paths have been longer than others, while some have led to dangerous, wild animals along the way—mostly turkeys! Lucky or educated choices have led some in more promising directions.

Sailors have supported, and most likely will continue to support, this gamut of path-walking designers who, in turn, can be expected to continue to produce widely diverse manifestations of the "perfect boat."

In trying to analyze some of the major factors that affect the design of boats, we will assume that you want to sail faster.

Yacht designers, whatever their skills and goals, must pay homage to certain basic principles. By examining these from the standpoint of their effect on speed, we will better understand the designer's dilemma and our own as we seek to sail our boats fast.

Nothing is more basic to a boat than flotation, and flotation depends on weight. The weight of the boat is referred to as its displacement, which is the weight of the volume of water that the boat will push aside, or displace, when floating. Saline water weighs 64 points per cubic foot, and fresh water weighs 62.4 pounds per cubic foot.

Given the hull form and the total weight of the boat, the lines on which it will float can be calculated because the submerged volume of the boat will be equal to the volume of water displaced by the boat. The waterline length is measured along these lines.

Now we are getting down to how all this affects speed. A displacement hull —which is one with a high displacement to waterline length ratio compared to a planing hull—has a practical limit on boat speed of 1.34 times the square root of its waterline length. This speed is referred to as a boat's "hull speed" (See Figure 1).

This hull speed of a displacement boat is limited by the length of the wave the boat creates as it moves through the water.

At slow speeds, the boat, which must push aside a volume of water equal in weight to her displacement as she moves through the water, makes a bow wave and a series of smaller waves. These smaller waves are distributed along the distance of the hull to the stern.

As boat speed increases, the bow wave gets higher and longer, and the number of the waves along the hull decreases at the same time because the distance between crests increases.

The distance between crests can be measured. For example, waves traveling at one knot are about six inches long, while at four knots waves are nearly nine feet between crests. Knowing the length of the boat, one can count the number of waves along her windward

Figure 1: When a yacht heels over, the waterline length is increased and that increases the yacht's speed potential.

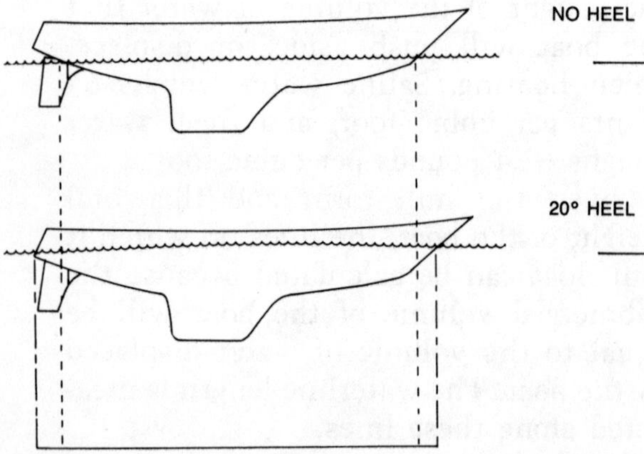

NO HEEL

20° HEEL

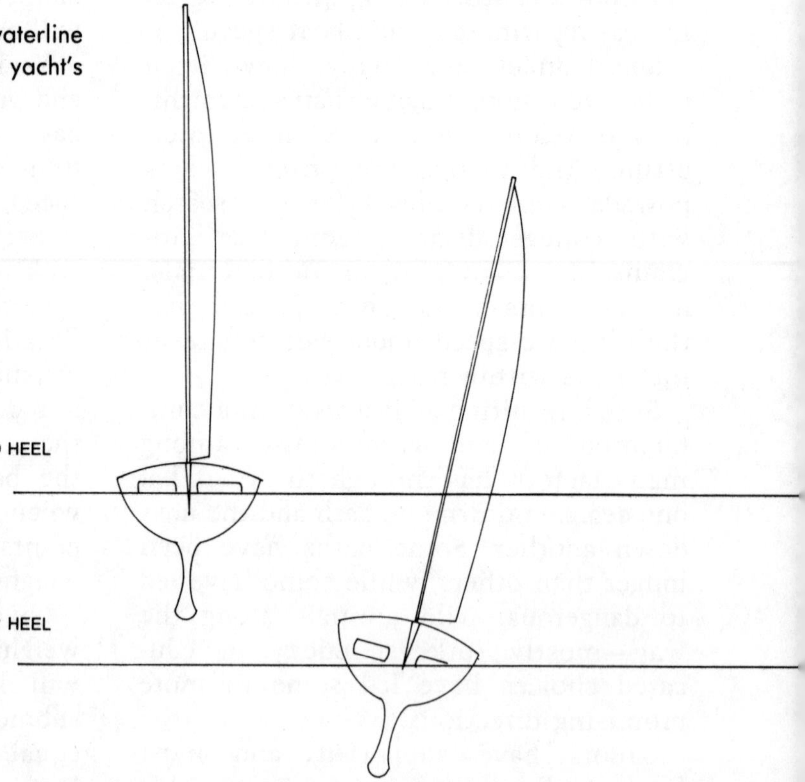

side in a photograph and estimate the boat's speed at the time the picture was taken.

Eventually only one wave remains, with crests at the bow and the stern and with a length equal to the waterline length of the boat. The waves are traveling at the speed of 1.34 times the square root of the distance between crests, and this distance is now the same length as the boat's waterline. The boat cannot generate enough power from the sails to climb over the bow wave, and so it is limited by the speed of that wave, at least upwind.

Downwind, different conditions sometimes prevail. Even a displacement hull can gain enough power from the pull of gravity while sliding down the front of a large wave to exceed hull speed briefly by rising to a plane. Of course, this will happen only if wind, wave, and helmsman are in tune.

A planing hull is much lighter than a displacement hull in relation to waterline length. If the light weight is combined with other characteristics—typically a flat stern and powerful sail plan—the boat will be able to develop enough power and lift to rise over the bow wave and ride on top of the water at greater speed than the waves because the boat no longer has to overcome the resistance caused by the hull trying to move through the water.

A planing hull, when planing, will sail faster than a displacement hull. Planing occurs most often and most easily sailing off the wind in moderately strong winds and fairly flat water. Some boat types, such as The Flying Dutchman, the 505, and the Australian 18's, will plane

upwind. Otherwise, the planing hull has no advantage over the displacement boat and in fact may suffer loss of speed from its design when not sailing in planing conditions.

The reason sailboards are fast is the lost displacement thanks to the lifting force generated from the angle of the sail. Light displacement is always fast if the stability is there, which it is on a sailboard.

Displacement/waterline length ratios may vary from 500 for an extremely heavy-displacement boat down to perhaps 90 for a planing hull, with infinite variations in between.

Other factors may restrict a boat's performance long before its theoretical hull speed is reached. These factors might be a fouled bottom, poor sails, improper sail trim, excessive heeling, weather helm, or poor crew work.

Resistance in several forms slows a boat down as it moves through the water. The types that make a considerable impact on boat speed are skin friction, eddy-making resistance and wave-making resistance (which are closely related), and windage or (air resistance).

Skin friction, the adhesion of particles of water to the wetted surface of the boat, can be combatted by both designer and sailor. The designer does his part by reducing the wetted surface as much as possible for a particular displacement. The owner's contribution is to keep the bottom clean and fair, and the bow, where the effect is most detrimental, free of even small projections, such as through hull fittings or transducers.

Our 12-Meters picked up a considerable amount of oil and dirt just towing from our berth in Newport through the harbor and out into the ocean. To help combat this, every 12-Meter had a liberal coating of some kind of soap, which was allowed to dry on the hull in several layers. This soap would disperse on the tow out to the ocean and help keep oil and dirt off the hull. If the 12-Meter was left in the water overnight, the growth was tremendous.

Skin friction becomes relatively more important at slow speeds, creating just one more problem for a skipper racing on a light-air day and knowing he has not washed the bottom in more than a week.

Exerting more effect at higher speeds are eddy- and wave- making resistance. These are the disturbances in the water caused by the movement of the hull through it. The results can be readily observed in the bow wave and wake, which are visible manifestions of force expended and lost to the greater aim of propelling the boat forward.

Eddy-making resistance and wave-making resistance are controlled by the distribution of the displacement and the lines of the boat.

Propellers, propeller apertures, and propeller struts are all important causes of eddy-making resistance on sailing auxiliaries. Don Street, in his book *The Ocean Sailing Yacht*, writes of increasing the speed of a 49-foot ketch by almost a knot by feathering the blades (See Figure 2) of the propeller in a straight fore-and-aft position. Another interesting statement Street makes is that a boat traveling at hull speed will slow down by as much as a knot if the propeller is allowed to windmill. Many ocean racing yachts are built today with see-through

Figure 2: By using a propeller with blades that feather, a yacht can gain at least one knot in added speed. It is critical that the propeller be aligned in a before and aft position with the keel.

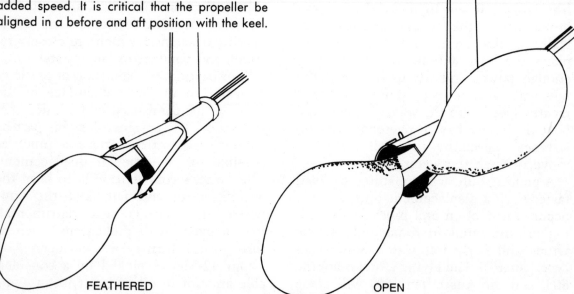

FEATHERED   OPEN

ports in the bottom of the boat so sailors can inspect whether the blades of the prop are feathered correctly.

Rudders, both by their form and by their use, enter into any discussion of eddy-making resistance. To be well designed and offer the least resistance, attention must be paid to the area, shape, and location. This optimum rudder will then make the least disturbance in the water when it is held on center line. When it is moved to one side or the other to steer the boat, eddy resistance is increased. So it may be seen that using a large amount of helm for control will slow a boat considerably.

Wave-making resistance is the principal factor when a displacement boat tries to break through its theoretical hull speed and when a planing boat is moving slowly. This resistance is largely influenced by a boat's prismatic coefficient.

Skene's *Elements of Yacht Design* defines prismatic coefficient as "a fancy term for expressing how fine or how full the shape of a hull is"; more technically as "a ratio between the volume of displacement and a solid having a constant section the shape of the largest section multiplied by the waterline length."

To give some common numbers for comparison, a prismatic coefficient of .54 has been considered a fairly normal number for cruising and ocean racing boats. Larger numbers indicate a hull tending toward a boxy shape. Prismatic coefficients of .53 and down signal finer ends.

The optimum prismatic coefficient for a hull varies with the speed. As speed/length ratio increases, a greater prismatic coefficient is desirable to ob-

tain the least resistance. However, as speed/length ratio decreases, a lower prismatic coefficient is better.

In his discussion of wave- and eddy-making resistance in his book *Yacht Designing and Planning*, Howard Chapelle contends that they cannot be entirely predicted and recommends use of the towing tank to find out how a certain design will be affected.

Windage or air resistance is created by the rigging and superstructure of a vessel. Windage can be minimized by eliminating unnecessary rigging, using the smallest standing rigging strong enough for its task, and fairing the spars to present the least windage possible. But theoretically, the best spar would be no spar at all, if somehow you could figure out how to support the sail. Winged masts on catamarans have proven successful because there is smooth air flow and no windage.

Reducing windage will improve a boat's performance to windward. But since air is only about 1/800th the density of water, air resistance has less influence on boat speed than water resistance.

Stability—resistance to sudden change—equates to a sailboat's tendency to roll, pitch, or yaw.

Two factors—the center of gravity (CG) and the center of buoyancy (CB)—control the stability of a boat. The more readily observed characteristics, such as hull form, amount of sail carried, the displacement, and the ballast affect these two factors to some degree.

The CG of a boat is the point around which a boat will spin if suspended in space. It remains constant unless the

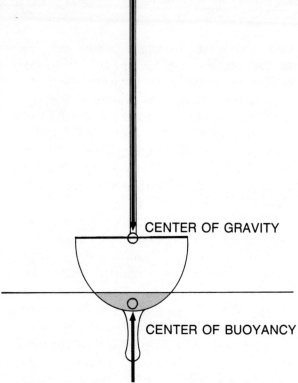

CENTER OF GRAVITY

CENTER OF BUOYANCY

Figure 3: When a boat is at rest, the center of gravity and the center of buoyancy are on the same vertical line.

configuration of the boat is changed. Gravity is always pulling down toward the earth along a vertical line running through the CG.

The CB is always at the volumetric center of the displacement of the hull. Buoyancy is the equal and opposite force counteracting gravity. The force of the buoyancy operates along a vertical line running through the CB.

At rest the CG and the CB will be found along the same vertical line (See Figure 3). When the boat tips, the CB moves in the direction the boat is tipping and away from the CG (unless the boat is round). The two forces then work against each other to right the boat.

In unballasted boats, the CG is located above the CB. To gain stability, this type of boat must have a broad, flat bottom or shallow V-bottom. Initially very stable, the center of buoyancy moves out in the hull in the direction in which the boat is beginning to tip (See Figure 4). The boat becomes progressively less stable because the horizontal distance between the CB and the CG decreases as the boat heels farther. When the CG is located directly over the CB, the boat loses stability and a capsize may follow. Beamier boats, therefore, have more "form stability."

In ballasted boats, the CG is below the CB, giving the hull positive stability, or the ability to return to an upright position after heeling. Commonly this type of hull has a more rounded bottom, less initial stability (heels more easily in the beginning), but greater ultimate stability (heels to a certain degree and then requires a great deal of force to go farther) (See Figure 5).

A boat with a deep, heavy keel will be very stable but will pay for the stability with greater displacement and wetted surface, which will in turn slow the boat down. A dinghy, which uses an unballasted centerboard for lateral plane and the crew for ballast, will be more subject to capsize but more lively and responsive to sail.

Naval architects studying the problems of monohulls capsizing in reaction to a breaking sea recommend that designers avoid flared topsides and extreme beam and locate the vertical center of gravity low in the boat to maintain positive stability.

Generally speaking, very stable boats tend also to be heavy, not easily driven

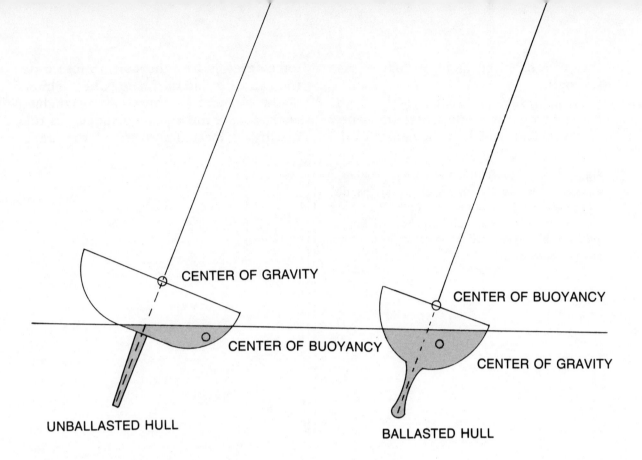

CENTER OF GRAVITY

CENTER OF BUOYANCY

UNBALLASTED HULL

CENTER OF BUOYANCY

CENTER OF GRAVITY

BALLASTED HULL

Figure 4: In unballasted boats, the center of gravity is located above the center of buoyancy. Beamier boats have more form stability.

Figure 5: In ballasted boats, the center of gravity is below the center of buoyancy, giving the hull positive stability or the ability to return to an upright position after heeling.

by their sails, to plow through the water rather than over it, and to have high wetted surface areas. These characteristics are counterproductive to achieving boat speed, though they may be necessary to some degree if other goals of the design are to be met, such as a comfortable ride.

When a designer creates the sail plan of a boat, he is concerned both with how much sail area is optimum and where to put it.

He can choose among a variety of rigs—schooner, ketch, yawl, cutter, cat, or sloop, for example. The sloop is most

apt to be selected because it performs best to windward. Some favor the cat rig now because it is easy to handle. Cutters have advocates among the cruising fraternity, as do yawls and ketches, where the area in any one sail can be kept to a more manageable size on a large boat.

If the designer does his job correctly, whatever the rig, the boat will be balanced under sail when trimmed properly and sail well with just a slight amount of weather helm. Two to five degrees are considered optimum. "She sails herself" is the brag of many a proud owner. In this well-balanced state, a boat is also sailing fast.

To achieve a well-balanced boat, the designer must properly locate the center of effort (CE), which is the center of the force developed by the sails, in regard to the center of lateral plane (CLP), which is the fore-and-aft center of the underwater area of the hull. In practice, the CE usually is located forward of the CLP,

Figure 6: The center of effort is usually located forward of the center of lateral plane. The distance between CE and CLP is called the lead. If the lead is too close, the boat will have a built-in weather helm. If the lead is too great, the boat will have a leeward helm.

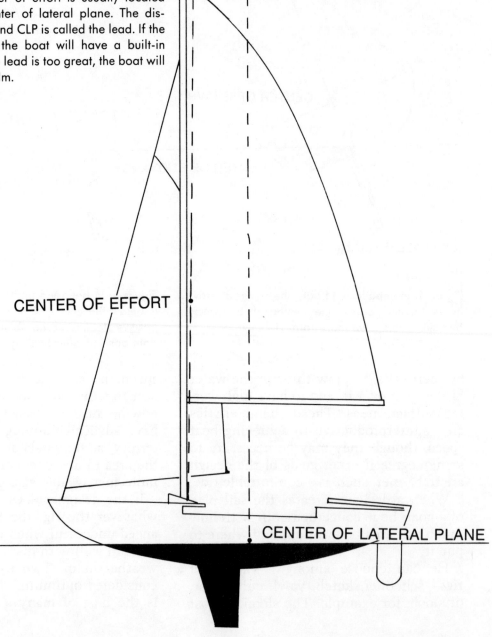

CENTER OF EFFORT

CENTER OF LATERAL PLANE

this distance being called the lead and usually expressed as a percentage of the waterline length (See Figure 6). If the lead is too little, the boat will have a built-in weather helm, or tendency to round up to weather. If it is too great, the boat will always have a lee helm, or tendency to fall off to leeward. The ideal lead cannot be expressed as a constant, because it varies with the hull form. Characteristics that indicate a shorter lead will produce a balanced boat are a fine hull, short keel, deep draft, high stability, and a low-aspect-ratio rig. Conversely, a long lead is required if a boat has a beamy hull, long keel, shoal draft, is tender, and has a high-aspect-ratio rig.

A sailor who wants to sail fast must balance his boat as well as possible, thereby reducing the need to steer with the rudder, which produces drag. Weather helm can be reduced by increasing the sail area forward (hoist a bigger jib) or reducing the sail area aft (reef or luff the main), moving weight aft, raking the mast forward, positioning the centerboard halfway up (to move CLP aft), and reducing the angle of heel.

The weather helm caused by heeling comes from two sources. The curved shape of the leeward bow of the boat, which has been forced down in the water, tends to turn the boat to weather. Second, because a large part of the sail area is now over the water instead of over the hull, the sails' force tends to twist the boat to weather.

To reduce the angle of heel, put the movable ballast (crew) as far out to weather as possible. Think about all those pictures you have seen lately of grand prix racing yachts with the crew of 20 or more huddled on the windward rails. The offshore racing council has recently put a crew limitation into the rule $(R \times .4) - 3$ = number of crew, where R is rating). For a boat rating 30, for example, you would multiply 30 times .4, equaling 12. Subtract 3; therefore your crew limitation would be nine people. If your crew isn't big enough or heavy enough to level the boat, reduce the sail area by reefing the main or hoisting a smaller jib. The boat will sail faster, will make less leeway, and will arrive at the windward mark sooner.

If the boat still has excessive weather helm, try one or more of the following: Move or rake the mast forward, recut the main to make it flatter, or modify the keel and/or rudder shape to move the CLP aft.

The complicated interaction of so many factors made yacht design an art in the past, practiced most successfully by a handful of geniuses with a "feel" or a "sense" for it. Today the art approaches a science as designers attack the challenges of creating boats that are fast, strong, and seaworthy by designing them with the aid of computers that can draw lines in hours (instead of the days that were required to do the job by hand) and that make calculations in seconds instead of hours, and by building boats with exotic, strong, and light materials.

Performance prediction programs analyzed in computers have made hull and sail design more scientific than it has been in the past. A combination of this knowledge and strict attention to detail during construction will give one boat the edge over another.

2
RATING FORMULAS

Four popular systems are currently used to handicap racing yachts: the International Offshore Rule (IOR), the Measurement Handicap System (MHS), the Performance Handicap Racing Fleet (PHRF), and the Midget Ocean Racing Club (MORC). Each is significantly different from the other three, but all attempt to do the same thing—evaluate the speed potential of yachts through observations, or by measurements and formulas to assess ratings so that all boats can be more or less equal on the racecourse. The intent is that the winner of any race be the best-sailed boat, not just the best-designed one.

Yacht owners and yacht designers never tire of trying to fool rating handicappers into thinking that their boat is slower than it really is and thus being awarded a lower rating than the boat's actual speed potential warrants. Fortunately, none of the rules penalize sailing skill, tactical genius, boat maintenance, preparation, and the ability to work together as an efficient team.

Ratings are a way of giving older and slower boats a fair chance of beating newer and faster boats, although no system is perfect. The IOR and MORC systems are developmental rules and require the best, most up-to-date equipment available and a keen, competitive spirit. Most of the successful boats racing under IOR or MORC were designed specifically to the rating rules. MHS is a newer, highly sophisticated system based on a large number of measurements and formulas and is considered by some sailors to be an innovative system for evaluating speed potential and assessing fair ratings. It is not the type of rule designers can design around, and it is geared toward sailors who enjoy cruising aboard their boats.

The PHRF system was developed to give weekend racers a rating system to equate a very broad range of boats. This system is based on performance and is more subjective than the other three.

No handicapping system is perfect. In fact, the 12-Meter rule was originally developed in 1906 so yachts could race on a one-design level. With a handicap there is always an excuse when you lose and, at times, arguments. We have enjoyed the IOR system because the racing is so close and it seems to us to be fair.

No rule is perfect, but the four rules discussed here are the most popular in the United States.

International Offshore Rule

The International Offshore Rule (IOR) replaced the Cruising Club of America Rule (CCR) in 1970 when English and American sailors combined their respective rating rules into one. It originated as a means of allowing a diverse range of yachts to race together and has enjoyed considerable success worldwide.

The IOR is a development rule and represents the grand prix level of the sport. It is the most expensive and competitive system to race under. There are more than 10,000 boats worldwide with IOR certificates; it is the system used at most international yachting events (Admiral's Cup, Clipper Cup, Sydney–Hobart race, SORC, etc.). To win at this level requires ample funds and plenty of talent.

The Americans race under a time-on-distance system, while the British use a time-on-time system. We prefer time-on-distance because we know exactly how many seconds per mile we owe competitors. Time-on-time handicapping is based on the amount of time a race takes. There is no way of knowing how you are performing in a race until all boats finish. Time-on-time handicapping tends to be unfair to small boats in heavy winds (the race is short in time) and unfair in light winds to big boats (too much time to cover the course).

The IOR is managed by the Offshore Racing Council, which meets once a year to discuss changes and make amendments to the rule. Some of the most recent changes to the IOR have dealt with the use of Kevlar in sails and with the "gorilla factor," the tendency of designers to use crew weight as a substitute for inherent stability.

Under the IOR handicapping system, a series of measurements is used to produce ratings for offshore yachts (ratings are expressed in feet). When combined with time allowance tables these ratings permit yachts of various types and sizes to race together.

The rule includes measurement of a sailboat's hull, rig, auxiliary installation, and stability characteristics. These measurements are used in formulas comparing the boat's speed characteristics with its drag characteristics. Speed is a function of length and sail area, while drag is a function of weight and beam.

The resulting number provides an assessment of a boat's speed potential expressed on the basis of length. This rating is in feet and is derived from putting length and sail area over beam and displacement and then multiplying that fraction by a series of factors. In many instances this rated length turns out to be less than the boat's actual length, a desirable result since longer boats are considered to be faster than shorter boats.

As a rule, designers are willing to sacrifice a little rating to get more speed. Through the years many conditional requirements have been attached to the original IOR formula in an attempt to head off efforts by yacht designers to take advantage of loopholes in the original rule. Understandably these efforts aim at camouflaging speed characteristics and exaggerating drag factors to achieve a low rating in relation to the true speed potential of the boat.

In addition to this exploitation of the rule's loopholes, the technology available to boat builders has advanced significantly. Consequently the rule has gone through several revisions to allow for designs that were unheard of when the IOR originated. The rule now in use was implemented in 1982. It is called the IOR Mark III.

Through its various revisions, the Ocean Racing Club (ORC) has endeavored to protect the value of the majority of the existing IOR fleet from rapid obsolescence caused by design trends, loopholes in the rule, and other developments that produce increased performance without corresponding increases in ratings. The ORC discourages developments that lead to excessive costs, or reduce safety or the suitability of yachts for cruising.

The ORC controls and moderates design trends by penalizing design features that depart significantly from fleet norms while boats near the norms are affected as little as possible. It also provides retrospective rating credits to extend the competitive life of older boats and to reduce the impact on the fleet of gradual improvements in design.

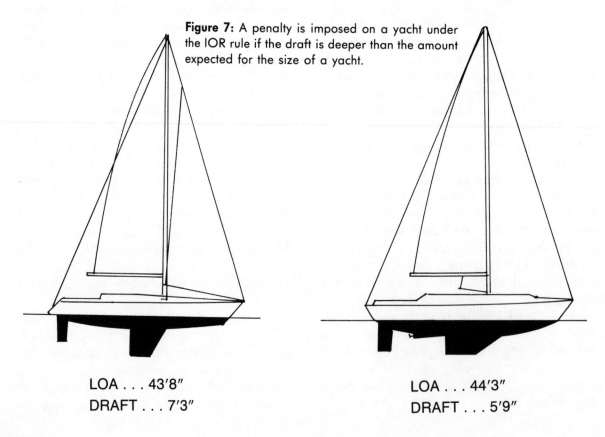

Figure 7: A penalty is imposed on a yacht under the IOR rule if the draft is deeper than the amount expected for the size of a yacht.

LOA . . . 43'8"
DRAFT . . . 7'3"

LOA . . . 44'3"
DRAFT . . . 5'9"

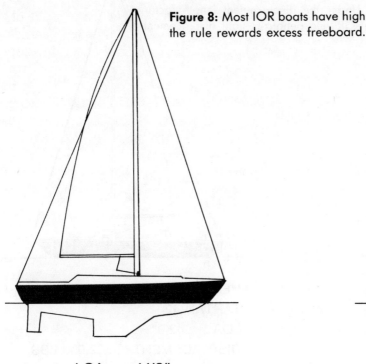

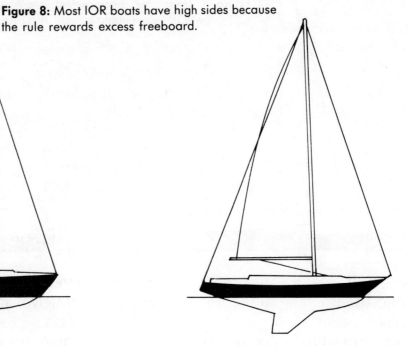

Figure 8: Most IOR boats have high sides because the rule rewards excess freeboard.

LOA . . . 44'3"

LOA . . . 45'0"

In the spirit of these management policies the ORC has implemented many correction factors to maintain fair IOR ratings. Briefly these are:

- Draft Correction (DC)—a penalty or reward for a deeper or shallower draft than the amount expected for the size of the yacht (See Figure 7).
- Freeboard Correction (FC)—excess freeboard above the IOR formula's base is rewarded by using a negative freeboard correction factor. This accounts for the high sides of most of today's IOR yachts (See Figure 8).
- Displacement Length Factor (DLF) —penalizes light-displacement yachts (See Figure 9).
- Movable Appendage Factor (MAF) (See

Figure 10) Spar Material Factor (SMF), Centerboard Factor (CBF) (See Figure 11), and Low Rigging Penalty (LRP) (See Figure 12) —all were designed to penalize unusual and controversial design features.
- Center of Gravity Factor (CGF)—relates to the IOR formula's tenderness ratio (TR) and is intended to measure sail-carrying power. Depending on your point of view, this factor either rewards tenderness or penalizes stiffness (See Figure 13).
- Engine and Propeller Factor (EPF)—compensates for the disadvantages of carrying the weight of an auxiliary engine and the drag of its propeller while racing.
- Drag Factor (DF)—based on the diame-

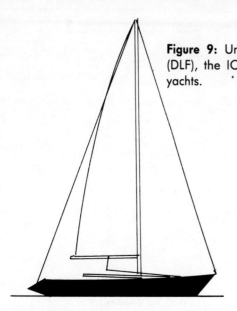

Figure 9: Under the displacement length factor (DLF), the IOR rule penalizes light displacement yachts.

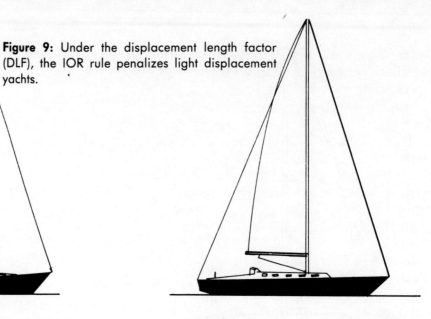

LIGHTER DISPLACEMENT YACHT
CHOATE 42
LOA . . . 42'0"
DISPLACEMENT . . . 17,000 LBS

HEAVIER DISPLACEMENT YACHT
TARTAN 42
LOA . . . 42'0"
DISPLACEMENT . . . 22,000 LBS

Figure 10: Movable appendage factor (MAF) is discouraged under the IOR rule.

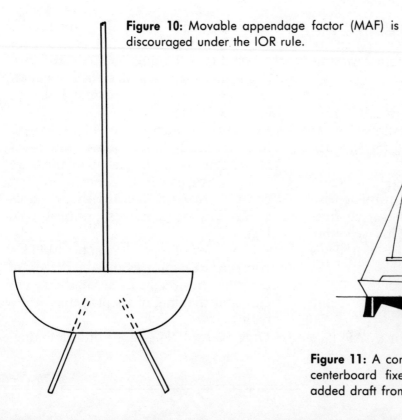

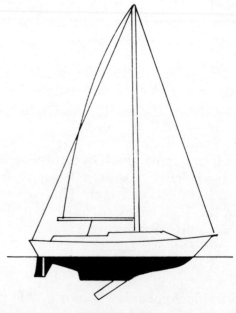

Figure 11: A correction is added to boats with a centerboard fixed in the keel because of the added draft from the movable centerboard.

ter, type, and installation of the propeller. For serious racing most designers favor a maximum-diameter folding prop on an exposed draft (See Figure 2).

It is easy to see why success on the IOR racecourse is greatly affected by designers. Since the IOR measurement system uses a very limited number of points to define an entire hull, a boat designed to fit into those points will be a much more successful IOR boat than one that is not. It takes some amount of design genius to disguise speed-enchancing characteristics in order to produce a fast boat with a low rating. So while top-flight sailors compete under the IOR, the competition among yacht designers to produce the fastest IOR boat with the best handicap is equally intense.

Naval architect Bruce Farr's example is a good one of the repercussions that innovations in design can bring. In 1975 Farr started concentrating on the stern areas of IOR boats, managing to reduce a yacht's rating while developing better all-around boat speed. A string of IOR racecourse successes prompted the IOR makers to close this loophole, severely penalizing broad sterns with rule changes made in 1976–77. Farr produced a new group of designs featuring retractable centerboards, and consequently in 1978 another rule change was implemented specifically to prohibit these.

Understandably, the chances of breakthroughs today are slim, although possible. Remember, the 12-Meter rule has been exploited since 1906, and the Australians sprouted wings in 1983.

Lately the magic comes from saving weight in the skins of the boat while re-

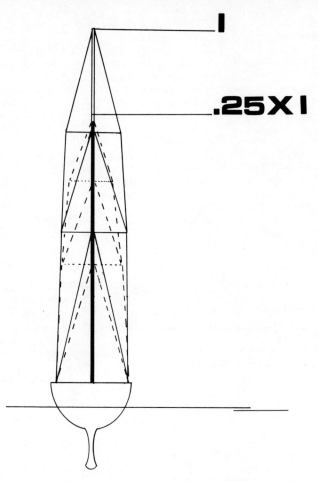

Figure 12: Yachts with low rigging on mast of the same size are penalized. Low rigging substantially cuts down on windage but can become unsafe. For this reason the rule penalizes low rigging on masts.

taining the hull's structural integrity. Exotic materials in hulls (such as Kevlar, carbon fiber, S-glass, E-glass, Plascore, and prepreg hulls) are holding court as one of the great unrated performance features. After undergoing its several major changes and rewrites, the IOR seems to have settled down, having lost some of its reputation for producing disposable boats that sail well in a narrow range.

The IOR encourages beamy boats with

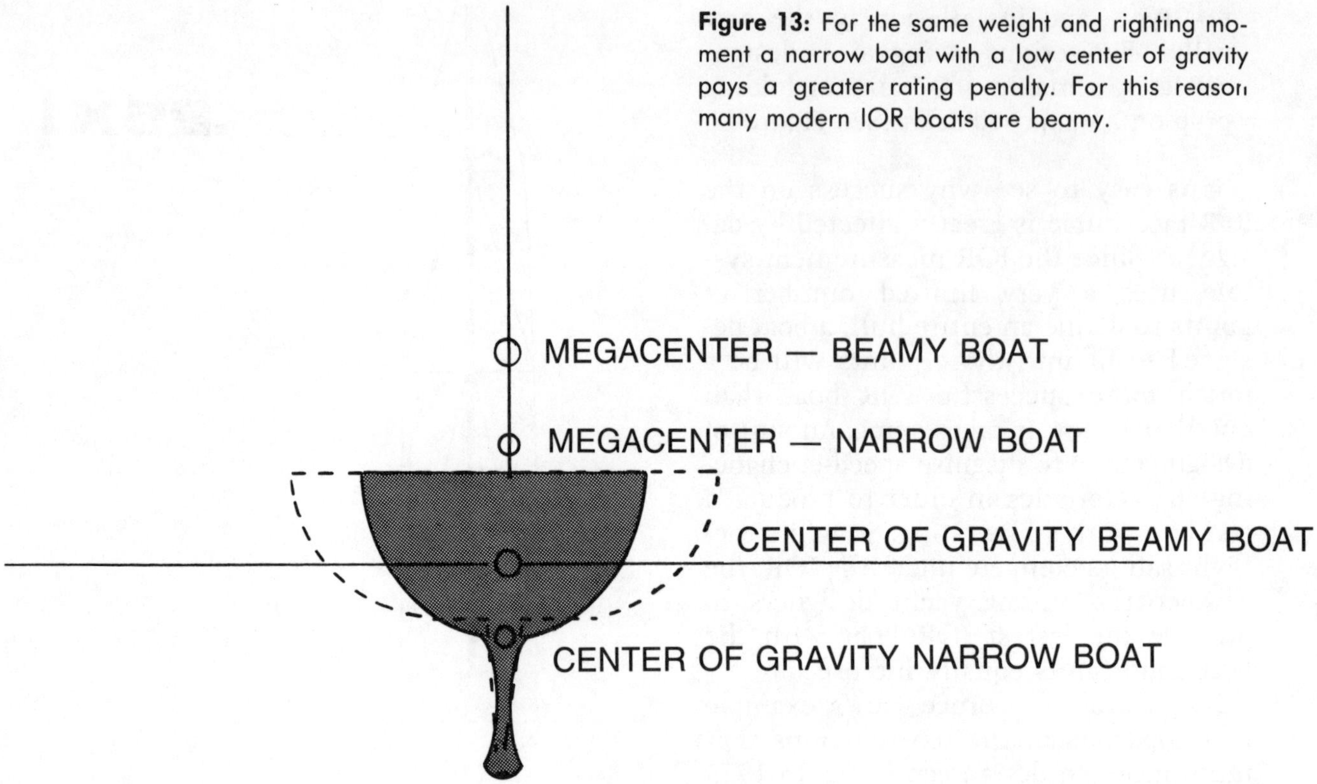

Figure 13: For the same weight and righting moment a narrow boat with a low center of gravity pays a greater rating penalty. For this reason many modern IOR boats are beamy.

MEGACENTER — BEAMY BOAT

MEGACENTER — NARROW BOAT

CENTER OF GRAVITY BEAMY BOAT

CENTER OF GRAVITY NARROW BOAT

low centers of gravity and moderate displacement. Most of the successful IOR boats today are relatively fine-ended, giving good upwind and running speeds. Narrow entries and moderate freeboards are other speed-enhancing features, offering good upwind speed. Keel shape and placement, and the hull's entry shape are speed-enhancing factors not reflected on rating certificates. And actual displacement, wetted surface, and keel area are not measured.

To protect the IOR's existing fleet and prolong their competitive life-spans, special adjustments have been made to the rule. Mark III answers the need to rate older boats fairly, those designed before the rule came into effect and those that have become outdated by new innovative designs and high-tech materials.

Any yacht is eligible for a Mark III rating (which gives a retrospective allowance to compensate for certain proportions and design features found in older yachts). Contrary to popular belief, the Mark III is not an "old age" allowance, rather it is a way of giving credits to different hull shapes that were popular during certain time periods. Boats designed before 1972 are in one section, boats from 1973 to 1976 in another section, and boats from 1976 to the present are in yet another section. Each type of boat is measured a bit differently.

To race under the IOR system, a valid rating certificate is required. This is obtainable from the United States Yacht Racing Union. Rating certificates must be revalidated annually by written application from the owner to the USYRU. Only official measurers appointed by the USYRU or the Offshore Racing Council are allowed to measure a yacht for rating purposes.

Principal hull measurements are taken when the yacht is ashore. Also, certain measurements must be taken on a single occasion with the yacht afloat in measurement trim.

Owners of IOR yachts must uphold several responsibilities while racing. These include:

1. Crew members must understand and comply with sail setting and sheeting limitations contained in the rule.

2. The yacht's owner is responsible for ensuring that when the engine is running for any reason, the propeller does not rotate.

3. Drop keels or any other movable appendages must be locked.

Kevlar sails, at first legal and then banned, are now permitted on a limited basis. Kevlar can be used as a reinforcing material along the leeches of sails, and it can be used in 110 percent genoas (#3) and aboard yachts rating 60 feet or over.

The IOR is the most expensive rating system to be measured under. Rating certificates are automatically invalidated by a change of ownership or by a change made to the yacht, its rig, or equipment that could change any of its measurements under the rule. A copy of the rating certificate must always be aboard the yacht. No yacht may have more than one valid rating certificate at one time. Changes to the hull may cause the yacht to lose the benefits of a Mark III rating and other age-protected concessions under the rule.

Measurement Handicap System

The Measurement Handicap System (MHS) is the newest system in existence. Speed predictions generated by a computer are used to derive fair ratings based on a yacht's performance on various points of sail and in different wind conditions. Through this scientific approach the MHS rule attempts to equate boats of varying sizes, ages, and designs.

The objective is to minimize costs, promote safety, and permit dual-purpose yachts to compete without a disadvantage relative to those yachts built specifically for racing. The rule rewards seaworthy boats and specifically excludes stripped-out hulls, bloopers, and bendy masts.

The MHS was developed to fill what some sailors perceived to be a gap left by the IOR. Many five-year-old designs were no longer competitive.

In 1976 the offshore committee of USYRU developed a handicapping system that would work alongside the IOR system. The result was the H. Irving Pratt Race Handicapping Project at Massachusetts Institute of Technology, from which emerged the very sophisticated program for speed predictions that is now the core of the MHS rule—the Velocity Prediction Program (VPP).

The VPP balances the elements of drag against the aerodynamic propulsive thrust of the sails. This calls for complex calculations involving a comprehensive set of measurements—the yacht's full hull line as well as rig, propeller, and flotation measurements. These are all entered into the VPP and enable the yacht's hull shape to be reproduced, the reverse process of what a designer does. By comparison, the IOR takes only a few measurements and guesses at what happens in between in order to assess a yacht's performance potential.

MHS ratings are expressed in seconds per mile. Time-allowance tables are not used. Speed potential is determined by evaluating the drive forces of the yacht (sail power). The drag forces are determined by measuring the yacht's physical characteristics (wetted surface, actual displacement, and full hull lines). Taken to the extreme, sail shapes would have to be rated as well, but luckily they are not.

The lines are taken with a field measurement instrument, an electromechanical device that stores on magnetic tape the hull line's coordinates. This tape and the manual measurements of the rig, propeller, and flotation are processed on the USYRU computer to produce the speed predictions and handicaps that appear on the MHS certificate. Several ratings appear on each yacht's certificate, and the matter of which to implement is left up to the race committee of each race.

The certificate also bears ratings for the following mixes of wind conditions:

BRR Average—Equal distances of optimum beat, 110 degrees true wind angle reach, and optimum run. Assumes 33 percent dead to windward. Usable for triangle courses with assured close-beat or Olympic-type courses not controlled by moving the marks as the wind shifts.

CR Average—Circular random, as though a boat circumnavigated a circular island with wind from a constant direction. Dead to windward beat content, 25 percent of the distance. Appropriate for closed-course races using government marks.

LR Average—Linear random, as though a boat sailed from point A to point B while the wind blew for equal periods from each direction. Dead to windward beat content, about 16 percent of distance (25 percent of the time). Appropriate for point-to-point races.

For events run under the sanction of a local club, the general-purpose rating printed at the top of the MHS certificate is generally used.

Some race committees are now using postrace determination of wind speeds and directions, considered to be a fairer alternative to the ratings mentioned above. Called "dynamic scoring," this system involves a sophisticated computer program that analyzes the finishers of the race, looking at what boats did well in order to determine what the wind speed on the course actually was.

There is also the Standard Hull Program under MHS. For those unmodified, series-produced yachts for which lines are already on file, it will not be necessary to field-measure the hull. A fee is charged for use of the lines, but it is still a considerable savings over field measurement.

Club measurement is an alternative, simplified measurement method that omits the stability test and the checking of penalty conditions in rig dimension. MHS club certificates are intended primarily for local racing and may not be accepted by some race sponsors. They are available only for production yachts included in the Standard Hull Program that are unmodified in shape, structure, ballast, or rig.

Under the MHS rule, no yacht may have more than one valid rating certificate at any one time, and owners are responsible for declaring any changes made to the yacht that could change its measurement under the rule. For example: changes in the amount or location of ballast or stores; change in tankage; changes in engine and/or propeller; structural modification; movement of measurement bands or change of spars; the addition of replacement of sales required to be measured.

The MHS class allows fine tuning to regional conditions (lighter winds than the U.S. average over water generally prevail on Chesapeake Bay, for example) without resorting to performance handicapping. A recent change requires that all MHS certificates display an additional set of handicaps for nonspinnaker racing, based on simulating the performance of a yacht without the use of its spinnaker. The class is administered by an elected eight-person executive committee and is sponsored by USYRU. MHS has been used successfully in the Bermuda Race sponsored by the Cruising Club of America, and the Chicago–Mackinac Race sponsored by the Chicago Yacht Club.

Performance Handicap Racing Fleet

The Performance Handicap Racing Fleet (PHRF) is by far the most popular method of handicapping yachts for racing. Throughout the United States there are more than 20,000 boats in nearly 100 fleets racing under the PHRF system. PHRF is an easy rule to apply and an inexpensive one to maintain.

Originated in Southern California in 1960, the PHRF concept rates boats based on their past performance on the racecourse rather than having them measure into a certain rule. When the IOR was created in 1970, older boats were no longer competitive. In 1981, the PHRF was recognized by USYRU as a full committee under its Offshore Racing Council; USYRU now acts as a central clearinghouse for United States PHRF.

PHRF ratings are based on performance, not on measurements, as with the IOR, MHS, and MORC systems. PHRF ratings are based on the speed potential of the boat, determined as much as possible by observations of previous racing experiences. In making their arbitrary calculations, the PHRF handicappers assume that every yacht is in absolute top racing condition. They assume that the bottom of each yacht is clean and smooth; the propeller is a folding type; the quality of sail is adequate for any race the yacht may enter. Furthermore, it is assumed that every skipper and crew are capable of racing the yacht to its speed potential as calculated from the past performance of yachts of the same design.

PHRF is an open rule. There are no limitations other than those listed here:

1. a monohull design of at least 20 feet
2. must be self-righting
3. must contain approved cruising accommodations with an enclosed cabin
4. must carry the approved safety equipment (the PHRF class has a list of such approved equipment).

Ratings are expressed in seconds per mile to be deducted from elapsed times to produce corrected times. The higher rating indicates the slower boats. If one boat is rated 150, and another 156, the former owes the latter six seconds per mile of racing. Over a 10-mile course the first boat would have to finish more than one minute ahead of the second to win. Ratings are expressed in six-second-per-mile increments, with the smallest increment of performance being three seconds per mile.

Observations of numerous races show that it is impossible to gauge a boat's potential performance more accurately than actual performance. Differences in skipper and crew skill represent a much larger factor than three seconds per mile.

All ratings are "based ratings" for standard, out-of-the-box stock or basic boats. Ratings are determined by a board of handicappers, each member of which represents an area or yacht club. The chief handicapper acts as chairman. Each area handicapper is responsible for handicapping boats in the region assigned to him. With time, the handicapper becomes familiar with the performance of all the more active boats and is able to evaluate their characteristics. Through experience, the handicapper becomes familiar with the wind and current conditions in his area and understands how much allowance to make for local conditions before evaluating boat speed in competition. Handicappers maintain a constant search for boats that require an adjustment of handicap to permit them to compete fairly with the balance of the fleet.

If you are unhappy with your handicap, it sometimes helps to complain. Take the handicapper racing with you and let him then determine whether your rating is fair.

A skipper with a boat from an established class is given the rating for that class, except that adjustments may be made for any deviation from the class standards. For new classes and custom boats, the rating is determined by comparing similar boats with established ratings. A determination will also be made as to whether the rig and hull comply with the approved guidelines set forth by PHRF.

PHRF base ratings are made on the assumption that (See Figure 14):

1. the spinnaker or whisker pole is equal to "J"
2. the spinnaker maximum girth is 180 percent of "J"
3. the genoa LP is a maximum 155 percent of "J"
4. the boat is in racing condition
5. the boat has a folding or feathering

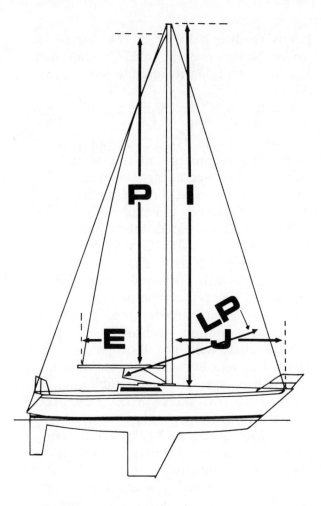

Figure 14: Sail plan measurements.

Some examples of modification adjustments follow:

No engine or auxiliary motor	6-second penalty
Inboard auxiliary option on small yacht	3-second credit
Spinnaker pole length over 100 percent of "J"	3-second penalty for each 10 percent of "J"
Spinnaker girth over 180 percent of "J"	3-second penalty for each 10 percent increase over "J"
Shoal draft version of standard	6-second credit
Tall mast, mast taller than standard class	3-second penalty for each 5 percent increase
Short mast, mast not as tall as standard class	3-second credit for each 5 percent increase

Because headsail size has so much to do with boat speed, PHRF uses this factor as a means of handicapping; boats rated for use with large or small headsails with 155 percent of LP are on the dividing line. Once a boat is rated with a large headsail (over 155 percent), this rating must be used, even though wind conditions may preclude use of the sail.

Local boards of PHRF handicappers meet once a month to evaluate and adjust ratings. At these meetings new boat handicaps as well as petitions for changes to existing handicaps are considered.

Decisions on new boats are effective immediately, while final decisions on

propeller, or a retractable outboard motor.

A skipper can experiment with different ways of improving the performance of his boat without remeasuring. If there are changes to the hull, rig, sails, or other factors upon which the existing rating is based, these must be reported to the local handicapper for evaluation.

Penalties are applied to the base for variations and modifications.

handicap adjustment are held over until the next meeting so that additional race data can be gathered and considered.

PHRF has more appeal among the masses, as it is inexpensive to get into and discourages the type of expensive boat modifications needed to be competitive at the IOR, MHS, and MORC levels.

Midget Ocean Racing Club

MORC is a measurement handicapping system for boats 24 to 30 feet long. It was developed by the Midget Ocean Racing Club and is based on scientific speed predictions. All ratings are issued by MORC International.

Organized in the early 1950s, the primary objective of MORC (as stated in its constitution and bylaws) is:

> to promote medium and long distance racing and cruising throughout the United States and internationally among sailing yachts below 30 feet length overall, to encourage the development of yachts suitable for this purpose, to formulate and administer rules for rating such yachts, to advance the tenets of safe seamanship and good sportsmanship, and to collect and disseminate information related to these ends.

There are 78 MORC fleets—called "stations"—across the United States. MORC currently has over 1,000 members.

The idea of a separate rule for smaller boats originated in 1954, when naval architects William Shaw and Olin Ste-phens modified the CCA rule for boats under 24 feet overall. In 1959, they had the rule expanded to include boats up to 30 feet.

MORC is a development rule very much like the IOR. A designer or builder can look at the MORC design parameters or development constraints and develop a boat accordingly. Because the rule is broad in scope, designers have been able to detect and exploit loopholes to produce lower-rated, faster boats. For that reason the MORC rule has gone through some 10 to 15 changes over the years and is still criticized for encouraging use of a specific type of boat.

MORC ratings are designed to give a fair approximation of how fast a particular boat will go. Ratings are expressed in feet and are used in conjunction with a time allowance table. Before adopting its own tables, MORC used the IOR time-allowance tables.

The Midget Ocean Racing Club maintains its own rating center and measurement rule committee. The club is administered by a board of governors comprised of the commodores of each active station together with the national officers. This board directs club policy, selects the members of the MORC rule committee, and approves all measurement rule modifications as well as other related regulations, including the required equipments list.

One of the unique aspects of MORC is sponsoring races for its members. In odd-numbered years the International MORC Regatta is held, and in designated areas, regional regattas are held in even-numbered years.

MORC ratings are simple, economical,

easy to measure, and easy to enforce. As a handicap rule, it attempts to equate speed-producing factors without prohibiting development or permitting design obsolescence; and at the same time it maintains the concept of encouraging the development of useful cruising yachts.

Certified MORC measurers are used to collect the yacht dimensions and sail measurements required by the rule's formula. One of the most unique things about this rule is that the boats are actually weighed, since they are small, using a hydraulic-crane scale rather than by mathematical calculations.

The MORC rule uses a model with certain dimensions. As the boat differs from the base model it is either credited or penalized. If the measurement rules committee thinks the change makes the boat slower, you receive a credit; if they think it makes it faster, you get penalized. Penalties and credits are then added together and multiplied by the rated length of the boat and a constant to come up with the final rating.

Using a typical 24-footer (Gotcha 24) as an example, let's look at how base boat differences are corrected as they relate to speed production factors.

Beam Correction—This factor is used to penalize or reward boats beamier or narrower than the base boat for a given size range. With a 10-foot beam—wider than the base boat's—the Gotcha 24 would have a minus beam correction factor.

Draft Correction—This adjusts the rating of a boat with more or less draft than the base boat. MORC allows for a boat with fairly deep draft, so at 5.05 feet of draft the Gotcha 24 gets a credit for draft correction.

Displacement Correction—If the Gotcha 24 is heavier than the base boat, she will receive a credit here. If not, a penalty is used to discourage light-displacement boats.

Freeboard Correction—MORC is very liberal on freeboards—its optimum boat has very high sides. The average freeboard on a Gotcha 24 is three feet, resulting in a very minor penalty. MORC encourages big boats with lots of volume, a good example being the S2 9.1.

Sail Area Correction—This factor reflects MORC's encouragement of moderately rigged boats. The Gotcha 24 carries 355 square feet of sail with 170 percent genoa, a 10-foot J, 10-foot boom, and a giant spinnaker. Consequently, a .2-foot penalty is taken. An underrigged boat would get a credit because it would not sail as fast.

Ballast Correction—This factor encourages use of well-balanced boats. A penalty is given for anything less than a 30 percent ballast/displacement ratio. There is also a live ballast correction (similar to IOR's new crew-member formula of $.4 \times$ rating $- 3 =$ total allowable crew) to be considered. With 1,700 pounds of internal ballast, the 3,825-pound Gotcha 24 takes only a .1-foot penalty on its rating. It takes a crew of five on the Gotcha 24's weather rail to keep her flat, and that is reflected by the minor penalty. Use of well-balanced, relatively heavy boats is encouraged under MORC, since most people race with their families.

Propeller Correction—Based on whether the boat has an inboard motor. A penalty of .1 foot is given for head-foils. Boats with more than one backstay are similarly penalized to discourage skinny masts supported by double-running backstays.

MORC does a good job of rating new designs fairly well, but it was not designed as a handicap system for old cruising boats, although it does contain an older-boat-credit factor. For all practical purposes MORC boats are racing boats with some cruising accommodations. The optimum boat is 25 to 26 feet in length overall, of moderate displacement and sail area, with lots of volume, deep draft, and high freeboard.

Several significant changes to the rule have attempted to make it fairer for heavy-displacement boats. In 1977 the 4 percent waterline measurement rule was adopted (in addition to waterline length, a length of 4 percent above the waterline was factored into the formula). But the most dramatic change was in 1979, when MORC implemented the 4Q rule. Up to that time a boat such as the J/24 had an inequitable rating, and it was almost impossible to beat. The new rule gave heavier-displacement boats a better chance against lighter-displacement boats. So far the 4Q is working.

Within the MORC rule are two additional rating systems that local stations may use if they wish: the 1979 MORC development rule and the MORC/PR rating (similar to PHRF).

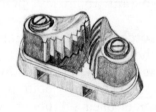

PART TWO

The Winning Team

This 470 crew shows good form on a heavy air windward leg. The crew is straight out from the wire without arching back. *Photograph by Daniel Forster.*

3

DEVELOPING YOUR CREW

A winning crew is made up of individuals who work together (See Figure 16). We believe that working in pairs with another crew member increases the efficiency of the whole boat. Two people working together benefit from collective wisdom and also act as a check on one another. Mistakes are cut down and new ideas on performance or tactics surface when crew members talk with each other.

The key to good sailing is communication. By organizing your crew in pairs, crew members will tend to work together and communicate continuously during a race.

Competent and experienced people are the most important assets of a crew. Winning is the common goal that holds any crew together. The secret is specialization. You will get the most out of your crew by developing people who specialize in specific areas and at the same time complement each other at other tasks. The best crews work better as a team than the sum of individual players (See Figure 15).

Teammates must rely on each other. The trick here is constant discussion between crew members, each sailor taking the attitudes "What can I do next?" and "If my job is done, how can I help my teammate?" If a mistake is being made, another teammate should be there as a backup.

A team must have one leader. The saying "Too many cooks spoil the stew" is appropriate on sailboats. Rule by committee seldom works. After all, how many statues have been built in your city honoring committees? It is critical that every crew member is satisfied with his position. We find that rotating jobs on a boat keeps each crew member fresh and also teaches the less-experienced sailors new techniques. Sailing is a sport best learned by doing; therefore, putting a sailor in a specific job, even if he is new at it, speeds up the learning process.

During critical maneuvers, such as the start or spinnaker takedowns, it is important to have your most talented crew members in the critical positions. During practice sessions, or while sailing in wide-open waters, use the time to talk through each function so your crew members have a clear understanding of what is expected of them. By reviewing things in advance, your team members become more comfortable during the ac-

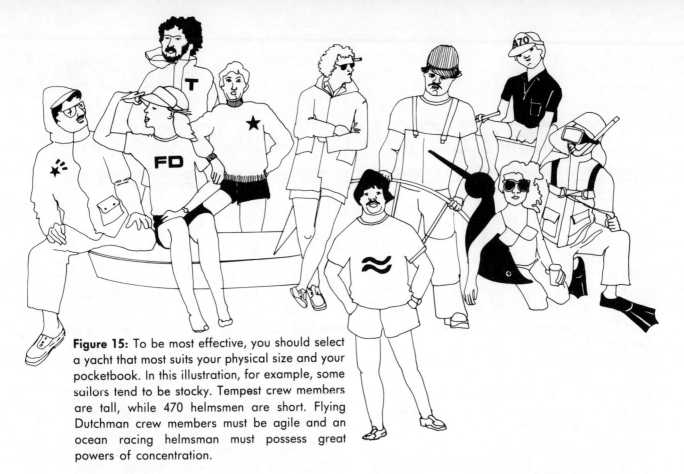

Figure 15: To be most effective, you should select a yacht that most suits your physical size and your pocketbook. In this illustration, for example, some sailors tend to be stocky. Tempest crew members are tall, while 470 helmsmen are short. Flying Dutchman crew members must be agile and an ocean racing helmsman must possess great powers of concentration.

tual maneuver because their subconscious tells them that they have been there before.

Before each race, think through your plan. Imagine yourself coming down to the boat in the morning, rigging it up, pushing off from the dock, conducting the crew meeting on board. Imagine the presence of your competitors, think about coming off the starting line with speed, sailing in light wind, sailing in heavy wind; even think about being over the line at the start, and imagine a quick and successful recovery. We find that the best time for these thoughts is the evening before the race. By actually thinking these things through, you will be more comfortable later during the racing.

Mental preparation in sailing gives you a better shot at winning.

While you prepare mentally for a race, convince yourself that not only do you deserve to win but also that you are going to win. Think of the race as a quest for excellence. How many mistakes can you avoid during the race?

Twelve-Meter racing, for example, is not a game of brilliance, it is a game of avoidance of errors. The team with the fewest errors will win the race.

There is a story of a basketball coach who successfully used mental preparation to improve his team's foul-shooting percentage. This coach divided his squad of 12 players in half. The first six players he asked to shoot 100 foul shots every night after practice. This group's foul-shooting percentage improved 10 percent after two weeks. The second six players on the team were asked also to shoot 100 foul shots after practice each night. But they were also asked to imagine themselves stepping to the foul line in Madison Square Garden during the final game of the NBA championship. This foul shot would bring their team victory. The coach asked each player to mentally shoot this crucial foul shot 100 times before going to sleep. The percentage improvement by the second six players was dramatically higher than that of the other group thanks to mental preparation.

When you sail, continuously try to predict what is going to happen on the racecourse. Then carefully review whether your call was right or not. As time goes on and you gain experience, you will make more successful predictions and therefore you will become more relaxed while sailing.

As a skipper, the toughest assignment is to motivate your individuals. Ted Turner does it by giving his crew a reason to excel and a reason to win. He assigns specific jobs to specific crew members. The desire to excel, however, rests with individuals. Motivation from leaders helps, but inner motivation is the key to achieving success. Give yourself a goal to reach. Use past victories as a reminder that you can and will be successful.

What really counts in any sport is being able to perform well under pressure. During practice sessions it is easy to excel, but during the actual contest it is usually the most prepared competitor who will win by using a combination of his skills, experience, and readiness.

Winning in sailing, however, is not the only thing. By just taking part in sailing you are a winner. What counts is doing your best at a particular moment and then making an improvement for the future. You can't afford to race in sailing if you can't afford to lose. No sailor can possibly win them all, but those who work hard by setting their goals early and practicing before an event will win their fair share of races.

Getting a regular crew to sail on your boat is hard work. You have to balance between experience and new people and make it fun for everyone. The key here is to let people participate in the decision-making process and also to rotate jobs so everyone learns. If you call a potential crew member at eight o'clock on Saturday morning out of the blue and expect this person for a noon start to perform well, you are mistaken.

Schedule your racing well in advance and get commitments from your crew as early as possible. This gives each crew member time to prepare mentally for the racing. Circulate your sailing schedule with regular psyche-up letters to keep your crew informed of your progress. Here are two samples of crew letters used for the *Defender/Courageous* team in 1982 and for the crew of *Jubilation* prior to the 1984 Southern Ocean Racing Conference.

TO: *Defender/Courageous* Crew
FROM: Gary Jobson
Plans for the first sailing session are going well. *Courageous* is currently at Newport Beach, California, and *Defender* is scheduled to leave on Wednesday, November 10. The

masts should be leaving Sturgeon Bay on November 11. Plan to arrive in California on November 29. (Housing is available November 28 at Park Newport Condominiums.) November 30 is a sailing day for all crew. You should plan to fly to Los Angeles; make your own reservation with the airline.

I believe our program has come a long way since we first met in June in Newport. The high-level talent that we have gathered is unique in sailing, and hopefully, it will be one of our strong points when we go into the trials next summer. Even with the greatly reduced sailing schedule, a number of our team have performed well throughout the world. Rod Davis won the Half-Ton World Championships. Paul Cayard and Tom Blackaller were first when they left Hawaii after the Pan Am Clipper Cup. Cayard, Keefe and Stuart won the St. Francis Perpetual Trophy. Stuart and I also squeezed in the Hall of Fame victory. Kolius and Stuart (that Stuart is getting hot!) won the J-24 Worlds last month, and, naturally, all of us were proud of Glenn Darden for finishing tenth at the Sunfish World Championships this year!

This next sailing session, November 30–December 20, will have two purposes. First, to begin our intensive sail development program. At present, Rod Davis has outlined nineteen different tests that we hope to achieve during this time period. Secondly, the crews for *Defender* and *Courageous* will be selected. It is anticipated that the two crews will be named prior to our second winter session starting on January 5. It is very important that you arrive in Newport Beach in shape and ready to go sailing.

TO: *Jubilation* Crew
FROM: Gary Jobson

Yesterday *Jubilation* was launched through the ice at Cove Haven in Barrington, Rhode Island. *Jubilation* is really special and all of us that attended the ceremony are anxious to start sailing next week. About 50 people braved the cold and freezing rain. Carol James gave a brief blessing and the champagne bottle was smashed on the bow with a little assistance from Jack.

The schedule for *Jubilation* is to be trucked to Florida on January 16. The keel has to be taken off for the trip. Our professional captain, George Varga, has done an outstanding job coordinating the project.

The deck layout is everything we hoped for and will allow for extra efficient sail handling and easy communication of the crew. Down below, *Jubilation* will be a comfortable boat particularly for a grand prix ocean racer. Every crew member will have individual stowage and the bunks have four inch foam cushions.

With good rest and good food, we will sail well. The night fighters are on their way. The spar is scheduled to be stepped on Wednesday, January 4 and we plan to be sailing the 6th.

Measuring will take place during this period. We expect the boat to rate within .1 of 43.0. Goetz Custom Boats have distinguished themselves with *Jubilation*. This boat is really strong and promises to be fast yet comfortable and all of us are going to be proud to be racing this great boat.

Mike Toppa has been working hard on our sails and we will have the latest technology learned from the America's Cup summer. We will catalog and test most of the sail inventory during our session on Narragansett Bay.

Jack James has put together the latest in yacht design, equipment, sails and technology in *Jubilation*, now it is our job to race with a vengeance. Get in shape. get psyched and mentally prepare yourself for the best SORC any of us have raced.

Letters like these make the recipients feel a part of the team and help to begin each crew member's mental preparation. By knowing a certain sailing effort is well planned and has been organized in advance, each crew member should arrive at the boat feeling confident and ready to sail.

4

CREW ORGANIZATION

The morning of a sailboat race is a special time. There is electricity in the air as sailors anticipate racing. Before the start, hopes are high.

Gary recalls many races on _Tenacious_ when skipper Ted Turner would show up about an hour before the boat was to leave and meet his crew, many of which he was meeting for the first time. Turner would survey the crew and assign jobs by each person's appearance. A large young guy would be put next to a winch, and a more elderly type with glasses and a beard probably would be handed a pencil to become the navigator. Sometimes the assignments grew chuckles from the veterans, but the point is Turner always made sure each man understood exactly what his job was.

Every race in which Gary participated with Turner there was a pep talk on why this race was important.

Big boat races often are decided by smooth boat handling and precise organization. To win, the big boat crew has to function much like a football team and

Ted Turner always psyches up his crews.
Photograph by Carol Singer

Figure 16: The best-sailed yachts are the ones in which the crew stays low and in their assigned positions.

execute maneuvers swiftly and efficiently. In what other sport do you have to coordinate the activities of twenty-four team players simultaneously as you might have to on a maxi yacht? In basketball there are five players, hockey six, baseball nine, and football eleven, but in maxi yacht sailing we have a unique team of twenty-four players. Any crewman can make an error that can spell disaster for the whole boat.

For every crew member you add to a boat, you square the potential problems. Therefore, good organization with a common goal is the key. All this takes practice. Organizing your crew for various boat-handling sequences can help offset lack of practice time.

Learning a crew position is more than memorizing steps by rote. You have to stay in touch with your surroundings, such as the boat's angle of heel, or the apparent wind.

But there are certain basics that the

entire crew must live by. Know your position well and be prepared well in advance of any maneuver. Talk quietly and keep your weight low and away from the ends of the boat. You can always spot a poorly sailed boat because the entire crew will be standing (See Figure 16). If there is a problem, crews on well-sailed boats will go to their stations, while on poorly sailed boats the whole crew dives at the problem. Remember, sail trim comes first, and every other function on board is secondary for crew members.

We have prepared the following lists to help crews understand their position and duties for racing/cruising boats. Competitive spirit is the lifeblood of sport, and the common goal of winning will help keep your crew's attention focused on racing the boat hard.

One Hour Before Leaving Dock—all crew on board

1. Afterguard strategy meeting
   a. review weather
   b. starting area on course?
   c. race instruction
   d. watch bill
   e. "all hands" station
   f. sail inventory
   g. check all instruments
   h. navigation equipment
   i. radios
   j. charts
   k. review meal schedule with cook
   l. stow all personal gear
2. Sail trimmers (main, jib, and spinnaker)
   a. check sail inventory and stowage
   b. select sails for start of race
   c. blend mainsail on boom with battens

d. lead and check sheets and guys
   e. check and service winches and blocks
   f. spray tracks
   g. stow all personal gear
   h. inspect all sails for telltales and tears
   i. check masthead fly; are the angles correct?
   j. lead mainsail reefing lines
   k. stow all personal gear
3. Grinder
   a. checks and services winches
   b. checks hydraulics
   c. helps stow sails
   d. helps bend mainsail on boom
   e. checks bilges
   f. stows all personal gear
4. Mastman
   a. helps stow sails
   b. services mast winches
   c. inspects halyards
   d. inspects mast, sheaves, and spreaders
   e. helps put main on boom
   f. packs spinnakers
   g. places telltells on shrouds
   h. stows all personal gear
5. Bowman
   a. checks all halyards
   b. checks spinnaker pole—put on mast with topping lift
   c. packs spinnakers
   d. checks all sheet and guy leads
   e. reviews sail inventory stowage
   f. assists stowage of sails
   g. checks boat's tools
   h. checks feeder and headstay, spray groove
   i. stows all personal gear

Belowdeck

1. Close and lock all hatches except main and forward hatches

This crew member keeps a lookout on the windward leg for crossing boats. *Photograph by Carol Singer*

2. Check fuel, lube, belts, etc., main engine, and generator
3. Check all batteries
4. Stow all food and beverages available and ice
5. Check all sails
   a. in proper bag
   b. spinnakers in turtles or put in stops
   c. stowage plan made and posted
   d. sheets placed on genoa staysail and spinnaker staysail
6. Check all bilges and bilge pumps
7. Remove cruising anchor and chain plus all other cruising gear
8. Have specific place for crew's gear (to be kept at a minimum), including foul-weather gear

After Leaving Dock

1. Skipper holds crew meeting
   a. assigns all jobs
   b. reviews watch routine
   c. reviews all safety requirements and equipment location
   d. reviews "all hands" position
   e. explains competition, the course, weather, and race strategy to crew (with time for comments)
   f. reviews sail inventory
   g. gives reason for performing well in this race
   h. ends meeting on positive note
   i. checks in with race committee before start
   j. records continuous wind readings, direction, and velocity
2. Sail Trimmers
   a. select and set sails
   b. check jib leads and halyard settings
   c. check mainsail setting and mast bend
   d. confirm correct sail for start and have next sail ready to set

3. Grinder
   a. helps set sails
   b. works with sail trimmers, grinding winches
4. Mastman
   a. hoists sails
   b. checks mast bend
   c. stows old sails
   d. checks for lines overboard
5. Bowman
   a. prepares for next sail change
   b. keeps bow lookout
   c. coordinates time to start with afterguard

Before Start

1. Continue with wind readings
2. Tune up on both tacks and not compass courses
3. Have short speed test with competitor
4. Make four racing tacks
5. Tune up on both jibes and note courses
6. Check for favored end of the line
7. Check for favored side of course

Sailing to Windward

1. Afterguard
   a. helmsman steers and concentrate on speed
   b. navigator/tactician
      1. plots progress on course
      2. records wind speed, course steered, and weather information in logbook
      3. computes apparent wind angle, wind speed, and the course to the next mark
      4. observes the performance of your competitors, continuously using a hand bearing compass
      5. plays main sail traveler
2. Sail trimmers
   a. trim sails
   b. check halyard settings
   c. check lead positions
   d. talk continuously with helmsman
   e. talk with navigator/tactician
   f. think about next sail
   g. shift weight in puffs
3. Grinder
   a. trims sails, grinds winches
   b. shifts weight with puffs
4. Mastman
   a. backs up grinder
   b. sets up halyards for set
   c. prepares for next sail change
   d. shifts crew weight to windward
   e. watches mast bend
   f. adjusts halyards
   g. hauls new sails on deck

HEADSAIL CHANGES

Notes on Headsail Changes: With the double-grooved headfoil systems currently in use on offshore boats, it's possible to hoist headsails to windward of the sail you want to remove, which won't disrupt critical leeward air flow. It's even more advantageous to conduct tack sets whenever possible. That way, the new sail goes up on the inside (weather side), and after the tack the old sail comes down on the new weather side.

The crew of *Quick Silver* shows good form with crew to windward and bunched together in the middle of the boat. The mainsail is being vang sheeted in this photograph. *Photograph by Gary Jobson*

The linchpin for the headsail change is the foredeck man, who must prepare the boat for the change by properly leading the new sheets, organizing the halyard, and inserting the headsail into the feeder at the stemhead. It's far better to have one person perform all these tasks. This will prevent confusion and unnecessary weight and movement on the foredeck. As the sail is being hoisted, it's important for the foredeck man to keep it under control and clear from shrouds or lifelines.

The mastman becomes important in removing the old headsail. At the precise moment the boat comes head to weather for the tack, he has to break the halyard on the old sail. During the tack, the foredeck man comes aft to the mast to assist with the Cunningham, babystay, or the new halyard, and then goes forward again to gather in the sail that has been dropped.

	1	2	3	4
Foredeck man	Leads sheet for new sail to opposite side of boat. Feeds sail carefully, making sure it is clear of shrouds, lifeline, etc.		Breaks halyard for old (now inside) sail just as boat comes head to weather	
Halyard man		Hoists the sail as quickly as possible (Hand over hand with another man tailing.)		Gathers old headsail.

TACKING

Notes on tacking: Obviously, proper steering through the tack is vitally important so that the boat won't pound into waves, slowing the boat considerably. The helmsman and the tactician (who also can be the mainsail trimmer) have to choose a "soft spot" in the chop for the maneuver. Also, it's easy to see that subsequent boat-handling procedures revolve around trimming the helm.

As the boat comes head to wind, the man working the halyards at the mast may want to throw off the cunningham, babystay, and lower the headsail halyard three to four inches, adding fullness to the sail on the opposite tack for added power. In addition, for the headsail to back properly, supplementing speed on the new tack, the old headsail trimmer has to be acutely aware of when to break his jib. In winds under 10 knots, the entire jib should be backed, which will force the bow five degrees below the intended course. In winds ranging from 10 to 20 knots, half the headsail is backed. For winds over 20 knots, the headsail is tacked immediately.

One technique for quick big boat tacking is the use of headsail sheet overhaulers for every tack. One or two members of the crew (*Ondine* used six, affectionately dubbed the "suicide squad") grab the new headsail sheet and run aft with it, taking it directly to the new block. The maneuver brings in the headsail much faster and takes a lot of pressure off the grinder.

	1	2	3	4
Helmsman	Rounds slowly at soft spot in waves, increasing spin as boat comes head to wind.			Steers 5 degrees low of intended course, then slowly up.
Mainsail trimmer	Slowly grinds main as boat tacks, helping boat to weather. Traveler is center line.			
Headsail trimmer	Slowly grinds in headsail as boat tacks, helping boat to weather.	Breaks jib when boat is head to weather. Takes jib clew forward and clears it around shrouds. Skirts foot.		New headsail trimmer fine-tunes new sheet. Boat at speed.
Mastman and bowman			1 to 2 men grasp new sheet and run aft, taking sheet directly to new lead block.	
Grinder				Takes in last 2 feet. Few wraps as possible for speed.

REEFING

Notes on reefing: Although the helmsman has no immediate function when installing a reef, he has one of the most difficult jobs. The boat wants to bear off when the mainsail is eased—which signals the start of the reefing maneuver—and he really has to fight to keep the boat sailing upwind.

Other than that, reefing is one of the few maneuvers in big boat sailing that follows any kind of real sequence. For instance, you can't fit the luff cringle to the horn at the gooseneck until the halyard has been eased, and you can't grind in the reefing line until the luff cringle has been fitted. To remove the reef, the steps are basically reversed.

Reef In	1	2	3	4
Mainsail trimmer	Starts maneuver by completely luffing mainsail.			Trims mainsail back to proper setting for upwind sailing.
Helmsman	Keeps boat head to weather at all times. (With main luffed, boat has tendency to bear off.)			
Halyard man		Eases halyard as soon as main is luffed. (Mark halyard with tape.)	Takes up halyard as soon as tack is attached at gooseneck.	
Tackman		Fits luff cringle to gooseneck horn as soon as halyard has been eased to mark. Then tails for reefing line grinder.		
	1	2	3	4
Reefing line grinder			Begins taking up reefing line as soon as tack is attached at gooseneck. Overtrims to offset stretch.	

Reef Out	1	2	3	4
Mainsail trimmer	Starts maneuver by completely luffing main.			Trims main back in to proper up-wind setting.
Helmsman	Keeps boat hard on wind.			
Halyard man	Eases halyard sufficiently for cringle to be removed.			
Tackman		Removes luff cringle from gooseneck horn. Assists main halyard man on rehoisting sail.		
Reefing line man			Releases reefing line to mainsail clew as soon as halyard is ready to be raised.	

SPINNAKER SETS

Notes on spinnaker sets: The four key positions for a clean spinnaker set are the foredeck, the helm, the guy, and the mast. The foredeck man, of course, has to prepare the boat for the set prescribed by the afterguard. The helmsman has to keep the boat sailing on her lines, which means he has to bear off, but not so much that bearing off will pull the apparent wind too far aft. So that the chute will be set utilizing the maximum apparent wind, the guy trimmer has to make certain that the pole is positioned only two feet aft of the headstay. Any farther aft and speed will suffer. The guy trimmer and the helmsman can then coordinate, sailing the boat farther off the wind, squaring the pole aft, and steering away. Last, the halyard man has to make sure the headsail is dropped quickly after the boat has rounded, even before the chute has filled.

Bear-away Set	1	2	3	4
Foredeck man	Prepares boat according to prescribed set and sail-chute flaked, sheets lead properly, turtle attached to stanchions, pole, topping life, and foreguy ready.			
Helmsman		On rounding, helmsman bears off to close reach. Calls for set.		
Mainsail trimmer	Selects sails.	Eases sail to close reach.		Releases Cunningham, outhaul, and flattening reef.
Spinnaker guyman		Brings pole only 2 feet aft of the headstay (boat will stay high to maximize apparent wind).		Once apparent wind has been established, coordinates with helmsman on bearing away and grinding pole aft.
Halyard man	Presets boom vang. Sets inboard end of pole.		Hoists chute as quickly as possible after rounding (generally when boat is sailing on her lines instead of heeled).	Douses headsail as quickly as possible, even before chute has been filled completely, then goes to assist foredeck man to gather in headsail.
Spinnaker sheet			Fills chute as quickly as possible. (May or may not need grinder, depending on size of boat.)	

Bear-away Set	1	2	3	4
Bowman	Has staysail ready. Hooks up spinnaker—guy, sheet, and fore-guy. Helps lift pole end.		Feeds spinnaker during hoist.	Gathers jib and makes it secure on deck. Halyard off the jib and on staysail, feeds up staysail during hoist. Clears for jibe. Helps adjust inboard end of spinnaker pole.

The tack set and the jibe are mere variations on the standard bear-away. Actually, it's best to avoid them both, as they can hamper speed, but if you're sailing in a tight situation, it's important to learn their subtleties.

The tack set means that your approach, if the mark is to be taken to port, is from the port side, necessitating a tack around the mark. The afterguard has key function. They must not call for the chute to be raised until the boat is well beyond the mark and sailing on her lines. (Obviously, then a tack set can sacrifice speed.) If the chute is raised too soon after the tack, there is a good chance the boat will be heeled excessively and the chute will be raised while dragging in the water, which can blow it out.

For a jibe set, there are two important functions. The mainsail trimmer has to ease the main completely after the mark has been rounded, in order to assist the boat in bearing off. Once the boat is dead off the wind, the mainsail has to be prejibed just as the chute is being hoisted. Also, so that the pole and topping lift don't tangle with the headsail and headsail sheets, the genoa must be placed completely on the new lee side as soon as possible. Then, as soon as the boat has been jibed, the halyard man can raise the topping lift, the guy trimmer can place the pole two feet aft of the head-stay to optimize apparent wind, and the usual spinnaker setting procedure can commence.

JIBING

Notes on the reach-to-reach jibe. The only way successfully to execute a jibe from one reach to another in big boat sailing is with the common dip pole jibe. Again, the helmsman plays a key role. He must steer the boat from one reach to another in one continuous, smooth motion within about three boat lengths. Each successive move by the rest of the crew is determined by the helm. For instance, as the helmsman begins to bear off, the guy trimmer gradually brings the pole aft as the boat approaches dead downwind. At the same time, the sheet is being eased, but not enough to send the leeward clew to the opposite side of the forestay, increasing the chance of spinnaker snarl. After the pole has been made on the new jibe, the old guy/new sheet trimmer has to continue trimming the sail up to a reach, the new guy/old sheet trimmer has to lock the guy at a position two feet aft of the forestay. The helmsman, again, steers up to that setting to keep the apparent wind far enough forward.

	1	2	3	4
Helmsman	Steering critical. Bears away, making one continuous motion from one reach to another. Uses 3 boat lengths for maneuver.			Steers up to course based on position of pole to maximize apparent wind, then slowly bears off in coordination with trimmers.
Mainsail trimmer	Eases mainsail rapidly through jibe to help boat around.			
Guy trimmer	Grinds pole aft (foreguy eased) as boat bears off until pole is 90 degrees to boat. (Uses primary winch. Boat is then dead off wind and actual sequence begins.		New guy trimmer makes guy fast 2 feet aft of head-stay.	
Old spinnaker sheet trimmer	Eases sheet to correspond with guy trim. Makes sure old leeward clew remains on old leeward side of forestay, preventing chute wrap. Becomes new guy trimmer.		New sheet trimmer continues to trim new sheet after pole has been jibed.	
Halyard man		Trips pole end fitting at command of pulpit, foredeck man. Lowers topping lift to pulpit/foredeck man.	Raises and secures topping lift.	

	1	2	3	4
Bowman	Removes staysail. Clears spare halyards. Takes lazy guy forward.	Gives mastman command to trip pole when boat is dead off the wind and pole is square. Makes new guy connection.	Uses only enough slack in the new guy to make connection. Places new guy in jaw. Makes sure lazy sheet is over pole.	Hoists staysail. Clears jib sheet over pole.

The crew of 5856 would be better off hiking over the rail as are their rivals on 5773. *Photograph by Carol Singer*

SPINNAKER DOUSE

Notes on the spinnaker douse: There are actually three spinnaker dousing techniques, each with its own particular flourish.

The advantage of the "forward" takedown is that it is most effective when the boat is approaching the leeward mark on a reach—reaching into the mark is the fastest way to sail the rounding. Also, because the forward takedown does not require the foredeck man to handle sheets, only the sail itself, the chances that he can lose a sheet and have the chute trail off to leeward are minimized. There are two critical points to the forward takedown. The halyard man has to lower the pole two feet off the deck so that the foredeck man can reach under the headsail and gather in the sail by its foot. In addition, the halyard man has to control the descent of the chute so that it doesn't go into the water.

The leeward douse can be used successfully if the boat is sailing more on a run than a reach. Of course, this is the more customary takedown, and the only caution is to make sure the chute is being gathered into the middle of the boat, away from shrouds and other gear.

The "floater" takedown is used when the boat is on a starboard jibe and must leave the mark to port, necessitating a jibe during the takedown. The key is to stow the pole as soon as possible, free-fly the chute (which may mean keeping the mainsail trimmed amidships to keep the chute full), and then have the foredeck man execute a forward or leeward takedown as soon as the boat is jibed and the mark rounding has begun.

Floater Douse	1	2	3	4
Foredeck man	Directs hoisting for proper headsail. Removes spinnaker pole early.		At jibe for rounding, has option of doing forward or leeward takedown.	
Guyman		Free-flies chute.		
Spinnaker sheer trimmer		Free-flies chute.		
Mainsail trimmer		Keeps mainsail amidships to help keep chute full.		Slightly overtrims main to help boat round mark.
Headsail trimmer				Lags jib to help boat round mark.
Helmsman				Rounds up, using 2-boat-length radius around mark.

Forward Douse	1	2	3	4
Helmsman	Approaches leeward mark on a reach to maintain speed as long as possible.			Rounds up, using a 2-boat-length radius around mark.
Foredeck man	Directs hoisting for headsail wanted on next leg. (Headsail is left partially luffing.)		Begins to gather chute in from middle to foot close to guy.	
Halyard man		Lowers topping lift so pole rests 2 feet from the deck against the headstay.	Lowers chute, keeping it out of water.	
Headsail trimmer		Slowly begins trimming.		Lags jib, helping boat round to weather.
Spinnaker sheet trimmer			Eases sheet completely. Assists foredeck man gathering chute.	
Mainsail trimmer				Slightly overtrims main to help boat round up.

Leeward Douse	1	2	3	4
Foredeck man	Directs hoisting for headsail wanted on next leg.		Gathers sail to middle of the boat, keeping sail away from shrouds.	
Spinnaker sheetman	Trims spinnaker sheet so foredeck man can reach it.			
Guy trimmer		Pops guy.		

	1	2	3	4
Halyard man			Releases spinnaker halyard, keeping spinnaker out of water. (Spinnaker has to be down before boat begins rounding.) Coordinates with mainsail trimmer to take up Cunningham, babystay, flattening reef.	
Headsail trimmer			Lags jib, helping boat round mark.	
Mainsail trimmer			Slightly overtrims main to help boat round up.	
Helmsman			Rounds up, using 2-boat-length radius around mark.	

After Sailing

1. Afterguard
   a. review race
   b. check on finishing times and results
   c. check in with race committee
   d. review broken equipment and assign people to fix
   e. clean up cockpit area
   f. shut down electronics
   g. remove personal gear
2. Sail trimmers
   a. flake, coil, and stow all sheets, guys, blocks, and winch handles
   b. repair torn sails
   c. dry out wet sails
   d. clean up tailing areas
   e. stow personal gear
3. Grinders
   a. fold and stow sails
   b. check and dry bilges
   c. assist repair of broken equipment
   d. check and service winches
   e. remove personal gear
4. Mastman
   a. helps fold and stow sails
   b. checks spar rigging, spreader, sheaves, and halyards
   c. removes personal gear
5. Bowman
   a. stows all halyards forward
   b. cleans up bow area
   c. helps fold and stow sails
   d. removes personal gear

THE CREW ON DECK

There is no perfect deck layout. Sailors change fittings, leads, halyards, winches, and blocks constantly. It is natural to want to improve a boat. When a new boat arrives, generally new gear is added onto the deck at a fast pace, but we believe that real progress is not made until you begin subtracting equipment from your boat.

Creating a deck layout is easy if you base your design on experience. During the development of the deck layout on *Defender*, several of our crew members traveled to Barrington, Rhode Island, where a number of the world's best 12-Meters were stored. We pulled back the covers on *Courageous, Freedom, Clipper, France,* and a number of older designs to study the different deck layouts. We believed that the best layout would allow the crews to have easy communication between the helmsman and trimmers, good visibility from the cockpit, standing weight in the optimum position, require the minimum amount of movement about the deck, and keep windage at a minimum. Our crew sat in the cockpit of *Clipper* and *Courageous* for a full day, making notes with designer David Pedrick on the possibilities.

Defender did have several good innovations in her deck layout, many of which were fine-tuned during the campaign. Perhaps the best innovation was what we called the "shuttle launcher." This device allowed jib leads to be moved easily on every tack fore and aft, and inboard. The "shuttle launcher" took a great deal of engineering and time, but Ken Keefe mastered the problems, and it worked flawlessly.

To sail your boat well, you can either learn to sail the boat by adapting to the existing deck layout or by adapting the boat to your style (See Figure 17). For some sailors it is more challenging to adapt to different boats, while others continually tinker with new ideas and never seem to settle down. A good starting point is to use the same layout the top sailors are already using and then adapt to your size. For example, in the Penguin class, which has a minimum weight of 275 pounds for two people, many adults sail with young children. These boats are set up so the skipper can make all adjustments to the mast tweeker, outhaul, Cunningham, and centerboard. Therefore, the crew simply helps with ballast and bailing.

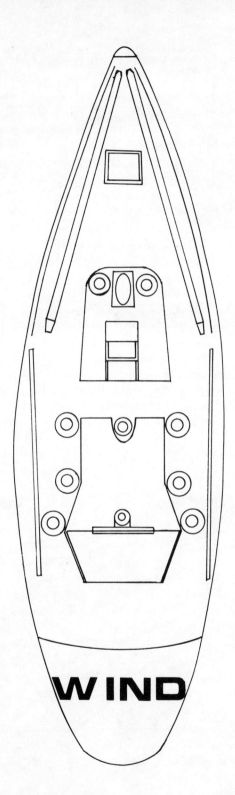

As tactician on *Defender*, Gary found himself continually calling for an ease or trim of the Cunningham, since he was in the best position to see it. Unfortunately, his hailing disturbed the crew between him and the mast. One morning he arrived at the boat and the Cunningham had been rerigged through the deck and exited right by the tactician's station so he could adjust it at will.

Dennis Conner felt it was so important as helmsman to communicate with his sail trimmers that he put his tactician and navigator behind his wheels so he could be closer to the trimming action.

Keeping the crew happy is essential on any sailboat. Several years back, Gary was racing on the 6-Meter *Ranger*, designed by Gary Mull. The crew sat belowdecks, even below the waterline, and had no visibility during the race. To make the crew happy, Mull designed into the hull two windows so the crew could peer out at the competition.

It seems the best boats to sail on are not only fast but also offer good food and have comfortable bunks. A rested crew is an effective crew. A crew that is wet, cold, hungry, and tired will not sail well. Belowdecks every crew member should have a dry place for his own gear, a bunk with plenty of foam that stays dry and remains quiet from deck noise, and have good meals available. Sailing to Bermuda on peanut butter and jelly is not the way to win sailboat races.

Bunks belowdecks should be installed

Figure 17: This clean deck layout will help the crew and encourage adjustments because there is plenty of room to work between winch stations and the helm.

THE CREW ON DECK

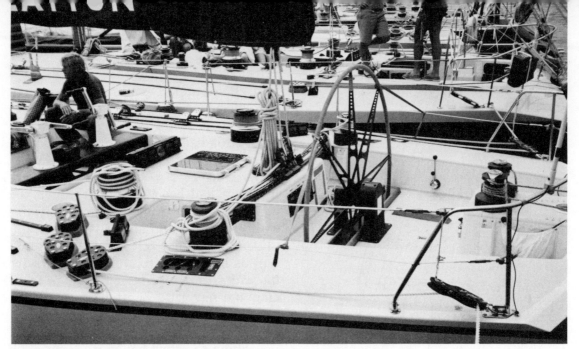

Jubilation deck layout: The layout is made so the helmsman, main trimmer, and jib trimmer are all together. Next to the mainsheet winch are the hydraulic controls for the vang, flat reef, and running backstays. The jib tailer's cockpit is small, but it allows him to keep his weight low and get the proper leverage in pulling the sheet off the grinder drum. *Photograph by Mike Toppa*

Morning Star deck layout: In an attempt to get more weight in the center of the boat, the steering wheel has been moved forward in front of the mainsheet station. The runners are set as close to center line as possible so they pull straight aft and not sideways, which they would do if they were set out on the transom's corner. *Photograph by Mike Toppa*

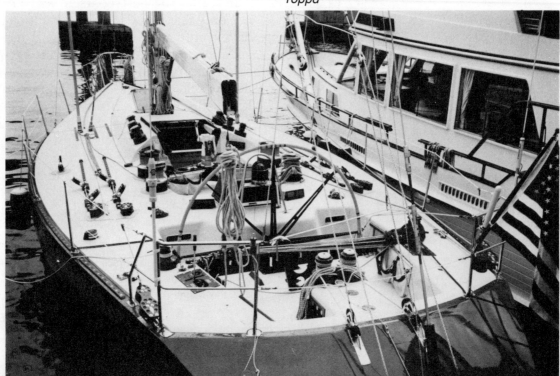

Retaliation deck layout: The large diameter wheel allows the helmsman to sit far outboard for better visibility of the genoa luff and waves. To reduce weight in the ends, the transom has been cut out and the backstay winch superstructure has been drilled out to the bare minimum. *Photograph by Mike Toppa*

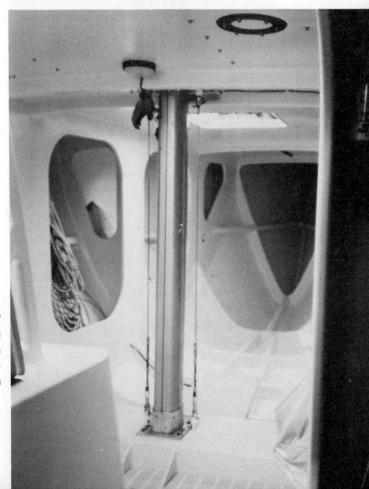

Brooke Ann belowdeck: The interior of this boat had all the corners and sharp edges of the joining work rounded off to make life below safer in rough weather. The cabin sole area was left uncluttered to allow the off watch to flake sails down below. *Photograph by Mike Toppa*

in the same position the crew is expected to sit on deck so the off watch is always keeping their weight in the same position on the boat.

On deck, try to have a backup for every system. If a winch, cam cleat, or block fails, have another way of using the sheet or line as a backup.

Teamwork in the Afterguard

The helmsman and the tactician must work together as a team to keep a boat

Figure 18: The helmsman and tactician must work together as a team to keep the boat sailing fast and going in the right direction. Collective wisdom of two people together is more effective than a single person calling all the shots.

sailing fast and going in the right places (See Figure 18). Continuous communication between them makes the difference between winning and losing.

While the helmsman steers and concentrates on speed, the tactician studies the wind, the competition, and boat speed. Both continually discuss performance. Often the helmsman is also the skipper and therefore the final authority, but the best decisions usually are made after discussing the available options. It should be agreed before the race what decisions will be made by whom, and a general game plan should be prepared and followed. After the race the plan should be evaluated and suggestions made for improving it for the next race.

The tactician should have a checklist in mind for every possible situation. He should be able to anticipate maneuvers and warn the helmsman well in advance in a calm and positive voice. But when a split-second decision has to be made, only one person can make it—the helmsman. Both tactician and helmsman should know that no one aboard should ever stop halfway through a maneuver. Always follow through once the decision is made to make a change in course or tactics. On larger boats, where different crew members rotate on the helm, a second person should always take the role of tactician. The duo complement each other much like a pilot who flies and a copilot who navigates and looks for traffic.

A tactician should be distinguished from a navigator but may be the same person. The tactician works on the local situation at the time—the next puff, the upcoming crossing situation, the inevitable luffing match developing, the deck preparation for the spinnaker set, or the next sail to be used. A navigator keeps track of the boat's position, the changing weather patterns, the apparent wind direction and velocity on the next leg of the course, and he continually updates your general game plan (long-range strategy).

The tactician has much to think about, and it is helpful to make notes. On *Defender* Gary used a grease pencil and made notes right on the deck to remind him of such things as compass course, the wind direction, or relative bearings on the competition. The tactician should watch the wind constantly and make notes. What is the course on each tack or jibe? Are patterns changing? Does the wind go light under the clouds? Are you heading more directly into the waves on port tack than on starboard, and therefore should the traveler be lower on port tack, or the sails fuller?

The tactician should also keep the crew updated on the boat's performance compared with the competition's. He should anticipate what sails may be set next and let the crew know what is coming so they are ready to change gears; for instance, he can let the sail trimmers know if the boat needs more speed (ease the sails) to drive over a competitor or to power through a chop.

The order of priority for the crew should always be sail trim and boat speed first, setting new sails second, and minor adjustments third. Part of the job of tactician also is to be tactful. In a way, a tactician is a coach psyching up the crew with enthusiasm, encouragement, and ideas on making the boat sail better.

If it is convenient, he should get a consensus from the rest of the crew before calling for a turn or a sail change, thereby making the crew part of the tactical action by soliciting their advice, asking others to watch the wind and look for the next mark or to let him know when another boat may have tacked. It will make his job easier, and other crew members will feel more a key part of the result.

While sail trimmers might be mesmerized by the sail, the tactician must be alert for a change in gear because he has been observing every pertinent detail. The tactician spends 70 percent of his time looking outside the boat. Brief the crew on your course with the chart and your weather forecasts so everyone on the boat has a clear understanding of what is going to happen in the race. It is also helpful and soothing to the crew to give a rough idea of what your tactics and options are. The larger the boat, the more time needed for a decision. On the maxi yacht *Condor*, any time a sail change was called for, we automatically waited five minutes before making the change just to confirm that our decision was correct.

Author Roger Vaughn, in his book *Ted Turner: The Man Behind the Mouth*, describes the relationship between the tactician and the helmsman in a very special way.

The Tactician is of critical importance on a 12-meter because to be successful, helmsman and tactician must function as one. Basically the helmsman steers and maneuvers the boat while the tactician literally calls the turns by evaluating his boat's position on the course relative to the competition and the weather.

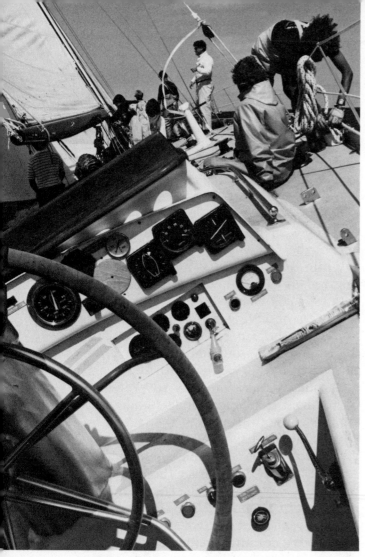

Crews should stay low so that the helmsman has as clear a view of the oncoming waves as he does of his instrument panel. *Photograph by Carol Singer*

The steering of the 12-meter is so demanding that if the helmsman were to continually take his eyes and attention off the boat long enough to make such evaluations, it would quickly cost sufficiently in boat speed and direction to lose the race. The tactician then becomes not only an extension of the helmsman's eyes but of his judgement as well, which is damn tricky business.

Because proper utilization of the tactician demands such ultimate confidence from a helmsman, who is usually the skipper, the combination most often falls far short of its goals. The problem is further complicated by the fact that the tactician must be a top ranking skipper in his own rights. He must have the experience and confidence to call the turns and it is against human nature for such a person not to harbor notions that he could be running and steering the ship better. So into the small cockpit of the 12-meter are placed two very competitive men with egos even larger than the outrageous lump of silver each of their accumulated sailing trophies would produce in a boundary and fragile as egg shells besides. Each of them is then supposed to give out a very delicate and precious piece of his soul to the other for the duration of this strange marriage at sea. The tactician bows and offers up his self image as number one. The skipper returns the bow, accepts the gift and vows to trust the tactician as much as he trusts himself. Mission impossible begins. Off they are supposed to glide like skate dancers, moving flawlessly together, smiling convincingly, like a brilliant doubles team in tennis covering instinctively for one another. Like a soloist and accompanist, the latter mostly following but ready to provide the lead at any time, blessed with an uncanny sense of where his prima donna is going, filling hesitations with such skill and subtlety that even the critics might not catch them.

In short the tactician must be extraordinarily able, supremely confident and practically incapable of being ruffled. In addition to the textbook job description, the peculiarities of each skipper places more abstract demands on the tactician. Aside from having his own head screwed on straight anyone taking on the job should have a degree in psychology as a prerequisite.

With a spirit of cooperation, a helmsman and a tactician working as a partnership will greatly increase the chances of winning and making racing more fun for all.

Figure 19: The sail trimmer and the winch grinder have to communicate to anticipate every change in the wind causing a change in sail trim.

The Trimmer-Grinder Duo

Aboard *Tenacious*, the spinnaker trimmer gives commands with a simple whistle, and the grinder responds depending on the whistle's shrillness. It's an effective system (although one of our competitors once tried to foil our signaling technique by blowing whistles of his own), and it helps to augment the coordination between the tailer and the grinder. The duo are partners, and much like a football running back and his blockers, they require cooperation to achieve success (See Figure 19).

The grinder need not be the strongest person on the boat. In fact, speed and endurance are the keys to grinding, not necessarily strength. Here are some pointers: Keep your winch handle path clear of all obstructions—lifelines, crew, and other sheets. Complete revolutions of the winch handle are preferable to back-and-forth motions because you are able to trim more line at a faster rate. Stand up to grind, keeping your arms rotating below your chest. This gives you the most power. Stand wide of the winch, allowing your tailer to have a clear view of the sail. It also helps to stand facing to windward. Keep your legs spread about four feet apart to distribute your weight for better balance. Always use both hands when grinding; two-handed cranks are best (lubricate your winch handles so they will spin easier). The longer the winch handle, the more power you will have; the shorter the handle, the more turning speed you'll be able to generate. Ball-bearing winch handles are the latest high-speed trimming craze.

Making adjustments at the end of the pole, as does this crew member on *Tenacious*, is preferable to bringing the pole to the deck. *Photograph by Carol Singer*

SERVICING YOUR WINCH

To keep winches working at the best efficiency it is important to service your winch periodically. The biggest culprit is salt. For this reason, winches should be washed with fresh water periodically. Sand, dirt, and salt are the chief factors cutting the efficiency of a winch. Winches should be broken down and checked once each season. Tear the winch down and clean with fresh water. Every winch can be supplied with a maintenance and service manual. If you do not have one, these are available through Barient. The drum should be taken off monthly and oil squirted on the pawls.

It is important not to use synthetic lubricants. There are no magic greases to use. Synthetic lubricants often conduct electricity, causing electrolysis between dissimilar metals such as bronze, stainless, and aluminum, causing a drum to seize. Winches need servicing like any mechanical machinery.

When you take your winch apart, look for salt deposits on the bearings. These should be cleaned carefully if salt is present. Crank the winch in both directions and check to see that everything is rotating free and smooth while the drum is off. Oil the pawl areas. *Do not grease pawls*—this slows down the winch operation. Clean and then regrease the drum bearings. You should clean with fuel oil or kerosene and wipe off before regreasing.

If your winch is not working, pawls are usually the biggest problem. Clean the pawl pockets and the gears. By looking after your winches you will keep them operating smoothly, making your sailing more enjoyable.

The efficiency of a winch is dramatically improved after servicing.

—courtesy of Barient, Inc.

The tailer always faces both the winch and the sail being trimmed. He must give the grinder room to turn the handle. Verbalize your instructions when tailing so the grinder knows what you are doing.

"I'm trimming the jib four inches." By putting your commands into exact terms (feet and inches), your actions will be easier to deal with. Keep your ear pointing toward and tuned into the helmsman. Use as few wraps of your sheet on the winch drum as possible. For normal trimming, four turns should do it. Wearing gloves will save your hands and give you a better grip on the sheet.

Anticipate tacks by clearing the sheet so it is free to run. As the boat rounds into the wind, the old tailer trims the jib in to force the boat to luff into the wind—keeping the sails full as long as possible helps to maintain your boat speed. Reduce the wraps on your winch on the old leeward side to a bare minimum just before you cast off; three wraps will do it on most boats, four on larger boats in heavy air. Use line that is roughed up slightly for better adhesion to the winch drum. New line tends to be slippery because of oils used in manufacturing. One method of roughing a line up is simply to drag it overboard for a mile. Be careful not to drag it for too long or it will begin to fray excessively.

The old tailer should ease the sail out quickly, but with a steady action. Work the turns off the winch by feeding it out and lifting the turns off the drum one at a time. Lifting the tail straight up off the drum will cause the line to form a corkscrew, which often gets trapped in the blocks.

To help the nose of the boat through the wind during a tack, cast off the sheet when two thirds of the jib is backed in light winds (three to eight knots); cast off after one third of the sail backs in medium winds (nine to 14 knots) and just after the sail begins to back in heavy winds (15 knots and up).

To avoid overrides while trimming the new sheet, keep the tail exiting off the drum just below the top of the winch drum and well above the other turns on the drum. As the drum turns, the wraps of the sheet work naturally down to the bottom of the drum.

Some tips: The tailer should make long, hard trims on the sheet. You gather more line with fewer long trims than with many short trims.

Have a spare short sheet ready in case of an override. Clip the short sheet on the clew of the sail and use it to trim the sail onto another winch.

Stow your winch handles within easy reach of both tailer and grinder. Have the handle facing forward so it can be pulled out of its rack easily.

Remember that the best exercise for trimming and grinding is simply trimming and grinding. The pair who do this, like no other pair on the boat, feels the real power in the sails.

The Mast-Bow Partnership

The fraternity among bowmen is a special order on sailboats. After all, not everyone enjoys working on the bow, where it's wet, cold, and confusing. But the often unwholesome conditions encountered in bowwork require special skills—strength, quickness, and agility (See Figure 20).

To run the bow of a modern offshore racer effectively requires a partnership between the man in the peak—the foredeck man—and the man at the mast, who has to sort out all the halyards, hoist, douse, gather, generally stay aware of the boat's maneuvers, and also pass along information from the cockpit to the bow. A solid relationship between these two vital functionaries contributes to overall teamwork, and the key to success is communication-coordination; anticipation, and a step-by-step approach when the going gets rough are also essential.

Although every racing boat has a slightly different layout from which the mastman and bowman operate, certain universal areas of cooperation can add a lot to the overall performance of the boats.

Taken individually, the tasks these two perform are essential to efficient boat handling when racing. The bowman, for instance, has to stay as far forward as is practical during a start to observe approaching boats and to gauge distance from the line. He then relays his information back to the cockpit. Going upwind, he has to direct headsail changes and plan upcoming moves. The bowman must also keep lazy sheets and guys orderly, hook up the chute (as far forward as possible so it won't interfere with the operation of the working sails), and direct the bow during jibes. A host of duties require the bowman's special mental and physical presence.

Many of those duties couldn't be performed if it were not for the cooperation of the mastman—keeping halyards ready for hoisting, flaking, gathering, and clearing and coiling line. Specifically, a mastman should also tend to proper

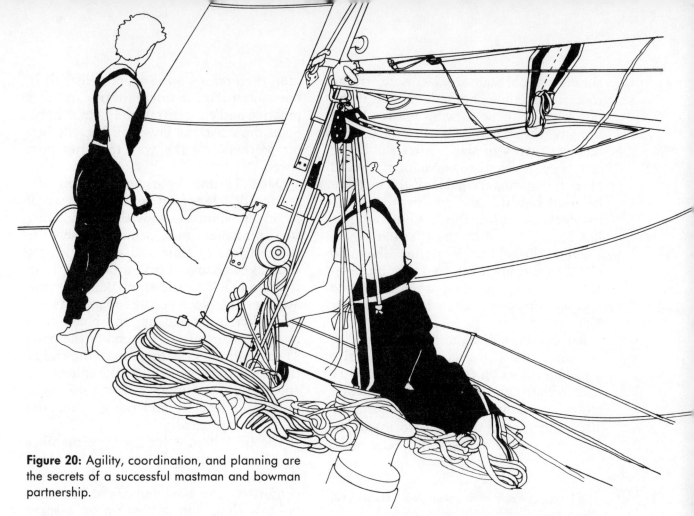

Figure 20: Agility, coordination, and planning are the secrets of a successful mastman and bowman partnership.

Cunningham and outhaul adjustment during all tacks and halyard tension, getting sheets ready for any auxiliary off-wind staysails and packing the chute.

There are many areas where these two roles converge and where cooperation should prevail. Imagine the usual hassles associated with raising a big, heavy spinnaker pole just before a bear-away set at a top mark. The topping lift has been attached, the mastman is standing by ready to hoist. The bowman has attached the guy in the jaws. Everything is set. So the bowman steps aft, the mastman hoists, and the outboard end of the pole

gets snagged on a stemhead fitting or comes up inside the bow pulpit. An extra minute taken to work together might have prevented this kind of minor annoyance; aggravations can multiply and rob a boat of her speed.

There are other examples of the mast-bow partnership. Communicating before a spinnaker set on the kind of sail required for a certain leg or condition is the most important. Also, the partners should question how the set will be done, which halyards are going to be used, which winch, etc. During the setup, the mastman and the bowman should watch each other closely, trying to anticipate one another's moves. If the bowman has gone forward to attach the foreguy, the mastman should make sure he's got plenty of slack. After the chute has been hoisted, the mastman should cleat the spinnaker halyard, uncleat the headsail halyard, and go directly to the foredeck to gather the headsail after it has been released by the trimmer.

After the chute is flying, the two should get ready for the next evolution—the mastman cleaning up around the spar and preparing sheets for a staysail or blooper.

Perhaps jibes demand the most precise coordination. The success of the entire procedure rests on the mastman's ability to trip the outboard end of the pole and simultaneously to ease off the topping lift, allowing the bowman to make the new guy on the opposite jibe. The mast-

The foredeck crew must act as lookouts as well.
Photograph by Carol Singer

man then rehoists the topping lift, all in one smooth, mechanical routine. It takes practice and concentration to get it right. Soon the mast and bow will become better partners, on the way to better boat speed.

Dana Timmer, our bowman on *Defender*, developed an innovative way of changing spinnakers without lowering the spinnaker pole, which causes the greatest loss of time and speed during a spinnaker change. Dana attaches a snap shackle block to the spinnaker tack and attaches the block to the foreguy. As the spinnaker is hauled up, the block rises up on the foreguy to the end of the pole. Then he climbs the foreguy to the end of the pole, trips away the old spinnaker, and the new spinnaker now rides right up to this foreguy and the guy and the sheet are attached.

The trick here is for the crew member to go out to the pole instead of dipping the pole to the deck. In rough weather conditions the bowman should be in a bosun's chair and hauled up on a spare genoa halyard to the end of the pole.

In testing on the 12-Meters we repeatedly found we could lose one boat length less distance when using this method. While making the change it is helpful to keep the sail with as much wind in it as possible by sailing on a reach.

It is best to change spinnakers in puffs and in clear air to minimize the distance lost.

During a heavy-air takedown, lower the pole and the halyard to get the pole down easier so the foredeck man can trip the spinnaker away, and the massive grinding operation to get the pole down via the foreguy is eliminated.

PART THREE

The Power Plant: Spars, Sails, and Electronics

6

BEFORE THE MAST

In general, the purpose of the mast is to support the sails aloft and to aid their shape adjustment. To do this it has to have the proper hardware to hoist the sails with minimum friction and be able to change shape and bend so the crew can vary the mainsail depth for different conditions. In theory, the performance mast should be small and aerodynamically shaped to minimize turbulence between the wind flow and the sail and also be light in weight, with a low center of gravity. But the aerodynamic benefits of a small mast may be overcome by the windage of extra rigging.

In practice, there have been masts designed which have been very small, but they needed extraordinary amounts of rigging. Such masts rely on multiple spreaders with normal diagonal and vertical rigging plus another set of shrouds that go from the inboard end of the lower spreader to the outboard tip of the upper spreader (See Figure 21). These masts also rely on swept-back spreaders put under static load from the multitide of shrouds. The idea behind the spreader sweep is to eliminate the need for ba-

bystays and running backstays. The drawback to this is that the spreader sweep-back prevents the main from being fully extended.

On the other side of the spectrum are the relatively new unstayed masts. These are big enough in diameter and strong enough (usually made of carbon fiber) to support themselves without shrouds, stays, or spreaders. Of course, eliminating the stays eliminates the ability to control mast bend while sailing.

Fortunately, mast builders have worked hard to design masts that are small, light, and perform well. In doing this they have been helped by advancements in technology that have produced lightweight, strong aluminum alloys and low-stretch rod-rigging. These new metals are used in composite building methods that take a lightweight extrusion and add internal stiffeners where the loads are greatest in the mast and produce high-performance racing spars.

Any boat can have a custom spar designed for it that contains all the latest high-tech components and features. Many top-of-the-line production boats now have mast options available. But most smaller

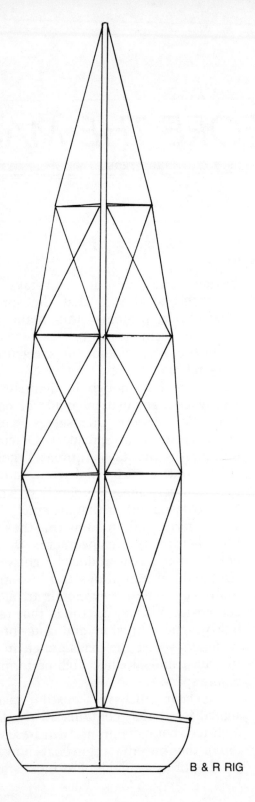

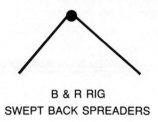

B & R RIG
SWEPT BACK SPREADERS

stock boats offer only a standard, production mast. These cruiser/racer boats usually come equipped with spars that are great for the cruising buyer but somewhat overbuilt for the person who wants the boat primarily for racing. However, things can be done to streamline a stock mast so it will perform better.

The two most important considerations in choosing a mast are weight and windage. Wherever you can eliminate weight in the form of unnecessary fittings you'll be lowering the center of gravity of the mast, which will help produce pitching in waves and make the boat go faster. And naturally, if you can take something off the mast, you'll be reducing windage.

Over the winter or when the boat's going through an overhaul, take the mast out and inspect it carefully for unnecessary items. Starting from the top, look at the sheave boxes for the halyards. Maybe the extra sheave for the spare halyard you never use can be taken out. On the aft side of the mast, look to see if the sail track extends above the black band. If it's an external track, you can cut this unused portion off.

B & R RIG

Going down the mast, look for a steaming light, which is supplied on many masts. In most states these aren't required on inland waters. This can be removed to eliminate windage and save the leech from catching it during a tack. Take a close look at the spinnaker pole track. Try to remember how much of the track you actually use. You may be able to shorten the track or remove it altogether and replace it with two or three spinnaker pole eyes.

You can further reduce windage by fairing in the existing fittings with Bondo or any similar body filler. Spreader bases, topping lift exits, and halyard sheave boxes all can be covered with Bondo and then smoothed down to fair them into the mast face.

Also check the halyard winches and cleats. On many stock boats, these are on the mast and become prime targets for jib sheets and leech lines to catch during a tack. If you have the room, relocate the winches from the mast to the deck, where they can be used more easily by someone standing in the hatch. Now, during sail changes, you'll have a pitman standing low instead of a mastman on deck obstructing your view as you round the mark.

Mast Tuning

When your mainsail is designed at the sail loft, much care is taken to calculate the exact amounts of broadseaming and luff curve so you get a sail that sets properly and is easy to trim. The broadseaming is applied to every seam and is matched and balanced by the luff curve in the front of the sail. All things being equal, you should get a smooth, fast sail, except when the sail is set on a mast that's improperly tuned. A mast out of tune can make your perfectly shaped mainsail look horrendous and take away from the boat's performance. But before you go running to your sailmaker to have him recut the main, take a close look at the mast to see how it might better be set up so the mast and main act in harmony.

There are no mysteries or hidden secrets to proper mast tune. Simply, the free-standing spar is supported by the shrouds and spreaders, which control the athwartships or lateral movement of the mast, and the stays (back-, head-, baby-, and running backstays), which control fore and aft movement. Fore and aft control and bend can be set up to change the mainsail shape for different conditions through use of adjustable backstays and babystays. Lateral bend and movement cannot be adjusted during racing according to the racing rules, so it is important that this aspect of mast tune be adjusted properly before leaving shore and that the mast remains the same for all sailing conditions.

The amount of lateral bend depends on whether you have a masthead or a fractional-rig boat. The top section of the fractional-rig mast above the hounds (where the headstay intersects the mast) is unsupported, so there will always be some sort of tip falloff. The masts are designed to bend to leeward in heavier winds to allow the top of the main to twist off, thus reducing weather helm and overpowering. Larger fractional-rig boats have jumper struts and an independent set of stays attached to them for exact control of the upper section. Most 12-Meters have hydraulic cylinders in the jumpers that tighten and ease the jumper stays. When the air is light, the cylinders are pumped out to stiffen the mast tip and to keep it straight. As the wind increases, the cylinders are eased in, slackening the jumper stays and allowing the tip to fall off and induce main twist. The loss by *Liberty* in the fifth race of the 1983 America's Cup was attributed to the failure of their hydraulic jumper system.

With a masthead-rig boat, lateral bend can cause problems because it's harder to control and affects more than just the leech of the main (See Figure 22). First of all, when the tip of the masthead rig mast falls to leeward, the headstay also will fall off. Not only does this rapidly decrease headstay tension and increase sag, but it also puts the center of effort of the sail plan to leeward, increasing weather helm. Most boats have more than enough helm in heavy air conditions, so adding to this would only hurt the speed. Lateral bend can also be dangerous to the integrity of the spar. The design of the mast and its ability to withstand high loads in rough weather rely on the stretch characteristics of the rigging and the angle at which the rigging intersects the mast. If the spar were to bend sideways, the angle of the upper shroud to the mast would get smaller. The smaller the angle of intersection, the more support is needed from the shroud. So the strength required to support the mast that is bending laterally increases rapidly. The shrouds begin to

stretch more, which adds to more bend. A still smaller intersection angle will cause more stretch, and so on. The ultimate result is an out-of-column spar and eventual failure.

Whether you have a fractional or a masthead boat, the mast has to be straight laterally to the hounds. You need to get the mast lined up along the center line of the boat and adjust the rigging so the entire mast stays in column

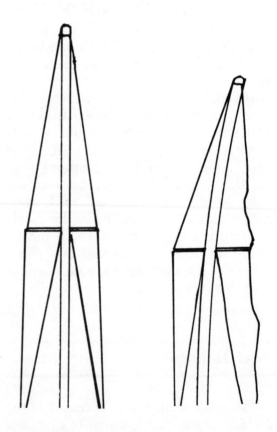

Figure 22: Lateral mast bend makes it difficult to control the leech of the mainsail and headstay sag.

when under load. To accomplish retuning of the mast, start at the bottom.

To begin, make sure your mast is centered in the boat. Measure the distance from the mast to the gunwale at the mast partners using a zero stretch steel tape measure. Believe it or not, we've seen stock boats come from the factory with the mast slot in the deck off center by as much as two inches. Once the mast is centered in the partners, wedge in some hard rubber chocks to inhibit movement.

The next step is to get the hounds centered over the mast step and partners. With the rigging fairly loose, hoist the tape measure up the main halyard (be sure to check if the halyard sheave is on the center line of the mast) and measure from the masthead to the gunwale. Adjust and tighten the rigging so the distances on both sides are equal.

Now that the mast is straight in the boat, the upper shrouds should be tightened. A good rule of thumb is to tighten the shrouds enough so the leeward shroud does not sag at 20 degrees of heel while sailing. Do this in a moderate breeze after you have done the dockside centering of the mast and have tightened the shrouds hand-tight. Start off on starboard tack and tighten the port shrouds on the leeward side. Make sure you count the number of turns you take with the turnbuckle so you can duplicate the adjustment on the other side after you tack. If you have centered the mast properly, both shrouds should come up to tension, with an equal number of turns on the turnbuckles.

The final step is to tighten the lower shrouds so the middle of the mast has the proper support and won't sag to leeward. Continue to sail on alternate tacks and tighten the lowers to eliminate any slack. Sight up the luff track to eyeball the length of the mast to make sure it's dead straight.

If you have both fore and aft lower shrouds, you need to tighten both in the same manner to get the mast from sagging at the spreaders. Having two lower shrouds enables you to influence the way the spar bends fore and aft at the lower section. If you need some prebend down low for an extra full main, tighten the forward lowers more than the aft. If you find your mast is too limber and bends too much between the spreaders and the deck, tighten the aft lower shrouds to prevent the middle of the mast from going forward.

Most smaller boats up to 30 feet have simple rigs with single spreaders, one upper shroud, and one or two sets of lowers. These boats may fall into one design category, such as the J-24, or MORC boats, where experimenting with different shroud tensions and mast positions has taken place. Check with your local fleet champion to find out his latest mast-tuning techniques. A good tool to have on board is a shroud tensiometer, which measures the actual load the shroud is under. Measure the shroud tension on the boats that are going fast and compare it against that of your boat. These devices are also handy if you trailer your boat to different regattas. When you restep your mast, you can use your tensiometer to duplicate your previous tension settings.

On larger boats with double or triple spreaders, mast tuning is somewhat more

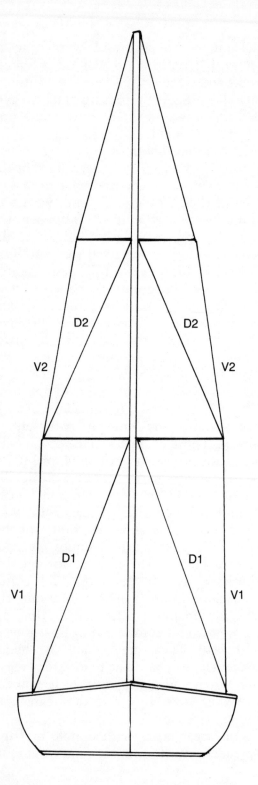

STANDARD RIG

complex because of the different intermediate shrouds between the spreaders. However, if you take the same logical approach to tuning the multiple-spreader rig as with the single-spreader mast, the result will be a perfectly straight spar.

To reduce confusion in identifying the different primary and intermediate shrouds, they have been labeled in the accompanying diagram (See Figure 23) with either the letter D or V. D is for diagonal, and V stands for vertical. They are numbered so that 1 is lower on the mast than 2. So the D1 is the shroud going from the deck to the inboard base of the spreader (the lower), and the V2 is the shroud going from the outboard end of the lower spreader to the outboard end of the second spreader.

As with the single-spreader rig, check to see that the mast is centered in the step, partners, and hounds. Once this is done, look to see that the spreaders are not drooping below perpendicular to the mast. Most spreaders are designed to be cocked above perpendicular so that the angle of intersection between the spreader and the shroud is the same on both sides of the spreader. Check with your boat dealer or the mastmaker to see which is better.

Now that the spar is straight and tensioned, adjustment has to be made to the

Figure 24

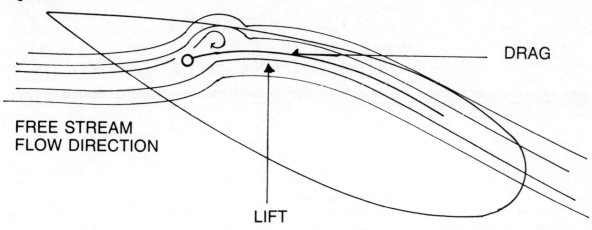

DRAG

FREE STREAM
FLOW DIRECTION

LIFT

D1's and D2's to keep the mast in column. Start with the D1's loose and gradually tighten them so the mast remains straight from the deck to the lower spreader. You'll find the final tension on the lowers will be less than on the uppers because the span you're supporting with this shroud gets extra support from the partners. However, when sailing, this area comes under tremendous compression load, so do the final adjustment when sailing in a good breeze.

The remaining shrouds needing adjustment are D2 and D3 if you have a three-spreader rig. Again, start with these shrouds loose and gradually tighten them to bring the upper spreaders in line with the top and bottom of the mast. Look carefully at the spar on one tack, consider the adjustments to make, tack over, and do them. Be careful not to put too much tension on the D2 and the D3. When this is overdone, the middle of the mast will be pulled to weather, and the tip will look like it's falling to leeward. A common mistake in this condition is to tighten the V1 to get the top back in line. But 95 percent of the time this only compounds the problem and pulls the whole mast off center. So at this stage, if the mast tip seems to be falling off to leeward but you have faith in the way you initially centered the rig, loosen the D2 and check again (See Figure 23).

7

TRIMMING THE MAIN

The fundamentals and fine-tune techniques of sail trim, from the basic straightforward Dacron mainsail to the exotic Kevlar/Mylar sails and the Mylar/Dacron composites, are all pieces of a puzzle that together make up the overall picture of sail trim technique. The boat's entire power plant must be looked at in terms of the many components that make it up and how these components interact and affect each other. For example, when you tighten the backstay to flatten the main, you change the headsail shape, and when you tighten the halyard to change the draft placement in the genoa, you affect the mainsail.

Every trim control on the boat directly affects the particular area of adjustment, and it also affects all parts of the power plant. To recognize this and to understand it is the key to understanding sail trim.

A well-made set of sails should be like putty in the hands of a good sail trimmer. They should be responsive enough to go the range from full-curving arcs to power the boat in the lightest of air, to flat, blade shapes for keeping the boat under control in heavy air. The sails should be able to do whatever you want them to do. They are the "engine" on a sailboat, they must be able to handle all speeds, and you must be able to handle them in all conditions. To do so, an understanding of technique, trim, shape, and mechanical controls is needed.

A sailboat moves through the water as a result of forces exerted upon its sails and hull. While the actual aerodynamics of all these forces and their reactions can be complex, a simplified view might be that the result of wind hitting sails is either lift or drag (See Figs. 24 and 25). Lift is the force exerted by the sail on the boat, and it acts in a direction perpendicular to the airflow. By trimming the sails correctly, you can maximize the lift and make the boat sail at top speed. Drag is the friction created by the interaction

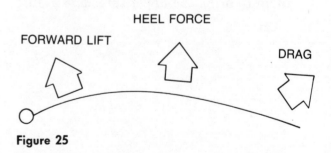

HEEL FORCE

FORWARD LIFT

DRAG

Figure 25

between the airflow and the whole sail plan, and it acts to retard a boat's speed. Let's take a close look at just how lift and drag are created and how they affect a boat's speed.

First, consider what happens when air first meets sail. Assume you're out in the middle of a bay or a lake and there's not a breath of wind. The sails are hoisted, but just hanging. The boat is just sitting there, the sun is beating down unmercifully, you're hot, and there's no wind. But then, off to the east, you see the water turning a darker color. The sea breeze is filling in, and just in time. The sails fill and the boat starts to move. You begin to feel pressure on the rudder.

What has really happened? The new wind was heading toward the sails in the form of free-flowing air, which happens to flow in parallel lines (See Figure 26). When it hit the mast, it couldn't go through it, so it was diverted to either side of the mast and along the sails. Since the sails are curved, the air on the leeward side of the sail bent around the sail until it reached the leech. The air on the windward side of the sail had little to keep it from going in its normal straight route. The leeward airstream had to travel around the arc shape of the sail and thus had to travel farther than its straight-flowing sister airstream on the weather side. To reach the leech at the same time, the leeward air was forced to travel faster.

This brings us to our first theory, formulated by the Italian physicist Giovanni Venturi: Since air is incompressible when forced into a smaller space, its velocity increases. In the case of the new air going

Figure 26

around the sail, the air is forced into a smaller space, which is bounded by the leeward side of the main and the free air-stream to leeward of it. This accelerated airflow on the leeward side of the main does more than just move faster than the air around it. It also creates a low-pressure area, illustrating Dutch physicist Daniel Benoulli's theory that the greater the velocity, the lower the pressure. It is this low pressure that actually sucks the sail to leeward.

When there isn't any wind, the broad-seaming (the curving of the edges of individual panels to produce shape) already manufactured into the sail gives it

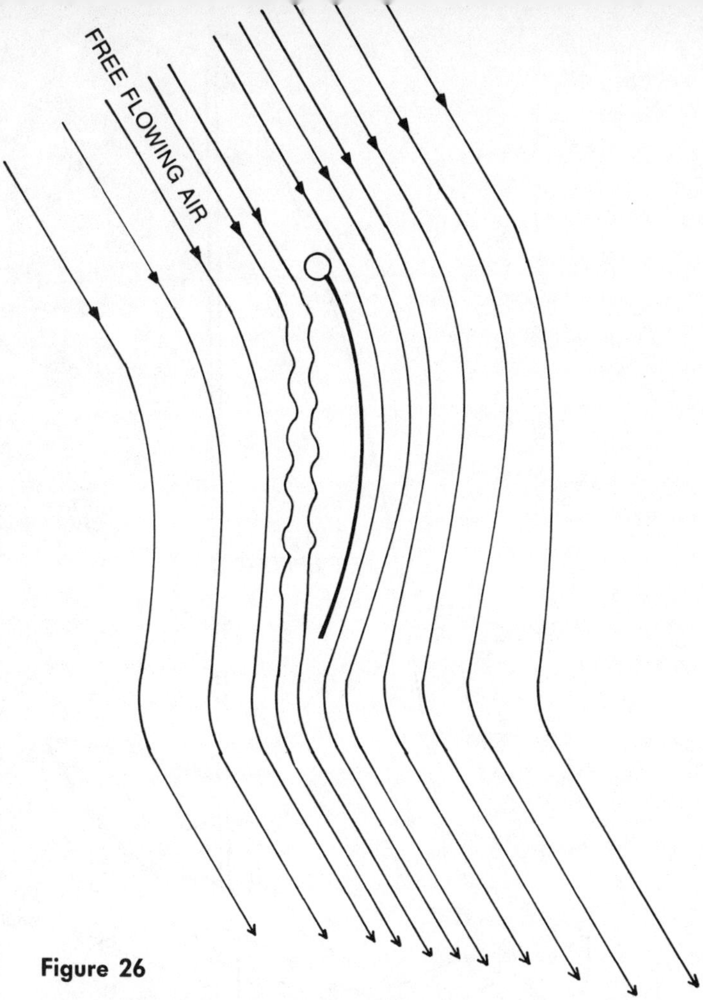

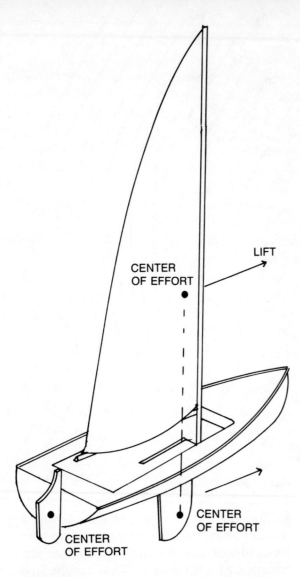

CENTER OF EFFORT

LIFT

CENTER OF EFFORT

CENTER OF EFFORT

Figure 27: The lift and drag components of boat speed formula also apply to the hull, rudder, and centerboard as well as to the sails.

On the other side of the sail the exact opposite is happening. The air is not being squeezed into a smaller space, so its speed has not increased. In fact, it has decelerated because of the general airflow, which is a clockwise circular flow around the main. The reverse of Benoulli's theory might be stated that if the air velocity is slower, then the pressure will be higher. This difference in pressure, the higher pressure on the windward side and the lower pressure on the leeward side, results in lift (See Figure 27).

While all this is going on above the water, the keel is going through the same energy-producing exercise as the water flows over it.

The keel also produces lift in the opposite direction of the sails and prevents the boat from going sideways. The resulting lift produced by the sail and the keel makes the boat go straight ahead (See Figure 28).

Consider how much attention and time are paid to trimming sails while the keel just sits under the boat doing its job. Maybe sailing technology in the future will take us to the point of having adjustable shape and depth of keel. Perhaps every boat will have an extra crewman sitting deep in the keel pushing and pulling it into the proper shape! Boats such as 12-Meters and 6-Meters already have trim tabs that change the depth of the keel to produce more energy in certain conditions. But for now, all we can do is make sure the keel is as smooth and as fair as possible.

We've looked at what happens to the mainsail when air first hits it, and the general circulation of the air currents that result. But what happens when you

enough shape to produce movement. However, you could go to the leeward side of the sail and easily push the sail with your hand. But when the wind is blowing even a little, there is enough airflow around the sail to require a good deal of pressure on the sail to push it to windward.

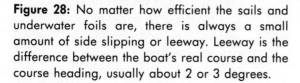

DIRECTION OF MOTION

LEEWAY ANGLE

Figure 28: No matter how efficient the sails and underwater foils are, there is always a small amount of side slipping or leeway. Leeway is the difference between the boat's real course and the course heading, usually about 2 or 3 degrees.

put the jib up in front of it? Now you've put the main in the back-wash of the jib and created a whole new aerodynamic picture. The interaction between the two sails takes place in the area between the two sails called the slot.

We know that there is a circular flow around the main that flows in a clockwise direction. The same circular flow also occurs around the jib. If you picture these two air patterns around the sails as one, you will see that they interact in an opposite way. The result is that the airflow around the jib slows the airflow around the main, especially at the leading edge and to leeward. So the air moves relatively slower through the slot, contrary to popular belief. This slower-moving air decreases the efficiency of the main by relieving the low pressure on the leeward side. If the jib is sheeted too much, it will increase this condition and reverse the whole process we just talked about. The flow on the leeward side will decrease further and increase the pressure until there is a high-pressure zone; this you see as a backwind bubble in the main.

The efficient sail that stood alone in the wind now has another sail in front of it and has been compromised. In addition to confusing the windflow pattern, the jib also slows down the apparent

wind speed, attacking the main. The main has to be sheeted at a much closer angle than the genoa. The genoa is sheeted to the tracks on the deck that are normally seven to 10 degrees from the center line, but the main is sheeted with the boom on the center line, or anywhere from zero to four degrees off it.

The mainsail's air circulation speeds up the airflow around the leeward side of the genoa, adding to its low-pressure system (See Figure 29). The easiest way to understand this is to sail with just the main alone, looking at the masthead fly or the instruments. Then take the main down, put the jib up, and do the same thing, again recording the wind data. Now sail with both sails up. You'll find you can sail at about the same angle to windward with just the main or jib up alone, but that you can sail four to five degrees closer to the wind with both sails up, working in harmonious fashion.

The sail plan is the center of effort of the boat; it's creating all the power and effort to drive the boat through the water (See Figure 30). In conjunction with this, the keel, which is creating its own lift in the opposite direction from the sails, resists their efforts to make the boat go sideways. The center of resistance is in the geometrical center of the lifting forces created by the keel, just as the

TRIMMING THE MAIN

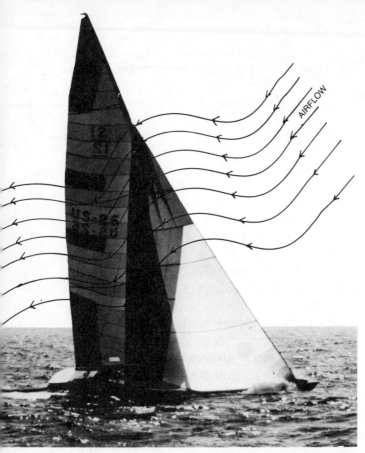

AIRFLOW

Figure 29: The 12-Meter *Courageous* sailing to windward. The air flow around the genoa slows the air flow around the mainsail.

boat had its center of effort ahead of the center of resistance, it would be pushing the bow away from the wind, forcing the stern to windward. This is leeward helm.

It would be hard to sail the boat effectively upwind if the boat itself kept wanting to go downwind. If, on the other hand, the center of effort is aft of the center of resistance, the opposite would happen. The driving force would be behind the keel, forcing the stern down, and the bow up into the wind. This windward helm situation is good because it keeps the boat in an upwind mode, and it automatically makes the boat take "bites" to windward, which is controlled by the force you put on the helm. Too much weather helm adds rudder pressure and counteracts the boat's ability to sail upwind. Too much rudder acts as a brake. A perfectly balanced boat will have just a slight amount of weather helm to keep the boat pointing upwind. This requires three to five degrees of corrective rudder angle. Any more rudder angle slows the boat down.

When the 12-Meter *Defender* was

center of effort is in the geometrical center of the lifting forces created by the sails. When these centers of resistance and effort are directly in line vertically, the boat will go in a straight line. If you let go of the tiller, the rudder will not move, and the boat will sail itself in a straight course.

If the center of effort is aft of the center of resistance, the boat would have windward helm. The opposite is true if the center of effort is forward of the center of resistance. Then the boat would sail off to leeward. To understand this, picture a boat on starboard tack. If the

CENTER OF EFFORT

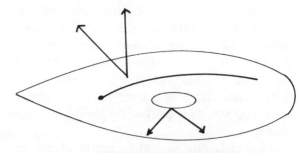

CENTER OF RESISTANCE

Figure 30: The counteracting forces on the sails and keel create the power to drive a sailboat through the water.

launched, it was found to have excessive weather helm. Something was not quite in balance. Either the center of effort was too far aft, or the center of resistance was too far forward. Moving the mast forward would have been an easy solution to the problem, but since the mast and headstay were as far forward as they could be under the 12-Meter rule, we had to look at the placement of the keel for the answer. By moving the keel aft eight inches, the center of resistance was realigned with the center of effort, and the boat became faster because less rudder angle was needed to correct the boat's course.

This same principle is in effect when a boat gets overpowered with too much wind. At 23 knots, the heavy #1 genoa may be too full and develop too much power. The main may be in constant backwind from the jib. Because the #1 is the only sail that's really working, the center of effort in the sail plan is in the genoa, which is too far forward. The boat becomes unbalanced and extremely hard to steer. In such a case, change to a smaller headsail, probably a #2 or a #3, and get the boat back in balance.

Now that we've discussed the theoretical side of sail trim to see how it produces the power to move the boat, let's see how to make the sails do what we want them to do in any given situation. There are many controls that can be used to manipulate the shape of the sails.

The important thing here is to be able to shape the sail right for the given condition. We want to be able to change gears without hesitation and to apply, or cut back, on the power when needed.

Sail trim should get constant attention until the finish line is crossed. Each control should be adjusted and the sail shape changed often in a reaction to the pressure on the rudder, the boat speed, the puff that just hit, or the light spot of wind into which you just sailed. Maximum power and maximum speed are achieved through this constant shifting of gears.

Mainsail Controls

Let's start with the mainsail. It is the most important sail on the boat. You cannot change mainsails as often as genoas; the same main is up when you're going two knots with the drifter as when you're going seven knots with the #3. It has to go through the whole spectrum of the wind range, from deep and powerful to reefed flat. The main can also act like the rudder, balancing the helm and keeping the boat on track. John Marshall, the mainsail trimmer on *Freedom* and *Liberty*, used to say that he had more control over how the boat sailed upwind than Dennis Conner, the helmsman. John was steering the boat through the waves and the puffs with the main, shaping it for the condition. "Dennis has his rudder that's five square feet, but my rudder is eighteen hundred square feet!"

A perfectly shaped main is a thing of beauty. The sailmaker has to be very competent to make a racing main that will be responsive to all the conditions it will sail in. It has to be made just right to be efficient both on a straight mast

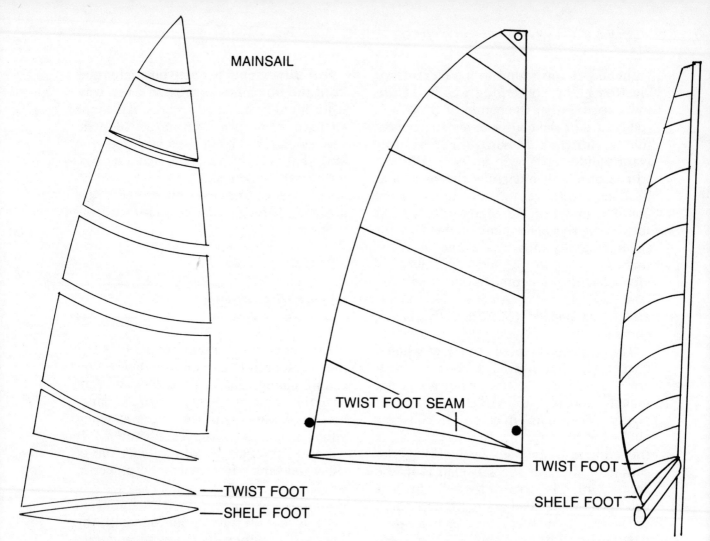

MAINSAIL

TWIST FOOT SEAM

TWIST FOOT
SHELF FOOT

TWIST FOOT
SHELF FOOT

Figure 31: The shape of a mainsail is controlled by the luff round, twist foot or draft control panel, and broad seaming or the overlapping of the seams to create draft in a sail.

Figure 32: Once a sail is sewn together, the trimmer can vary the shape by adjusting mast bend and sheet tension.

and when the mast is at its maximum bend. The cloth has to be just right to handle the heavy leech load, especially on today's high-aspect rigs, but not be too heavy and add excess weight to the rig.

When the sail is built, all the straight edges of the cloth are curved and shaped to the designer's specifications so that,

when sewn together, the flat pieces of cloth will take shape (See Figure 31). This broadseaming of the panels of cloth is done in a way that will make the sail form a constant foil shape from head to foot. If the cloth is Dacron, the designer has to correct these shape-producing broadseams to account for the inevitable stretch when the sail is under load. This is the reason materials such as Kevlar and Mylar have replaced Dacron. These new materials don't stretch, so the sail designer can produce the desired shape more precisely without the unknown factor of stretch adding to the formula.

In addition to the broadseaming, the sailmaker cuts luff curve into the sail to match the bend of the mast. Giving the luff a positive curve similar to the curve the mast will take, will make the sail perfectly. But the delicate balance of broadseam and luff curve must be kept. Too much of one or not enough of the other will produce a main that is impossible to set and trim in all conditions.

Before the onset of computer-refined design and nonstretch materials, the sailmaker used to rely on the material stretching to form the desired sail shape. Shape was added only in the luff curve, which would put most of the depth of the sail pretty far forward. When the sail came under load, the material would stretch and the draft would automatically move back about halfway. But we're beyond that stage now. Any sailmaker worth his salt will know exactly how each kind of mainsail fabric will stretch under different kinds of loads, and precisely how much broadseaming and luff curve will be required to form the perfect sail.

Mast bend is probably the most effective way to change the shape of the main while sailing, so it's really important to have the luff curve of the sail fit your mast just right (See Figure 32). If you're sailing on a boat that has a fractional rig or a masthead rig with a fully adjustable backstay, then you have the ability to bend the mast.

One way to ensure that your main and mast will match is to measure the way the mast bends and give these measurements to your sailmaker. To do this, all you need is a one-foot-long piece of luff tape that fits your mast track, and an old batten. Mark off the batten in one-inch increments with a Magic Marker, then sew this into the section of luff tape so that when the luff tape is inserted in the mast groove, the batten sticks out perpendicular to the mast. Run a tape measure up to the masthead, measure the distance from the top of the mast to the gooseneck, and find the quarter points at 25 percent, 50 percent, and 75 percent of the height. With the backstay at its maximum tension and the mast fully bent, raise the piece of luff tape to one-quarter height and measure the distance from the afteredge of the mast to the tape measure that has been pulled tight to the gooseneck. Record this offset and then raise the batten to one-half height and three-quarters height, recording the offsets as you go. Repeat the procedure with the backstay at one-half maximum tension and with the backstay completely slack.

On many smaller boats you may have the mast set up with a small amount of bend in the mast when the backstay is loose, so this last set of measurements is just as important. Give these offsets to your sailmaker so he can check them with the design of your main and build or recut your sail more precisely so it's right. Eliminating all the variables like this will make sure you have a fast sail on your boom, instead of a slow sail that is always in the loft getting recut.

Besides mast bend, which changes the

12-Meter light air mainsail. The shape here is fuller than the medium and heavy air mainsails to develop more power in the lower air speeds. Note the way the leech curves back to windward in a smooth arc to help induce weather helm. This sail was named Frankenstein because of all the different pieces of cloth that went into the sail. *Photograph by Mike Toppa*

shape of the whole sail, there are other controls that affect different, more localized areas of the main. The outhaul puts tension on the foot and controls the depth of the lower third of the sail. The tighter the outhaul, the flatter the lower part of the sail will be. Every good sailmaker will cut the foot of the main straight and add an elliptical wedge of cloth that is lighter in weight than the body of the sail. When the outhaul is eased, this small panel will form a shelf next to the boom and add considerable depth to the bottom of the sail for sailing in light air or off the wind. When the outhaul is tightened, this shelf will automatically close and the straight-cut foot will come up next to the boom, flattening out the sail.

After the outhaul, there's the flattening reef. This is a reefing cringle placed on the leech, right on top of the first seam above the clew. This seam, which is known as the twist foot seam, has three or four more times the amount of broadseaming in it than the rest of the seams because it does not start at the luff like the other seams but originates at the tack. Because the shape of the sail here is not controlled by luff curve, this seam has more shape added. The flattening reef sucks out the depth created by the twist foot. When the outhaul is tightened to its maximum and you still need to flatten the foot out, you can pull on the flattening reef and pull the twist foot seam out straight, eliminating the shape.

The Cunningham (named after Briggs Cunningham, who invented the device in 1958 on the 12-Meter *Columbia*) is used to adjust the draft location through luff tension. The tighter the luff tension, the farther forward the draft will come. The main should fit perfectly between the black bands when the halyard is fairly tight, with little room to spare. When you bend the mast to flatten the sail though, the effective height of the mast becomes shorter so you have to readjust the Cunningham to get back to the original luff tension and draft placement.

The leech line is the small line that runs inside the leech fold, from the top of the sail to the clew, where it exits out of the sail. Most people use it to control any flutter of the leech between the bat-tens, but it also can be used to help shape the after end of the sail. Most mainsails are built with the maximum amount of roach possible. Since the roach is extra material extended outside a straight line between the clew and the head, it is relatively unsupported. That is the job of the battens. If you were to pull hard on the leech line, you would be forcing that extra material back into the sail. Since it can't go directly into itself, the leech and the roach get pushed up to windward, making the sail deeper. This is a nice trick to know when you are forced to sail with a main that's too flat, or one that's old and has a loose leech that falls off to leeward.

The other controls for the main are the mainsheet, traveler, and boom vang. When sailing upwind, you use the main-

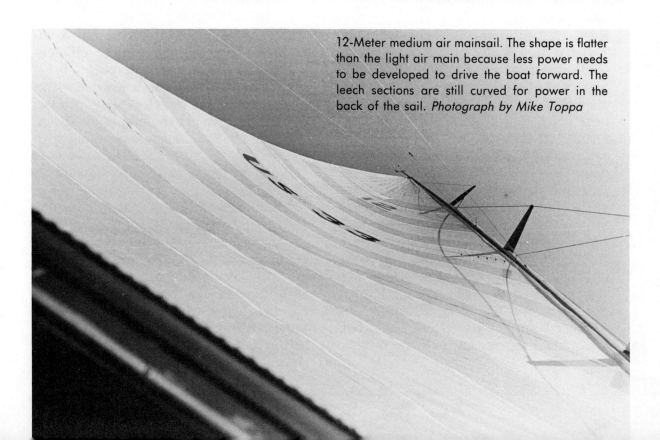

12-Meter medium air mainsail. The shape is flatter than the light air main because less power needs to be developed to drive the boat forward. The leech sections are still curved for power in the back of the sail. *Photograph by Mike Toppa*

12-Meter heavy air mainsail. The bottom 20 percent is board flat from max outhaul tension. The sections are flatter and the leech is straight for undisturbed air flow exit. Note the increased back wind. *Photograph by Mike Toppa*

sheet to control the twist of the main. Twist is the change of the angle of the cordlines in the sail from top to bottom. Since the apparent wind angle is farther aft at the top of the mast than it is at deck level, the sail has to be angled differently at different heights or else the sail would be in a constant state of overtrim. Once the mainsheet is set and the main has the proper amount of twist, the angle of attack can be changed by easing the traveler down or pulling it up. Sailing in puffy wind can be pretty tricky, especially when you are just on the edge of being overpowered. On a smaller boat the helmsman plays the traveler. Drop it down when a puff hits to relieve the weather helm and to keep the boat flat. When the puff recedes, pull the traveler to windward, increasing the angle of attack, making the main more efficient and giving the boat more power.

On bigger boats, or on boats that aren't set up to play the traveler easily, you can use the vang to get the proper leech tension and change the angle of attack with the mainsheet. Vang sheeting upwind is fast and efficient. Put gentle pressure on the vang to get just the right amount of leech tension and twist in the main. The leech will be set up. When the puff hits, the mainsheet is eased out and the angle is decreased, making the main less powerful and decreasing the weather helm that the puff creates. The front half of the main gets backwinded and doesn't provide any power, but the leech is still set up and is still giving the helm some bite. If the whole main were let go and the leech luffed as well as the front part of the sail, the helm would go neutral, and it would be very hard to keep the boat under control.

These are the controls to use to trim the main. Now let's see how the main should be set up in every condition and how to use these controls to do it.

Trimming the Main

Every racing main should come out of the loft with draft stripes (or speed stripes, as they're sometimes called) installed on the sail. You can use them as a guide to help you see how the draft in the sail is set, and the relative change in their shape as you begin to change the sail for different wind conditions. The draft stripes provide a contrast in color within the sail and help you see the exact shape of the sail at each stripe. You should have three in every sail positioned at the quarter points of the sail. Not only does this help when trimming the sail, but it also gives you a clearer illustration when you take pictures of the sail, or when you need to measure them.

In light air, the main needs to be as full as possible to give the boat maximum power to go upwind. When you have the drifter or light #1 genoa up, you want to create the most lift that the sails can provide, because you won't have any problem with being overpowered.

The main should be as full and as powerful as possible, so everything should be eased up. The outhaul should be relatively slack so the bottom of the main is curved and full and the shelf is partially open. The luff should also be slack so the draft of the sail is about halfway back. This means that there should be no Cunningham tension, and the main halyard might even have to be eased a couple of inches. Remember to look at the shape of the sail. If you have to ease the main halyard to get the draft back, you may create wrinkles in the luff, but that's O.K. The mast should be pretty straight. Any luff curve in the sail should be used to its maximum to put the most shape into the sail. Thus, the backstay should be loose enough to give the headstay sufficient tension for pointing and should not bend the mast. You may even want to tighten the running backstays if your boat has them. On a masthead-rigged boat, this will pull the middle of the mast aft, taking any bend out and making the mast dead straight from top to bottom. If your main is particularly flat and you need fullness, you may even go to the extreme of pulling the running backstays tighter so the middle of the mast is aft of a straight line between the top and the bottom. Once you have the main as full as possible, it's time to get the mainsheet tension and the twist set. This part is critical because it's very easy to overtrim and stall out the main in the lightest conditions. Stall is more likely to occur when the air is flowing at low speeds over the sail, so the sail should be full but not tight-leeched. One rule of thumb that always seems to work is to trim the mainsheet so the upper batten is parallel to the boom. If you trim the mainsheet too tight the top batten will poke out to windward, eliminating the twist in the main and decreasing boat speed. When the mainsheet tension is just right, look up the leech to see how the battens twist off toward the top of sail. The bottom battens will be hooked to windward in relation to the boom, but the top batten should be parallel. The traveler should be set so the boom is right on the center line of the boat, or more precisely, the leech of the sail at the clew should be on the center line of the boat. They are not always the same. To double-check the trim, look at the telltales on the leech of the main. They should all be streaming back behind the sail. In the lightest of air or in lumpy water, the telltales may not stream back, especially the top one. If you can't get them just right, recheck the angle of the batten to the boom and try letting the mainsheet out a little bit. If you still can't get it, don't worry. This simply means the air is too light to get any flow to attach all the way to the leech. You've done everything you can. Above 10 or 11 knots apparent wind, though, there should be no excuse!

There are times when you may need to bend the rule. On a fractional rig, the top batten might not be parallel to the boom. The top part of the mainsail is in free air because there is no jib in front of it; it can be trimmed differently. The top third of the sail is not placed in a relative header by the jib so it can be trimmed looser. Be sure to check the telltales on the top of a fractional-rig main to see that they aren't stalled when the main is trimmed with the top batten parallel to the boom. If they are, ease the sheet so the telltales work.

There are also a few times when the main should be set with the top telltale stalled a little bit and the top batten slightly to weather of the boom. The tightness of the leech controls how much side force the sail contributes to the power of the boat and therefore how much helm it gives. A slightly tight leech will give the boat more helm and more feel. A little bit of weather helm helps tremendously to get the boat upwind. But in light air there may not be enough power generated by the sails to provide the helm, so you may have to induce weather helm artificially by overtrimming the main a bit. Some boats are designed with a slight amount of neutral, or lee helm, and in light air you need to overtrim the main to get some feel into the helm and help the boat to point. The J-24 is a good example. The keel is pretty far forward on the J, so everybody in the class sails with the mast raked way back to get the center of effort behind the center of resistance. In light air this isn't enough, and you have to overtrim the main to get the center of effort even farther back. The same is true on bigger boats, too.

Remember that the main puts the genoa in an apparent lift, so the tighter it's trimmed, the more lift it gives the genoa. In this case the positive aspects of pointing higher outweigh the negative aspects of partially stalling out the main.

As you're racing upwind, continuously check the trim of the main. In a constant condition, such as flat water and no tacking, there's no reason to change things too much, but very rarely do things stay constant in sailboat racing. There's always something happening: a spot of rough water, a powerboat wake, a starboard tacker you have to duck slightly, a light spot or puff—all these changes necessitate a change in sail trim. Always think of the sails as the power plant of the boat. If you need more speed, step on the accelerator—ease the sails out, ease the outhaul, make the sails full and more powerful. When you don't need the extra power, trim them back for maximum upwind efficiency.

Now you're halfway up the first beat, and the sea breeze that filled in before the start is continuing to build. You've just changed from the light to the heavy #1, but the main is too full. You've pulled the mainsheet tighter, but that just appears to make the sail deeper. The boat is building too much weather helm. It's time to start to depower the sails. Everything you tried to do before in achieving maximum power is starting to work against you. The boat is developing too much power, and the side forces and excessive helm are too much for the keel and rudder. Not only that, the sailcloth is starting to stretch somewhat under the increasing loads, automatically making the sail deeper. Use the controls in the sail and on the boat to counteract these forces, to get the mainsail shape, and balance of the boat, back under control.

In doing this we have to reverse the actions we did to make the main fuller. The textbook approach to this is rather simple, but to know how much to do it depends on your feel for the boat and the balance of the helm. The more experience and time you spend in the boat, the better your feel for the way it sails will become.

Start with the outhaul and pull it tight enough so the clew is out to its max-imum extension at the black band. This will flatten the bottom part of the sail, pulling the shelf close and straightening the twist foot seam. It also opens the lower leech.

Next, you need to attack the middle and upper portions of the main by bending the mast and taking out luff curve. On smaller boats this can be achieved only by tightening the backstay. By doing this, the mast bends, and the luff moves forward farther away from the leech, leaving only the broadseaming to give it shape.

When you tighten the backstay, the mast is compressed because of the downward force of the pull. The center of the mast gets pushed in front of its vertical center, which is the bend, but the top of the mast gets closer to the deck. The effective luff length of the mast then is shorter, loosening the luff and the leech. Now you will have to tighten both the Cunningham and the mainsheet.

When the backstay is pulled tight and the luff gets loose, the draft goes back toward the leech. By pulling the Cunningham down, you reintroduce luff tension, which pulls the draft forward to its 45 to 50 percent mark. The sheet is then pulled back down to get the leech firm, adding that little bit of weather helm you need. Now look at the telltales. Make sure the leech isn't too tight so the flow is stalled. Let them flow! Also look at the speed stripes. They should show a much flatter, less rounded cross section than before, when the wind was lighter. The draft should be deepest at the midpoint of the stripes.

It helps here to have a set of telltales placed at the 50 percent mark on the stripes, not only to show where 50 percent is, but also to check the flow in the middle of the sail. These telltales are hard to read on the weather side because, as we saw, there is little attached flow on the weather side and because the mast creates turbulence that extends more than halfway back. But the lee telltales can be useful in seeing the flow. If these telltales are not flowing smoothly, it usually means that the main is still too deep. Try a little more mast bend.

The idea behind the new Frisbee-cut mainsail is to flatten out the middle of the main in the initial design stage so there would be more attached flow within the sail during the midwind range (See Figure 33). Instead of the usual arc shape, these mains are designed with a flattened center, so, in cross section, they appear more elliptical, like a Fris-

bee. Whatever the name, this kind of shape is much more efficient.

By now there may be some backwinding in the main from the genoa. A small amount of backwind is generally O.K., and there's really very little you can do about it, but excessive backwinding only makes the mainsail inefficient and slows the boat. Backwind is acceptable when the lower section of the main is aback 20 to 30 percent of the boom length. Any more of this will slow the boat. If the mast bend is already at maximum, which means the leading edge of the main is as straight as possible, it's time either to move the lead of the genoa outboard, or change down to a smaller jib. Backwind also distorts the view of the mainsail when looking at the draft position, so it appears that the draft is farther back than it really is. Keep this in mind

Figure 33: The Frisbee cut mainsail has a flatter middle section. The theory here is that the wind creates a more attached flow within the sail.

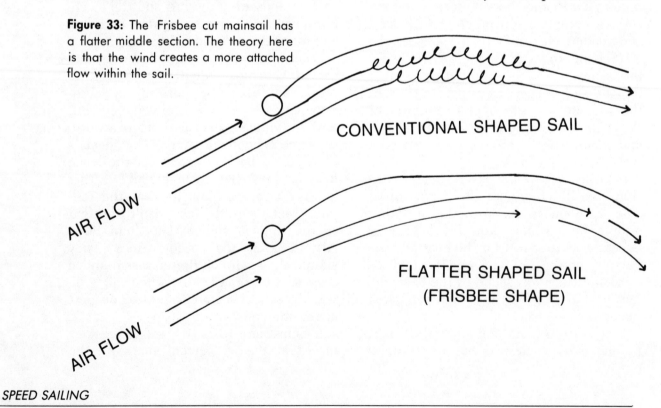

CONVENTIONAL SHAPED SAIL

AIR FLOW

AIR FLOW

FLATTER SHAPED SAIL
(FRISBEE SHAPE)

and train your eye to take this into account.

On larger boats there is more to bending the mast than just the permanent backstay. On many boats over 35 feet, there are babystays and running backstays. Modern, offshore racing rigs have evolved from using babystays to help bend the mast, to running backstays to keep the mast from pumping in the waves, and now to eliminating the babystay and just using the runners. This evolution has come about because of the new materials and techniques in mast construction. Babystays were introduced because the older masts were relatively stiff and hard to bend. Simple backstay tension was not enough to induce bend, so the babystay was invented to pull the middle of the mast forward. As masts were built lighter and thinner, they became easier to bend (and in many cases, *too* bendy). So the running backstays were invented to counteract the bend provided by the babystay and the backstay. But at this point it was found that the lighter masts bent with just the pressure of the backstay, and the babystay wasn't needed; it just kept the genoa from clearing the mast when tacking.

On a masthead-rig boat, running backstays give the mainsail trimmer fingertip control over the shape of the main without going through a series of . . . if this is changed, then this, this, and that must be changed also. Once the main has been set up for the average condition you're sailing in, you can fine-tune the depth of the main with the runner. Tightening the runners will pull the mast straighter and add depth to the sail. Easing them will allow the mast to bend more and

thus flatten the sail. The amount of adjustment is very slight; on a boat with a direct purchase of one to one on the runner, the adjustment should be only two to three inches. A little bit goes a long way here. And once the backstay is set up to provide the proper headstay tension and general mast bend, then trimming the runners should be all that's necessary. You don't have to adjust the mainsheet or the Cunningham, because the small amount of runner adjustment isn't affecting these.

During the 1981 SORC on *Midnight Sun* in the Miami-to-Nassau race, we had a beat to Fort Lauderdale in some pretty big Gulf Stream waves before we headed east to Nassau. The wind was pretty puffy, from 20 to 26 knots, and the waves were irregular. We had a heavy #1 up, but we were really pushing it in the puffs. All the boats in the class were pretty close in speed, so a change to the #2 would have put us in the back of the pack. We had the genoa trimmed out to the rail, but the key to how the boat went in these overpowering conditions was the way the main was trimmed. The backstay was at maximum tension, the Cunningham was tight so the draft was at 50 percent, and the mainsheet was just tight enough to keep the leech set, despite the backwind from the genoa. The boat deck layout was set up superbly so the main trimmer had all his controls within easy reach. To the right was the running backstay self-tailing winch, and between his legs were the mainsheet self-tailer and the traveler controls. When a puff would hit, the trimmer would ease the runner slightly, to bend the mast more and relieve the helm. If the puff were really big and we were about to go down the back of a particularly big wave, the trimmer would ease the runner all the way, and also drop the traveler. This would really keep the boat on its feet and help maintain the boat speed. When the puff receded and we got into relatively flat water, I would crank the runner back up, shaping the main and restoring the power. In this mode the boat was really flying. This was the only time we were able to beat *Williwaw* to the weather mark during the whole regatta.

In these heavy-air conditions, just before changing down, the main trimmer should be very conscious of how the boat feels and how hard a time the helmsman is having steering the boat. Using these instincts, he should set up the main so that the boat stays on its feet and does not get slowed down despite the overpowering conditions. In these conditions, the main becomes the most important sail on the boat, and the main trimmer becomes the most important crew member. In many cases he may have to let the main luff entirely for the duration of a particularly big puff to keep the boat from heeling too much. He must do whatever he can until either a smaller jib is hooked on or the weather mark is cleared.

There are times when the boat will need a smaller mainsail, so it will have to be reefed. It's important to know when to reef, because if the boat is reefed down at the wrong time, she will go slower than when she felt overpowered.

Most modern, medium-displacement boats usually sail much faster upwind with a full main and reduced-size headsails. Modern #2, #3, and #4 genoas are

Sail testing on *Defender.* The leeward boat stays behind so both boats stay in free air. Note the luff and foot shelves opened up to expose more area and fullness. *Photograph by Mike Toppa*

high-aspect sails made with the maximum luff length, as the #1 is, but their area is reduced by decreasing the foot length. The center of effort, then, is pretty far forward. When the main is reefed instead of changing down in headsail size, sail area is reduced, but the center of effort is moved forward, increasing lee helm. All of a sudden the helm and sailing characteristics of the boat change radically. There is less sail up, so there is no longer that all-important tug on the tiller to keep the boat pointing, and to help steer her around the waves. The solution would be to unreef the main and put the next smaller headsail up.

In the old days (five years ago), the smaller headsails were shorter on the hoist, but their foot length was still pretty long. The idea behind this was to lower the sail area to stop the heeling forces. The main could be reefed with these shaped headsails up, and the center of effort would become lower. This seemed to make sense. But when sailmakers began to pay more attention to aerodynamics, they saw that a more efficient headsail had a long leading edge. More lift and drive could be achieved from a full luff-length sail than from one that was short and stubby. The high-lift advantages were much better than lowering the heeling angle.

It's better to keep the main up and to change to a smaller headsail so it keeps the power on and gives you the full benefit of the mainsail leech to help steer the boat. However, when you do reef, there are some important things to consider.

First, the reef must be taken in as quickly as possible. At this point, the main is luffing and the center of effort is all in the jib, giving the boat lee helm. The helmsman should steer the boat upwind just when the main starts to luff as the reef is taken in. Otherwise the boat would slide off to leeward and would lose valuable distance upwind.

Second, it's important for the main trimmer to coordinate the reefing process on the boat. At his word, the main halyard should come down, the new tack should be secured, and the new clew should be pulled in. After all this is done, the main can be sheeted back in. The process should not start with easing the mainsheet but with slacking the main halyard. Once the halyard is let go, the main will luff. Then the trimmer can ease the sheet enough so the reefline can be pulled in. Easing the halyard first saves valuable seconds; the reef will be put in and the boat will be back on its feet, sailing that much faster.

Once the reef is put in, the controls available to trim the main are limited. The Cunningham has now been eliminated, and so has the outhaul. The runners still can be used, but not as effectively, since the main has been lowered. This will affect the luff curve more in the top of the sail than in the bottom, creating an imbalance. So basically the halyard reefline and mainsheet are the only controls left to shape the sail. But you should still work hard at trimming. You still want maximum lift and all the telltales working. Adjust the halyard so the draft is at the 50 percent mark. This is harder to locate when the sail is flatter, so study the speed stripes carefully. When in doubt, ease the halyard. Also, make sure the outhaul tension from the reef line is not too tight.

If the fairlead blocks for the reef lines are located correctly on the boom, they should trim the clew from a 45-degree angle. If the fairlead blocks are too far aft along the boom, the foot will be too tight. It's a good idea to tie a small piece of line through the clew and around the boom to keep the clew as close as possible. With this done, any adjustment to the reef line will cause the clew to move fore and aft along the boom, acting like a true outhaul. This gives you much more control over the shape in the bottom of the sail and also acts as a safety valve if the reef line breaks.

Once the main is reefed, tie up the extra sailcloth that's around the boom. Roll and tie it neatly, especially near the luff, since this is where the windage and visibility are most important. Make sure the ties aren't so tight that they pull the sail into the boom. They should be just tight enough to keep the reefed portion of the sail from getting loose.

Using the Main Downwind

Off the wind, the main is easier to trim because the headsail does not affect it so much. Although the wind is still being bent by the reacher or spinnaker, the airstream that hits the main is more direct. The telltales should all be streaming, especially the ones in the middle of the sail.

As in light air, the outhaul should be eased so the shelf opens up, deepening the bottom of the sail. The Cunningham can be eased completely and the main halyard can be eased to keep the luff loose and the draft at 50 percent. If this causes wrinkles to appear, don't worry. It's more important that the draft placement be correct than to try to eliminate wrinkles.

To put maximum depth in the sail, the mast should be as straight as possible. Ease the backstay, and if you have running backstays, tighten them so the mast is perfectly straight. Have one of the crew sight up the mast to determine when it's straight as you crank up the runner winch. If the main is particularly flat, tighten the runners to put in a reverse bend and to make the main fuller.

The most important aspect of offwind mainsail trim is the twist. Use the telltales as your indicators. The top of the sail will luff if there is too much twist. If there is too little, the telltales will not stream, indicating stall. The best way to ensure that the twist is correct is to set the leech tension so the main luffs evenly from top to bottom. Since the outboard end of the boom is over the lifelines and not under the effect of the traveler, use the boom vang to set the twist. A powerful and easily adjustable vang is important. If you don't have a hydraulically controlled vang, you should have enough purchase in it to make any adjustment easy to do.

When reaching with a staysail, you will have to change the twist because the staysail will affect the free airstream around the main. The bottom of the main has to be trimmed flatter because the staysail will create a relative header. The top of the sail will not be under the effect of the staysail, so it still has to be trimmed loosely. Again, you want to trim the main so that it luffs evenly, but in this case there will be much more twist. The boom will be trimmed much closer to the center line, while the top is more open. One trick here is to flatten the bottom of the sail with the outhaul. This has the same effect of trimming the boom closer to the center line, allowing you to keep the boom out farther.

When sailing dead downwind, there isn't any windflow across the main, so the telltales are of little use. The sail is in an unavoidable stall. The goal now is to expose as much mainsail area to the wind as possible in the form of a deep pocket. The mast should be straight, the luff loose, and the leech just tight enough so the top batten is parallel to the boom. To increase exposed area, tighten the leech line, which will kick the battens to windward, causing the sail to fill. Then pull the outhaul a couple of inches farther out toward the end of the boom, to lengthen the effective foot distance. Because the leech is now farther to windward, you can ease the mainsheet out.

In heavy-air conditions, flatten out the main to depower it for the same reasons you did upwind. Too much power will cause excessive helm and a possible broach. Any more power than what's needed to keep the boat at full speed will cause trouble. So again, reverse the process used to get the main full as the helm built up. But now it's O.K. to reef the main and keep the big chute up. It's important to keep the rudder angle needed to steer the boat to a minimum. Reefing the main will bring the center of effort forward and take the load off the rudder.

Headsails

We've seen how to trim the main for power, and more importantly, how to trim it for helm balance. The mainsail causes a lift in the genoa due to its up-wash, so the genoa can be sheeted at a wider angle to the center line of the boat. The lifting forces act in a direction perpendicular to the chord line of the sail. Since the jib is sheeted farther off the center line, the forces are more in a forward direction than the main (See Figure 34). Also, the genoas are the leading edge of the sail plan. There are no mast or shrouds or halyards to interfere with the free airflow that would create turbulence.

There are fewer controls available to shape the genoa than there are for the mainsail, so the sail shape built in at the sail loft is critical. And unlike the main, the genoa is supported only by the luff; both the foot and leech are controlled by the sheet alone. The controls are few, so they have to be used with the greatest of

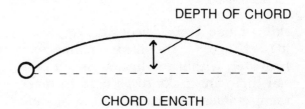

DEPTH OF CHORD

CHORD LENGTH

Figure 34: Sail shape is often discussed in terms of chord length and draft. The chord length is the distance from luff to leech. The chord depth is the deepest point of the sail along the chord length, commonly called the draft. Position of the draft along the chord length is critical to proper sail trim.

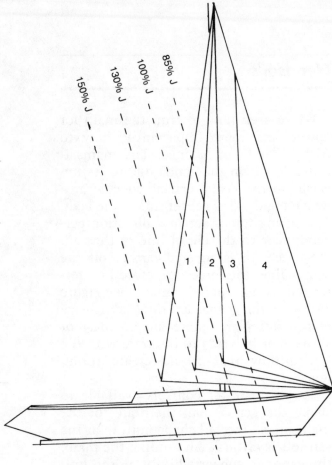

Figure 35: The standard size reduction of genoas on bigger boats starts at 150 percent for the number 1's, goes to 130 percent for the number 2's, 100 percent for the number 3's, and 85 percent for the number 4's.

skill. If one genoa becomes overpowering, change to the next smaller one. However, within the limitations of each sail there are tricks to be used to make them efficient from the bottom of their range to the top.

A normal sail inventory might consist of a light #1, heavy #1, a #2 and #3 to be used through most sailing conditions (Figure 35). Since you now have four sails to get through the range of zero to 30 knots, the sail designer has more lati-

tude in shaping these for a specific function. By knowing exactly what conditions and wind strengths each sail will be used in, he can build in the proper shape for the job.

Cloth selection is critical. It has to be tough enough to take the beating of being slammed against the mast during the tacks, but light enough not to add too much weight aloft. It has to be strong and not stretch so that the designed shape stays in even when the wind blows hard. The idea of Mylar laminates was initially developed for use in genoas to control stretch. Only later were they used to make mainsails.

Mylar headsails are far and away superior to Dacron sails. Because of the limited stretch, the sailmaker can build in more shape and depth with Mylar headsails, increasing the lower end range capabilities of the sail. To be competitive, anyone racing with a Dacron headsail should seriously consider purchasing a Mylar sail. The difference between the two is similar to the difference between the cotton and the Dacron sails 20 years ago!

The low-stretch qualities of the cloth allow the sailmaker to build in a predetermined shape that the sail will take every time it is used. The shape is "locked in," so there's less trimming required to set the sail. Newer Mylar sails are made to be set in a relaxed state. You need to put only enough tension on the halyard to remove the wrinkles.

So many times we've seen new sails returned to the loft because they have been seriously stretched beyond the yield point when the halyard was set too tight. The sail becomes delaminated and stretched, or the telltale windows are elongated. Many times the owners of these sails are first-time Mylar buyers who either weren't told or didn't know the difference between the new sail and their Dacron counterparts. The lesson here is if your sails are made with Mylar, use a little less muscle on the halyard.

Once the correct sail has been chosen, it's time to set it and get it trimmed properly. First check the fore and aft lead position so the proper amount of twist is established. As the apparent wind angle changes from the deck level to the masthead due to wind sheer, the angle of the sail must change also. And the twist in the genoa is important because it sets up the flow pattern of the wind not only for itself but for the main also. The mainsail twist relies on the airflow off the genoa, so it has to be just right. Again, the telltales will be the prime indicators of airflow at the leading edge of the genoa. If there is too much twist, the top of the sail will luff, causing the telltales to become out of control. If there is too little twist, the sail will stall, and the lifting forces within the sail become inefficient.

To judge the proper amount of twist, move the lead fore and aft until the telltales lift evenly from top to bottom as you slowly head up into the wind. If the lead is too far forward, the leech will be tight and cause more backwind in the main than normal. Also, the bottom telltales will lift first. If this is the case,

This is a Kevlar/Mylar heavy air genoa. The shape is flatter than the other lighter air sails and like the heavy air main, it is straight in the back to allow easy air exit. The Mylar side and Kevlar side are "flip-flopped" so the stresses on each side of the sail remain the same even though they are composed of different materials. *Photograph by Mike Toppa*

move the lead aft one hole on the track, and sheet the sail in. If the top telltales lift first, then there is too much twist, and the lead should be moved forward.

When all the telltales break evenly, you're ready to go upwind. However, there are times when you will want to change the twist in the sail for conditions that aren't ideal. If the wind comes up so you are overpowered and you can't change the jibs right away, you can move the lead back to induce more twist. This will let the top of the sail luff, spilling off the extra power while still deepening the bottom trim. Also, by moving the lead aft, you've flattened out the bottom, making it more efficient for a higher wind velocity.

This technique works well on smaller boats such as the MORC fleet or J-24's that have limited sail inventories. We once saw Tony Parker sail his J in a class race off Annapolis. The race started in a puff, and the wind filled in from the southeast. Every boat started with 150 percent genoas up, but as the wind increased, most boats changed to the 100 percent jibs, but not Tony's. He worked his way through the fleet with the big genoa still up despite puffs building to 26 knots. After the race he explained that all he did was move the lead back to twist the sail more and depower in the puffs. Not only did he gain by not having to change jibs, but also he had the bigger sail up in the lulls, which gave him more power than the other boats. In this case, the disadvantage of having a bigger, depowered sail up in the puffs was overcome by having the extra power in the lulls.

There will be times when you get caught with a sail that's too small. If you can't change right away, you can move the lead forward to remove twist and make the sail more powerful until a change can be made. Most sails are designed with a certain amount of twist built in. Naturally, the more wind the sail will be used in, the more twist is built in. Say you're sailing with the #3 and the wind has dropped to 24 knots apparent. You can't change yet because the halyards are fouled. By moving the lead forward, you will close the upper leech, making the sail deeper. Also, the bottom will get fuller because by moving the lead forward you move the clew forward toward the tack. It's much like easing the out haul. Unlike the mainsail, the draft in the headsail should be moved fore and aft depending on the tactical situations. Both halyard and headstay sag contribute to draft placement.

Optimally, the draft should be 35 to 40 percent aft. Tightening the halyard will move the draft forward, while easing it off will move the draft aft. With the halyard tighter than normal and the draft at 25 to 30 percent, the leading edge of the genoa forms a round shape, while the back of the genoa is straight. This should be done when the steering gets hard or you need extra speed. With the draft forward, the sail is much more forgiving and the boat is easier to steer. The wider leading edge makes the genoa harder to stall because the windflow stays attached longer and farther back into the body of the sail. You can see this on the telltales as you go from an average upwind course to one slightly higher. The telltales will dance lightly at the luff, but they won't fly about madly, as if the

BROAD SEAMING

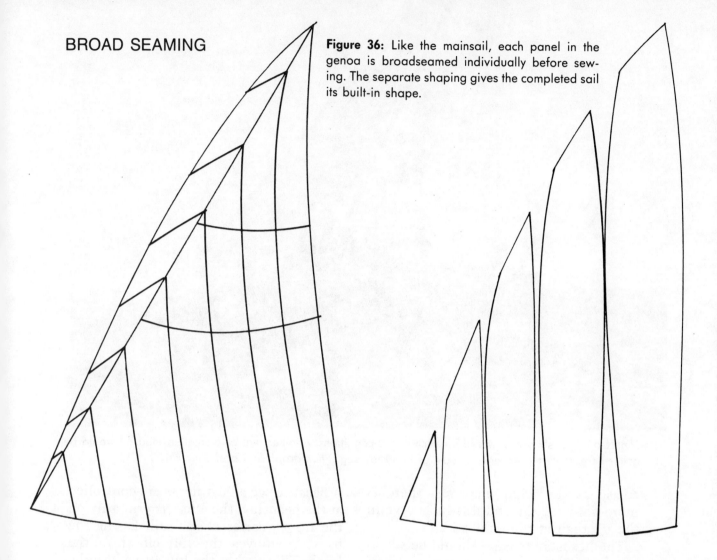

Figure 36: Like the mainsail, each panel in the genoa is broadseamed individually before sewing. The separate shaping gives the completed sail its built-in shape.

flow were unattached altogether. This feathering of the boat, sailing on the high side of the groove, is necessary when sailing in waves.

When you adjust the halyard, always check the lead position afterward to see if you still have the desired amount of twist. Usually when you tighten the halyard, the sail gets lifted off the deck, and the leech gets tighter. If you ease the halyard down, the lead should be moved forward because the leech gets loose and more twist develops.

The other factor that contributes to the draft location is the headstay tension. Most genoas are designed and shaped with just broadseaming (See Figure 36). The luff curve built in is to offset the headstay sag that will occur in increasing wind. Because the forces in-

Limit Up is grossly overpowered for such heavy conditions. Another reef or a smaller headsail would be better here. Note the extreme amount of headstay sag. *Photograph by Carol Singer*

crease as the wind increases, there is more headstay sag and less luff curve in the #2 than in the light #1.

The headstay tension should be set so the draft is at its optimal 35 to 40 percent placement. In changing conditions, or when you want to change the draft so it's more forward or more aft, you can adjust the amount of sag in conjunction with the halyard. Tightening the backstay will straighten the headstay, sucking out the luff curve, bringing the sail draft aft, and allowing you to point higher. Easing the backstay will have the opposite effect, creating a powerful draft forward.

Because sag adjustments are controlled at the headstay, the effect is primarily on the front quarter of the sail. Easing the backstay moves the luff closer to the leech. This pushes the luff curve into the sail, making it slightly deeper and creating more draft forward. Taking sag out pulls the luff farther away from the leech, making the sail flatter and creating more draft aft.

Control of the draft with the headstay sag is best used when coming out of tacks. After the tack, keep plenty of sag in when the heading is still low and the apparent wind hasn't built up to the maximum. As the speed increases and you come up to the close-hauled heading, take the sag out and get the sail back into the upwind mode trim.

Just as you measured the mast bend offsets to get an exact reference on the main for the sailmaker, you should measure the amount of headstay sag under different conditions so you can get the luff curve of the genoas correct. Each boat has a different backstay tensioning device and different-size rigging, so the amount of sag on two similar 30-foot boats might be different under similar conditions. You should take some pictures of the headstay sag for each genoa you would use in a race. Set the sail up with the backstay tension you would normally use and then take a picture from a couple of boat lengths away. It's important that the picture be taken from an angle perpendicular to the leading edge of the sail and not from directly in front of it. The headstay sags aft as well as to leeward, so a picture from this angle will take it all into account. With a fine-point pen, draw a straight line with a ruler from the tack to the head. Then measure the greatest amount of sag and divide it by the length of the straight line. This will give you a percentage of sag for each sail. This information will allow the sailmaker to design the sail without guesswork, and it will indicate to you if you are putting enough tension on the backstay for each genoa (See Figure 37).

The genoa sheet is the most important control for the sail. As mentioned earlier, the genoa doesn't have a boom to support the foot, so the sheet has to act as the boom, vang, outhaul, and traveler, as well as the sail-tensioning device.

More than any other control, the sheet has a greater proportional effect over all the aspects of the genoa trim.

Once the halyard has been set and the lead positioned properly, the in-and-out action of the sheet will change the shape of the genoa in reaction to the changes in wind velocity. When a puff hits, the genoa will stretch and distort somewhat. The draft will slide back, the leech will open up, and the sail will become deeper. By trimming the sheet more, you will reverse these reactions by tightening the leech and moving the draft back forward.

In the lulls, the opposite happens. As the apparent wind decreases, the sail becomes more relaxed and tightens up into an overtrimmed shape. Here the sheet must be eased to compensate for the shape change.

Exact sheet tension for upwind conditions is hard to specify for each rig. But as a rule, the maximum sheet tension should be so the genoa just kisses the upper spreader. Never should it be so tight that the sail will jam against the spreader and bend around it.

The maximum eased position is impossible to define and really depends on the wind speed, the general conditions, and the feel of the boat. If you feel slow, ease the jib out a couple of inches and bear off a few degrees to power things up and reattach to the sail the airflow that was lost when the sail was overtrimmed.

The genoa trimmer must be good and experienced. His is a full-time job that should be coordinated with that of the helmsman to help get the shape right for course changes due to steering around big waves. The genoa trimmer should also be in communication with others in

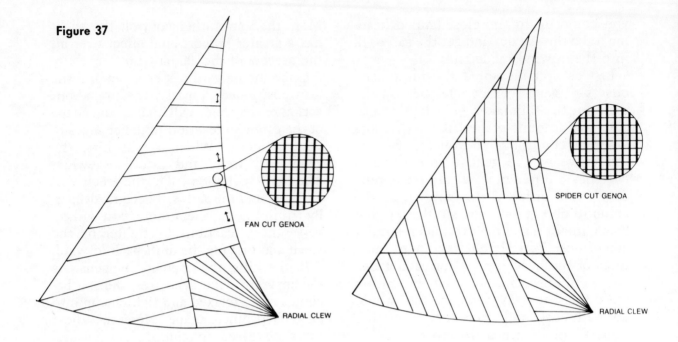

Figure 37

FAN CUT GENOA

RADIAL CLEW

SPIDER CUT GENOA

RADIAL CLEW

the crew who are hiking out, calling when the puffs are going to hit and when the boat is approaching light spots so he can anticipate the upcoming conditions.

Also, the genoa trimmer should be talking to the main trimmer so both sails are in perfect coordination and balance. On a 12-Meter, the deck layout is set up so that the jib trimmers, main trimmer, and helmsman are as close together as possible to make communication easiest.

A typical conversation in light or moderate conditions on *Defender* would be as follows:

PAUL CAYARD (windward tailer): "There's a puff coming a couple of boat lengths away."

TOM BLACKALLER (skipper): "Here it is. The wheel's over a couple of degrees and I'm bringing it up slowly."

MIKE TOPPA (leeward trimmer): to Rod Davis (main trimmer): "The jib's out a few inches, Rod. You might be able to let the main out some."

ROD DAVIS: "Yup, I eased when you did. Let me know when you start to bring it back in."

MIKE TOPPA: "I'm starting to bring it back in now." To the grinders: "A little trim, guys."

ROD DAVIS: "Main's coming in now."

PAUL CAYARD: "Another little puff's coming, looks like a slight knock...." And so on.

In puffy, high wind conditions, the sheet can be used as a safety valve to quickly release power that is overcoming the boat. In too much wind and when all else fails, you can ease the sheet a couple inches to twist the sail and flatten it out to help keep the boat on its feet. By doing this the sail twists off at the top, spilling power and automatically flattening itself. Since the jib is farther out, the helmsman can't point as high, but he shouldn't bear off. Instead, he keeps the same course and feathers the boat high. The front of the jib is soft, while the back half is still full to drive the boat. The boat stays relatively flat and under control instead of heeling beyond its sailing lines. Only in extremely overpowered conditions will this be effective, but it does work and will keep you in control in the severest of conditions.

When all the controls are set up so the genoa is in perfect trim, take a close look at the sail to determine if the depths are correct for the job. Study carefully the speed stripes and see that the draft is at 35 percent. (If you don't have speed stripes, get them!) Now look closely at the depth. The light #1 should be the fullest sail on the boat, and each heavier sail should get progressively flatter. Once a month during the racing season you should take a picture of all your genoas taken to keep track of possible distortion or permanent stretch. Measurements can be taken from the pictures and compared to the sailmaker's recommended numbers to ensure that your sails have the right shape.

Looking at a sail and determining if it is too full or too flat takes a trained and experienced eye. As a guide in learning to recognize correct sail shape, North Sails has designed the Sailscope, to be used on board to measure sail depths while racing. It's a small, transparent plastic card with a sighting grid superimposed on it. When the grid is lined up with the ends of the speed stripe, you can measure the sail using the corresponding numbers on the grid. It's a smart idea and a great aid in training the eye for the subtle differences in sail shape.

Upwind, the genoa is constantly trimmed within its windward trim mode. But there are times when you will use the genoa close reaching when the wind is too far forward for the spinnaker. A fresh look should be taken at what happens when the apparent wind is back to 40 degrees off the bow.

Naturally, when the wind is farther aft, the sheet can be eased out. Since the sail will twist as the sheet is eased, the lead should be moved forward so again all the telltales will break evenly. When you ease the genoa, the lifting forces are rotated more in front of the boat than to the side, so the healing and leeway effects are less. So it's possible to make the sail fuller and more powerful in the same conditions as upwind without worrying about becoming out of balance. Because the sail is under less load, it will become more relaxed and the draft will move too far forward. So the halyard should be eased to get the draft back to 40 percent. The lead should be moved outboard to the rail to open the slot and prevent backwinding of the main.

Now more than ever the jib trimmer should be in constant communication with the helmsman and the main trimmer to get all the sails working in perfect coordination. As the jib is trimmed in a heading puff, the trimmer should tell the mainsail guy what he's doing so the main can come in before it starts to backwind.

On most boats #1 genoas are high aspect in design, meaning the leeches are

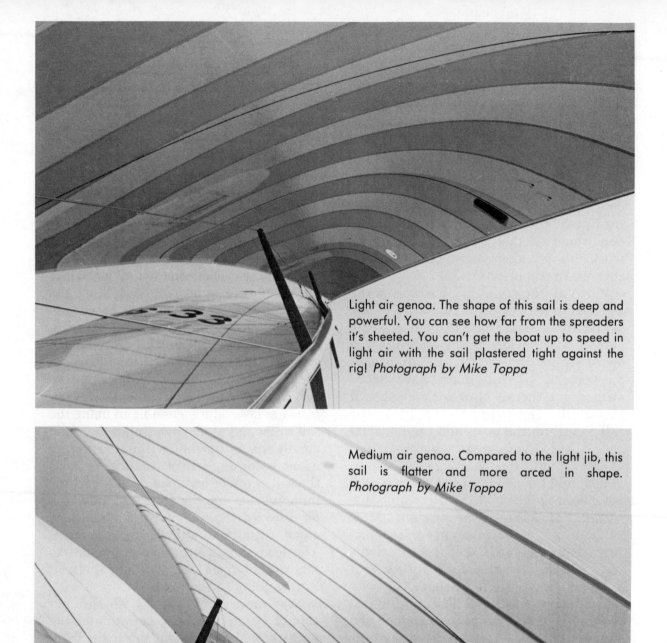

Light air genoa. The shape of this sail is deep and powerful. You can see how far from the spreaders it's sheeted. You can't get the boat up to speed in light air with the sail plastered tight against the rig! *Photograph by Mike Toppa*

Medium air genoa. Compared to the light jib, this sail is flatter and more arced in shape. *Photograph by Mike Toppa* much longer than the foot. When you are reaching, the lead has to be moved forward to minimize the twist, but many times you have to move the lead so far forward that the bottom of the sail gets too deep for the conditions. The end result is that the genoas get out of balance. The lead is forward to get the top of the sail trimmed, but the bottom is so full it luffs and the sail has to be overtrimmed.

The sailmaker's answer to this dilemma is the reacher, which is designed with foot and leech lengths that are close to the same length. So when the lead is set, any sheet adjustment affects them both. The sail can be trimmed with the sheet eased. The top and bottom of the sail will have the same angle of attack to the wind, producing much more power than the genoa in similar conditions.

Even though it has the same area as the #1 genoa, the reacher has a high clew, so there is much more area aloft, where the wind is less disturbed and fresher. The higher clew means the lead is much farther aft, usually at the transom, where the spinnaker leads are. Even though the measured angle of this lead is relatively narrow, the effective sheeting angle is quite wide because the clew is still farther outboard.

The reacher is more efficient than the genoa at about 35 percent apparent and can be used to the point where your closest reaching spinnaker is effective. Because it is sheeted farther out, it can be designed with a fuller shape than the genoa. The draft should still be at 40 percent, so the halyard and headstay sag should be set accordingly.

Because of the high clew and wide sheeting angle, there is between the deck and foot of the reacher a wide gap, which can be filled with a staysail. The added sail area can create an efficient double-head rig that can add up to .5 knot of speed.

The staysail is about 40 percent of the area of the reacher and should be tacked about a third of the way between the headstay and the mast. The sheeting angle should be such that the slot is equal between it and the main and reacher so the staysail could be sheeted out around the shrouds and to the rail on a relatively wide reach, or inside the shrouds and under the spreader to the genoa track on a tighter angle. As with all other headsails, the telltales should be watched, and the twist and sheet tension should be adjusted constantly.

When adding the staysail to the sail plan, you must consider the effect on the mainsail. Under most conditions, this will cause backwind in the lower third of the mainsail, because the staysail will bend the wind into the mainsail. To compensate, the main has to be trimmed with much more twist than before. The top has to be kept open and free, while the bottom has to be trimmed quite tightly, almost as if the boat were going to windward. Despite the excessive twist, you'll know it's trimmed properly when the front of the main will again luff evenly from top to bottom when the sail is eased.

8

FLYING THE SPINNAKER

Over the past decade there have been significant changes in mains and genoas with the introduction of Mylar and Kevlar and vertical panels. It used to be easy to determine if your competitors had a current inventory by watching them sail. If their sails were just Dacron, then you could consider them pushovers. If the sails were shiny, brown, or had vertical panels instead of horizontal, then you would know the boat was up-to-date and would be tough on the racecourse. But downwind, who would know the difference between a new spinnaker and an old one? Who knows the difference between a good spinnaker and an inferior one simply by looking?

Of all the boats we have raced, we cannot recall one where the crew's knowledge of spinnakers equaled their knowledge of mains and jibs. Upwind, there is constant talk of sail shape and draft placement, halyard tension and sheet lead. But after the weather mark, the wind is coming from behind instead of hitting you in the face. No more grueling tacks and sitting on the weather rail. The foul-weather gear can come off, and the boat is on an even keel. Crews tend

to relax, and concentration often wanes. Anybody want a beer?

Downwind sailing is certainly more enjoyable—especially when the wind is blowing hard and the waves are high. But it is also a time when the distances lost and gained can be greater than sailing upwind, depending upon the crew's attitude and aptitude. Speed differences are greater, and unlike sailing upwind, there is no definitive groove the boat falls into. The greater the speed differences, the greater your chances are to gain or lose a lot of time.

To be competitive, however, you have to be fast. To make big gains downwind, you have to have properly shaped spinnakers and know how to use those shapes to their full advantage, in the upper range as well as at the lower end. So let us concern ourselves with the correct spinnaker choices and trim techniques you can utilize to put yourself in the passing lane and gain some places on the racecourse.

Spinnaker inventories closely parallel genoa inventories in their size and purpose. From smaller one-designs to maxi boats, there should be a spinnaker on

Super flat reaching spinnaker. This sail had no horizontal panels for added shape. All the broad-seaming is in the head gores. *Photograph by Mike Toppa*

board for every wind range and for every purpose for which a genoa is used. The smaller one-design boat has one all-purpose jib and has one all-purpose spinnaker. A bigger offshore boat will have three #1 genoas of varying weights, and then smaller jibs right down to the storm sails. Much the same, it will have three full-size spinnakers, of .5-, .75-, and 1.502-ounce cloth; special reaching chutes; and small storm spinnakers. The difference in spinnakers on a big boat, compared to a smaller boat, is the same with everything else on the boat; when

the boat gets bigger, every item becomes more specialized. But regardless of the boat size, the basis of the spinnaker inventory is the all-purpose chute.

Because most boats have only one or two spinnakers, the all-purpose spinnaker must be designed, constructed, and used to its maximum potential of withstanding a full range of conditions, from the high reaching angles in super light air to the heavy running conditions in a blow.

There have been many changes in cloth, construction, and design of the all-purpose spinnaker over the past 10 years, although it is not as apparent as the changes in mains and genoas. The appearance of the spinnaker still looks the same, with all the pretty colors, but panel layout, cloth construction, and design sophistication all have advanced to produce a more versatile and longer-lasting sail.

The only type of spinnaker you should use is a triradial. The performance difference between a triradial and a crosscut or even a radial-head chute is like the difference between Dacron and Kevlar. The idea behind the triradial is just like that of the vertical genoa—aligning the strongest threads in the cloth with the greatest loads. In the case of nylon spinnaker cloth, the strongest threads are in the warp direction. Since the directions of the loads radiate from the corners of the sail, the panel's highest-strength threads are laid out in the same direction. Any crosscut sail would load the cloth on the fill threads, or the bias, causing stretch and shape distortion. Since the stretch is proportional to the amount of wind, the sailmaker cannot compensate for it in the design. Only when the sail is laid out for minimal stretch can the designer accurately build in the correct shape and be sure it will be seen in the sail (See Figure 38).

In designing the spinnaker, the sailmaker has two objectives: first, to build the fastest all-around shape into the sail, and second, to build in that shape so the sail flies in a stable manner and is easy to trim. A sail that has a fast shape will not produce speed if it is continually bouncing around and needs to be over-trimmed to settle it down. Speed and stability go hand in hand.

Stability comes in the form of the overall depth of the sail and the shape of the leading edge. If the sail is too flat, or if the leading edge is too straight, the lift needed to support the sail and make it project will not be produced. The luff will "wash out," and to maintain a constant curl in the luff would be difficult. An unstable sail will collapse right when the sheet is eased and a slight curl is seen. If you see these symptoms in your sail, have your sailmaker take a look.

No matter what size boat you have, or what weight the all-purpose chute is, the chute must be designed for all-around conditions, including running and reaching. The optimal shape of the all-purpose spinnaker, both in depth and cross-sectional shape, is difficult to define and more difficult to build in because of the ever-changing conditions in which they are used. Where the shape of the genoas are designed within specified parameters defined by a certain wind range and an exact wind angle, the spinnaker has to be used in much broader ranges of wind speed and angle.

This crew should raise the inboard end of the spinnaker pole to push the spinnaker away from the boat. *Photograph by Carol Singer*

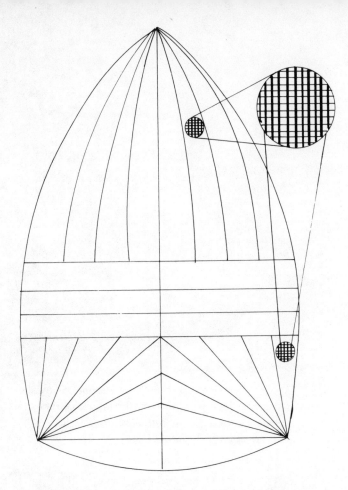

Figure 38: Load factors on sails cause stretch and shape distortion. Since stretch is proportional to the amount of wind, the sailmaker cannot compensate for it in the design. Only when the sail is laid out for minimal stretch can the designer accurately build in the correct shape and be sure it will be seen in the sail.

In his attempt to do this, the sailmaker designs the sail to a midrange of about 100 degrees apparent wind angle. The depth of the sail should produce enough lift and power to get the boat to maximum speed for the conditions.

This design shape is built into the sail, and the result is seen in the flying shape. In all the design work, picture analysis, and sail testing that has been done to find the optimal shape for displacement boats, there is a flying shape that is common to all boats that is best for all-purpose conditions. In measuring pictures of fast spinnakers in boats ranging from J-24's to IOR boats to 12-Meters, the fastest spinnakers always measured equally. Although their design is different, their flying shape is very similar.

The difference between design shape and flying shape is the cloth. Nylon is not as stable as Mylar or Kevlar; nylon's weave moves and stretches, depending upon strain by wind strength and sail size. So the sailmaker's dilemma is to design the best shape that will produce the optimal flying shape.

Because the loads are not that great, smaller boat chutes can be built more precisely and the designer can build the sail pretty much the way he wants it to fly. However, to achieve the same shape in a bigger sail, or one that will be used in more wind, he must compensate for

ABOVE: The foredeck crew has tripped away the spinnaker tack from the end of the pole, and the sail is starting to be retrieved by the lazy guy. *Photograph by Andrea Olsen*

BELOW: The spinnaker is brought aboard in the middle of the boat behind the mainsail. *Photograph by Andrea Olsen*

ABOVE: The mainsail blankets the free flying spinnaker and the halyard is lowered. In retrieving the sail from the middle of the boat instead of back aft, the cockpit is kept clear for trimming the jib. Also the helmsman's view is unobstructed. *Photograph by Andrea Olsen*

BELOW: The rest of the spinnaker is brought on deck, the cockpit crew trims the genoa, and the helmsman starts to turn the boat upwind for the next beat. *Photograph by Andrea Olsen*

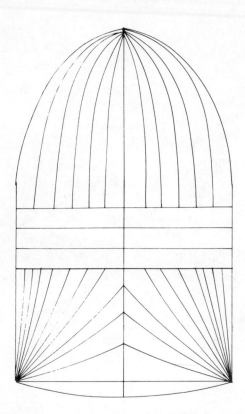

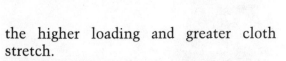

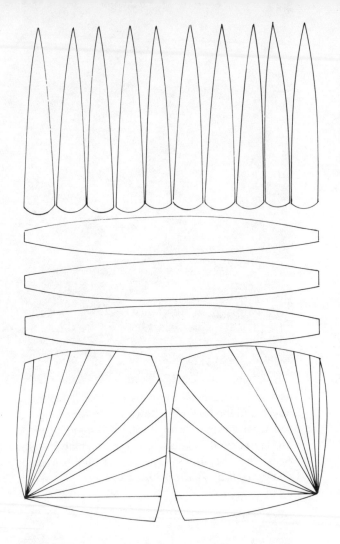

Figure 39: Here are the many parts of a spinnaker, before seaming and after. Each panel is broadseamed and then each side of the clew. Horizontal panels and the head are shaped prior to the final joining.

the higher loading and greater cloth stretch.

Once the sailmaker has decided on his design, it is translated into the sail by means of broadseaming the vertical head gores, horizontal midpanels, and radial clew gores (the tapered panels of cloth) (See Figure 39). The head gores are most important because their shape determines the way the sail lifts and projects away from the mast. The top 40 percent of the head gore usually is straight, with most of the broadseaming in the bottom half of the gore, so the sail will fly straight off the mast and then turn out and down, spreading itself for maximum exposure. The straighter topped head panels also reduce head angle. Common head angles are now 85 to 95 degrees, as opposed to older ones, which were over 106 degrees. Spinnakers with full heads and large head angles were fighting a losing battle because it took plenty of lifting power to support the larger angle and shoulders.

The larger amount of broadseaming in

the bottom of the head is matched in the top horizontal section, and then the broadseam amounts decrease as you go lower in the sail. The clew panels are pretty close to straight wedges, with small amounts of broadseaming added to keep the shape smooth and consistent with the rest of the sail.

The best way to judge spinnaker depth is to view the sail from off the boat. The broadseaming put in the sail gives it a certain vertical profile that is a determinant of how the sail will perform. From off the boat and to leeward, you can line up the leeches and see the vertical profile of the curve from the head, along the center line, to the middle of the foot. This vertical curve should be smooth and constant, without any bumps or distortions.

The next consideration to look into is the cross-sectional shape of the sail—the outline shape of the curve from luff to leech. Ideally, it should be as circular as possible, with a nice, fair curve from tape to tape, as opposed to an elliptical shape that is flat in the center with the leeches turned in. The shape here is critical because, unlike a genoa (which is designed to have a specific leading and trailing edge), the spinnaker is symmetrical, and what would be a perfect leading edge on one jibe would be the worst on the other (See Figure 40).

A pure circular shape is hard to fly because the leading edge of the sail is straight and the angle of attack on the spinnaker is too small. When you ease the sheet just a little bit, the sail will fold and collapse. On the other hand, the elliptical shape, while slower, makes for a more forgiving sail that is easier to

Susan shows good form because her spinnaker pole is perpendicular to the mast and the clews are even. *Photograph by Carol Singer*

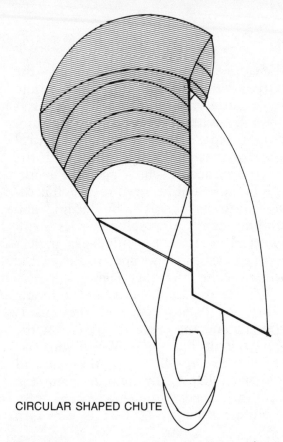

CIRCULAR SHAPED CHUTE

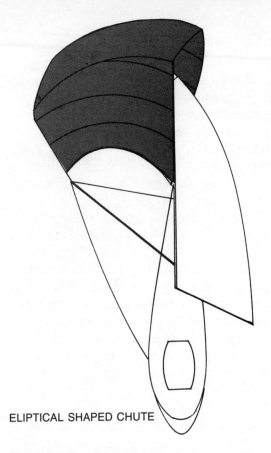

ELIPTICAL SHAPED CHUTE

Figure 40: The circular shape in a spinnaker is more of an even curve through the center of the sail. This shape is best for reaches because the leeches stay open and allow the air to exit from the sail undisturbed.

Figure 41: The elliptical spinnaker is straight in the center and curved at the leeches. This cross-sectional shape is good for running chutes because it exposes the most sail area to the wind.

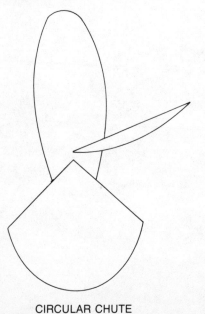

CIRCULAR CHUTE

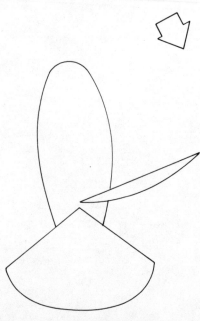

ELIPTICAL CHUTE

trim. So a compromise in the cross-sectional shape must be made so an efficient airfoil shape is presented to the wind, but also one that is easy to use (See Figure 41).

The most common weight for most boat chutes is ¾ ounce, although this depends on the size of the boat you are sailing. Stronger cloths and triradial construction have pushed up the maximum loading limits and wind strengths so you can use lighter chutes in more wind. In many cases, the all-purpose chute on a 25-foot-masthead boat or a 30-foot fractional rig can be ½ ounce. Chutes of ½ ounce are used up to 11 knots apparent on 12-Meters!

Trimming

Aerodynamically, the spinnaker becomes a foil, producing lift whenever there is airflow across the sail. Unlike the main and genoa, which are attached to a rigid stay or mast, the spinnaker is completely free-flying and relies on its own lift to stay aloft. Because of this and the fact that the cloth is not as stable as Mylar and Kevlar, the shape of the chute can be changed more drastically than for any other sail. The height of the spinnaker pole, the sheeting angle, and even bouncing over waves change the shape. Be aware of the small changes in wind velocity and angle. The smallest change in either of them means a change in the way the sail should be trimmed. Remember that unlike sailing upwind, when the helmsman changes the direc-

Overtrimming and undertrimming. The sail here is overtrimmed and as a result much flatter in cross section than is needed to make the boat go fast. *Photograph by Andrea Olsen*

Same sail, same angle. The sheet is eased out and the sail becomes fuller to its originally designed shape. *Photograph by Andrea Olsen*

The vertical profile of this sail is near perfect. The sail exits from the mast and away from the blanketing effects of the main but lifts high enough to have the rest of the sail fly away from the boat. The horizontal and clew sections are shaped to form a vertical wall to the wind. Note how the halyard is eased to help get the sail away from the mainsail. *Photograph by Mike Toppa*

tion of the boat to the changes in the wind direction and velocity, downwind there is no perceptible groove, and reactions to wind changes come slower. The trimmer is responsible for changing the pole angle and height to keep the angle of attack on the spinnaker constant. Do not be content with just keeping a slight curl in the luff; the whole attitude of the sail must be considered.

First, let us consider the spinnaker pole's use as a control. In addition to the masthead, the pole is the only other fixed point to which the spinnaker is attached. The pole's importance must not be overlooked. Do not just set the pole height to the old rule of keeping the clews level. If properly set, many times the tack will be lower than the clew.

The vertical component of the pole determines the draft placement and leading edge shape of the luff, while the fore and aft component determines the angle of attack. Remember, the spinnaker is a lift-producing foil just like the main and the genoa, so the pole control should be used to achieve the sail shape needed.

Because the spinnaker has to be symmetrical, the deepest part of the sail is in the middle. But because you want the chute to act as a foil, the draft has to be moved forward. The pole acts like a Cunningham in the sense that the more luff tension applied, the more the draft will move forward. Draft placement through pole height is combined with having the sail luff evenly. Just like the main or the genoa, you want the luff of the chute to break evenly. If the pole is too high, the top of the chute will be allowed to lift and it will twist off, collapsing over itself. If the pole is set too low, the bottom of the chute will be pulled too tight, causing the break to be low. Adding telltales to the luff of the spinnaker will help you see the windflow across the luff, just as on the genoa, and can be used much the same way to determine correct pole height and luff twist. A word of caution: The telltales will read windflow only on a reach. When running, the sail is in a stalled condition and there is very little attached flow over the luff (See Figure 42).

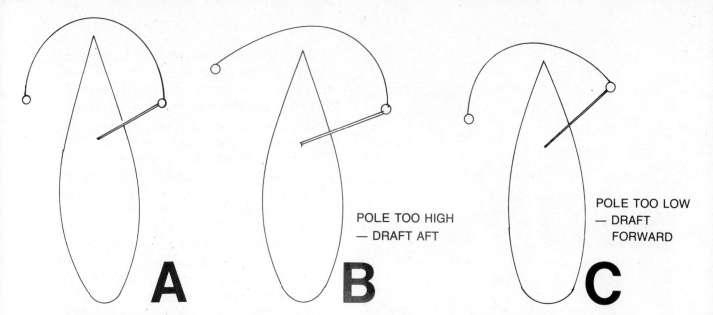

POLE TOO HIGH
— DRAFT AFT

POLE TOO LOW
— DRAFT
FORWARD

A **B** **C**

Figure 42: In these diagrams, spinnaker shapes change due to different pole height settings. When the pole is at its correct height (A), the luff will curl evenly when the sheet is eased out. When the pole is too high (B), the draft slides back in the sail and the leading edge straightens out. This shape is good for pointing high with the spinnaker because it presents a straighter leading edge to the wind although it makes the sail more unstable and harder to fly. When the pole is too low (C), the luff gets tight and the draft moves forward. This shape is good in lighter air when you need a deeper leading edge to create drive in the sail.

When the pole is too high, the luff, or "break," will be too high. The top of the sail twists off and folds over itself. When the break is high, lower the pole. *Photograph by Andrea Olsen*

Here the pole is set too low. The spinnaker is not allowed to lift at all and the luff is too tight, causing the break to be in the lower half of the sail. When this happens, raise the pole. *Photograph by Andrea Olsen*

Here the spinnaker pole is set too high. The bottom of the sail looks good, but the top of the sail is lifting too much and exposed area is lost. The head length of this chute is half the total length of the spinnaker. As you can see, most of the head area is going straight away from the mast. Not very fast! *Photograph by Andrea Olsen*

When the pole height is just right and the sheet is eased a bit, the sail will maintain a smooth, even curl throughout the middle of the luff. However, within the range of the sail, the pole height will be lowered and raised from this medium setting depending on the sea conditions and wind strength. When the wind strength is less, or decreases over the leeward leg, the pole has to be lowered to keep the luff tension and draft placement in the right spot.

As pole height affects luff tension and draft placement, it also affects the stability of the sail. As mentioned earlier, a curved luff cross-sectional shape makes for an easily trimmed sail. To help out a sail that is hard to fly, you can lower the pole and move the draft forward to give the sail more stability. In light air and sloppy sea conditions, this is most effective in getting the chute to settle down instead of oscillating with each roll of the boat.

To illustrate how pole height controls stability, try sailing with a pole a few feet on the high side and then lower it so it is too low. When the pole is too high, you will see that it is impossible to keep a constant curl in the luff. When the pole is too low, you can sail with a curl in the luff that is almost half the width of the sail.

Knowing how the sail reacts to different pole heights can be used in your strategy on the racecourse. Say you are on the reaching leg of a triangle and the current has forced you down below the reach mark. You can raise the pole, move the draft aft, and provide a finer entry to the spinnaker, allowing you to point higher and get back up to the mark.

Pole height should also be adjusted during the jibe. As you bear away, the pole should be lowered to counteract the apparent wind drop. After the pole is tripped away and you are on the new jibe, keep the pole low and draft forward for maximum acceleration out of the jibe.

Pole position, fore and aft, will determine just how effective your spinnaker will be. It controls the angle of attack on the luff of the chute. If too far forward, the angle will be too great, and there will be little attached flow. If the pole is squared too far back, the angle of attack will be too narrow, causing you to oversheet the sail and create stall. Basically, the spinnaker luff should be vertical and at right angles to the pole. If the luff of the sail is angled toward the bow and away from the end of the pole, then the pole should be eased forward. If the luff

When setting the pole height, don't go by the old rule of keeping the clews level. As you can see here, the clew is about 18 inches higher than the pole end, but the sail breaks evenly and is in correct trim. *Photograph by Andrea Olsen*

When the pole height is correct, the break on the luff when the sheet is eased will be even from top to bottom. Pole height is determined by positioning the lead of the genoa: When the luff breaks evenly, it's right. *Photograph by Andrea Olsen*

is going too windward and away from the pole, it should be brought aft.

Proper trimming requires not only trimming the sheet when a slight header comes, but also easing the pole forward to maintain the proper angle of attack. The whole sail should be rotated around the boat to the changing apparent wind changes. When doing this, it is important to realize that it is the luff of the chute you want to keep square to the wind—not the pole. In light air on a 90-degree reach with the pole on the headstay, the luff is too far to leeward. The pole should be brought back so the luff of the sail is even with the headstay.

On the other hand, when going dead downwind in a heavy breeze, you can ease the pole forward slightly to decrease the efficiency of the luff and depower the sail.

ABOVE: The spinnaker is two blocked and the pole is pulled aft to the proper angle to fill the sail. *Photograph by Andrea Olsen*

ABOVE LEFT: The spinnaker is full and drawing except for some disturbed air at the head and foot caused by the genoa. Note the flaked jib halyard on deck below the genoa clew ready to be released. *Photograph by Andrea Olsen*

LEFT: The genoa halyard is released and the foredeck crew brings the sail down on deck. Notice that he tries to do this without going directly to the bow of the boat in an effort to keep the weight back. Total elapsed time from spinnaker up to jib down: 18 seconds. *Photograph by Andrea Olsen*

Clear air and
full speed are
the key to
good starts as
shown by this
SORC fleet.

PHOTOGRAPHER KAREN OLSEN.

The concentration of
these collegiate
sailors at the annual
Timme Angsten regatta
in Chicago is apparent
during starting maneuvers.

PHOTOGRAPHER CAROL SINGER.

Teamwork between helmsman and tactician is essential for smart decision making. Here Gary Jobson works as tactician for Bob Tetterman on the 12-meter *Gleam*.

PHOTOGRAPHER JOHN MECRAY.

Crew of *Defender* shows intense concentration during starting maneuvers.

PHOTOGRAPHER DAN NERNEY.

Jubilation (US-53221) being drafted by *Golden Eagle*, *Brooke Anne* and *Gem* following the start of the 1984 Miami-Nassau race.

PHOTOGRAPHER DAN NERNEY.

This dinghy crew is searching for every breath of wind during this light air regatta.

PHOTOGRAPHER CAROL SINGER.

The crew on *Pinta* has completely lost it following a broach. Perhaps not flying a spinnaker would have been safer.

PHOTOGRAPHER DAN NERNEY.

Innovations in new sail cloth have taken many forms in recent years.
Here *Intuition* is sailing with a clear Mylar light wind headsail.

Gary Jobson is the last man up on the rack as the Australian 18
crew scrambles to get *Silhouette Vodka* under control.

PHOTOGRAPHER CHRISTOPHER CUNNINGHAM.

This Bill Tripp-designed yacht shows four kinds of cloth with a black Kevlar mainsail, dacron leech and Mylar luff headsail and a new Kevlar headsail being hoisted underneath.

PHOTOGRAPHER DANIEL FORSTER.

Australia in 1980 gained considerable sail area with a bendy top spar made of fiber glass. The boat showed great speed in light air.

PHOTOGRAPHER DAN NERNEY.

The quest for speed often takes many forms as the heaviest crew members on this Bahamian work boat sit on a hiking board to keep the boat level.

PHOTOGRAPHER CHRISTOPHER CUNNINGHAM.

Australia II's winged keel may have been the difference in the 1983 America's Cup.

PHOTOGRAPHER DAN NERNEY.

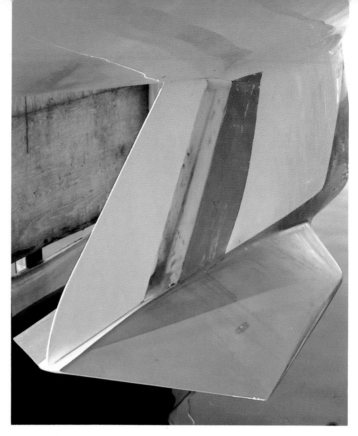

Slingshot, one of the fastest boats in the world, includes two crew on hiking platform trimming sails during the English speed trials.

PHOTOGRAPHER CHRISTOPHER CUNNINGHAM.

It is difficult to understand how these yachts maneuvered themselves into this position during the Pan Am Clipper Cup.

PHOTOGRAPHER PHIL UHL.

**Foredeck man, John Edgcomb, takes the brunt of a wave
on *Courageous* during 1980 America's Cup trials.**

PHOTOGRAPHER DAN NERNEY.

A crewman on *Bumblebee* is hoisted 15 feet off the deck to adjust leechline during close reach.
PHOTOGRAPHER DANIEL FORSTER.

This crew member helps the sail trimmer by putting his full
weight on the jib sheet as it is trimmed in.

PHOTOGRAPHER CAROL SINGER.

Sun poisoning is an enemy of many sailors.
This sailor has taken drastic action or perhaps
he's just preparing to steal a race!

PHOTOGRAPHER CHRISTOPHER CUNNINGHAM.

Maxi boats require two dozen crew members.
Seventeen are shown here as powerful *Condor* comes off a wave.

PHOTOGRAPHER DAN NERNEY.

Every crew member you add
to your boat squares your
potential problems. The light
winds *Condor* has been
sitting in for forty-eight
hours is evident by the
enthusiasm of this crew.

PHOTOGRAPHER GARY JOBSON.

The positioning of the spinnaker sheet lead has its effect on the shape and efficiency of the chute also. Just like the genoa sheet, the spinnaker sheet lead controls leech twist, and it should be adjusted for the different wind conditions. Most boats sheet the spinnaker to the back of the boat and leave it there, but by changing the sheeting angle you can add or take away power from the sail as conditions warrant.

In lighter air, moving the lead forward decreases twist and gets the clew closer to the tack, making the sail deeper and more powerful. In medium and heavier air, move the lead back to open up the leech and prevent any air stall. In the heaviest conditions, you need to depower and twist off the leech as you would a genoa. Of course, the aftermost lead position is limited by the length of the boat, but you can twist off more by getting the sheet up over the boom. This will raise the clew, open up the leech, and spill off air that would normally overpower the boat.

To make it easy to move the lead under load, rig a tweeker line along the rail near the stern. Simply, this is a block that is attached to a line secured to the rail. The block is attached to the spinnaker sheet between the lead and the clew. To move the lead forward, pull down on the tweeker, and the block will redirect the sheet lead farther forward.

When running, the foot of the chute can get too deep (which is the opposite of what you want). You want to expose the maximum amount of sailcloth to the wind as possible. However, the length of your pole limits how much of the foot you can spread out. Usually the pole is

the length of "J," while the spinnaker width is 1.8 × "J." When the pole is out square to the boat, the sheet eased, and the clew near the headstay, the bottom of the sail will be too deep. You can open up the foot by putting the sheet up over the boom, getting the sheet farther outboard, and widening the sheeting base.

On some reaches, when the wind angle is right, you can set a big staysail, or even the genoa, inside the spinnaker for extra speed. Newer spinnakers like this one are designed to fly farther away from the boat to allow for more room to accommodate an inside sail. *Photograph by Andrea Olsen*

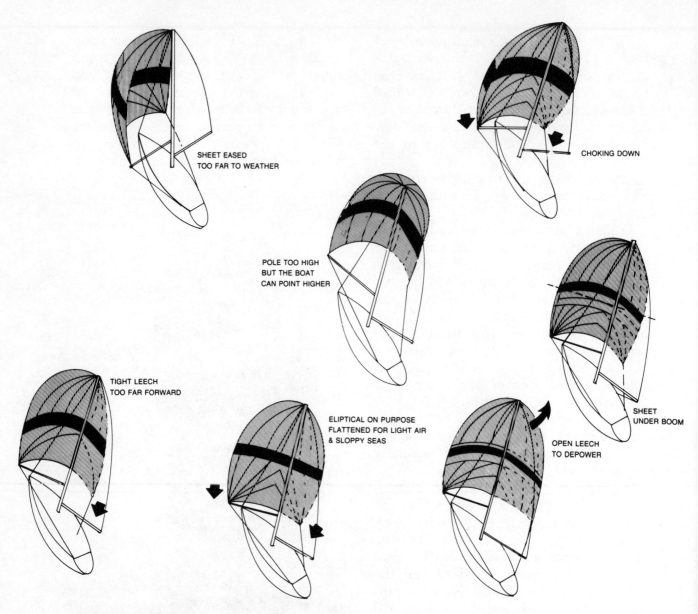

SHEET EASED
TOO FAR TO WEATHER

CHOKING DOWN

POLE TOO HIGH
BUT THE BOAT
CAN POINT HIGHER

SHEET
UNDER BOOM

TIGHT LEECH
TOO FAR FORWARD

ELIPTICAL ON PURPOSE
FLATTENED FOR LIGHT AIR
& SLOPPY SEAS

OPEN LEECH
TO DEPOWER

Figure 43: Normally, the spinnaker sheet should be led to the back corner of the deck and transom so the leech will not close off and affect the air exit.

This works well on most boats with high-aspect mainsails and short booms but not on fractional-rig boats with longer booms, because you would be forcing the clew too far outboard. In this case you can move the lead forward in the widest part of the boat (See Figure 43).

Trimming in Heavy Air

When trimming in heavy air, the trimmer and the helmsman must work together to keep the boat at top speed but not overpowered enough in the puffs to cause a broach. This is difficult because the irregular waves and puffs that cause broaching come at random. Only the helmsman can counter the waves, but the trimmer can deal with the puffs to help keep the boat on its feet. If the conditions that cause broaching are understood, he can fly the sail more effectively and reduce the spinouts.

Picture your boat on a puffy, heavy-air reach with the true wind angle at 90 degrees. The speed at which the boat moves through the water increases the apparent wind speed and also pulls the apparent wind angle forward. The helmsman is working hard to keep the boat on its feet, and the trimmer is trying to keep the chute on edge without having it overtrimmed.

When the puff hits, the boat heels over, adding to the weather helm. The helmsman tries to steer down, and the boom vang is released, luffing the main and moving the center of effort to the spinnaker. Now the trimmer can ease the sheet—not to luff the chute, but to keep it from being overtrimmed, because contrary to popular belief, the increased wind velocity draws the apparent wind angle aft. The boat is already going at hull speed, so the forward component in the apparent angle vector remains the same. As the puff hits, there is more wind velocity relative to boat speed, and the wind angle goes aft. It is as if the

This heavy air reaching chute was used in 20 + knots of wind. Note the open leeches in the main and spinnaker to let the air spill off the sails and keep the boat flat. *Photograph by Mike Toppa*

This spinnaker has two-ply leeches in the head of the luff and leech to help control stretch and maintain the sail shape. The loads in the spinnaker are much like mains and jib in that the leeches are heavily loaded while the body of the sail remains relatively unstressed. *Photograph by Mike Toppa*

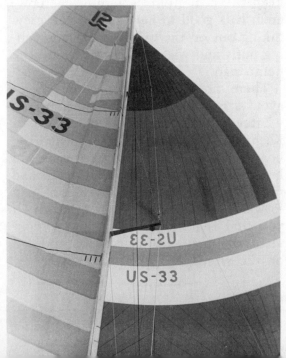

Spinnaker sets. The pole is set, the halyard is attached, and the tack has been pulled out to the end of the pole. *Photograph by Andrea Olsen*

lost area from the reef with a short genoa staysail set under the spinnaker. The extra area forward will help keep the bow down. It is important that this staysail be a low-aspect sail, as a tall one would add too much to the heeling forces.

Specialty Spinnakers

There are a few specialty spinnakers worth having on board if your budget and sail limitation rules permit. A reaching chute can be devastating to the competition when used in smooth water and light to moderate wind. Often called a starcut, or flanker, these sails can do what jib tops do but at close to twice the sail area and provide more power. These special reachers are flat and spread more area than the all-purpose chutes. The pole should be kept low to prevent the sail from lifting high into the air. Check the lead position also because the sail sets lower, the clew will be lower, and the lead might have to go forward.

Super light Mylar spinnakers have been used effectively in the lightest of air. Weighing .402 ounce, these sails are great in winds ranging from zero to five knots. They are also good when used during rain or heavy fog. Since it is not a woven material, it does not absorb moisture and gain weight. Because it is Mylar, there is no stretch in the material. The woven nylon in the free-flying spinnaker absorbs the shocks of bouncing through the waves and stays somewhat stable, but the Mylar spinnakers do not have the shock-absorbing ability, and

wind speed remained constant and the hull speed decreased. So when the puff hits, the trimmer can ease the sail out to match the apparent wind going aft and keep the boat from becoming overpowered. It is good to have one of the crew hiking out on the rail to spot approaching puffs and warn the trimmer and the helmsman.

There are times when you cannot avoid a broach. In these conditions, do whatever necessary prior to the event. Keep someone on the vang so when the boat begins to lose control, the vang can be released. This luffs the main and moves the center of effort in the sail plan forward to help pull the bow down. If you find that the main is luffing constantly, put in a reef or two to cut down on the windage. You might replace the they tend to bounce around in any but the smoothest conditions.

Like a #2 or #3 genoa, have smaller storm spinnakers for heavier air. These sails should be at least one step up in weight than your heaviest all-purpose spinnaker and be smaller in girth. Most storm chutes or "chicken chutes" are 85 to 95 percent of maximum allowable girth, depending on the stability of the boat. In heavy conditions, use these sails—they're about 3 percent flatter than the all-purpose spinnakers. These sails are designed flat with open leeches to reduce heeling power and are made to set well away from the boat, keeping the slot open and allowing for the main to be well eased.

The bow is at the mark and the chute is being hoisted. Easing the jib and main is important as the boat bears away so the boat keeps in trim and the spinnaker stays blanketed and won't fill until it is fully hoisted. *Photograph by Andrea Olsen*

The blooper is a special downwind sail that is often misunderstood because of the many things it does and the ways it is trimmed. Sometimes it is used to stabilize the boat in heavy air. In lighter air, it is used for speed.

The blooper is designed with a high clew and generous luff hollow so the area flies as far from the boat as possible. It is measured as a genoa, so its size is limited to the boat's maximum LP. In light to moderate wind speeds of six to 13 knots, the blooper can be used from 135 to 160 degrees apparent. In these broad-reaching conditions, the airflows to the sail are fed from the leech of the spinnaker. You trim the sail as you would a genoa. When the sail luffs, trim it in. Sailing any higher than 135 degrees creates too much side force and pressure on the helm. In the lighter air, you cannot sail dead downwind with the blooper because the apparent wind speed will be too low to support the sail.

In winds above 14 knots, you can sail dead down with the blooper, although now the airflow comes from the leech and flows across the sail to the luff. Trimming requires watching the leech. If it is sheeted too much, the blooper will collapse, so you have to ease it until it fulls.

When sailing dead down in wind speeds above 20 knots, the blooper can be set as a counterbalance to the spinnaker to help control oscillation. A big spinnaker will tend to pull the boat to windward, and the blooper set to leeward would balance this out and keep the boat going in the desired course.

9
CRUISING SAILS

While the racing sailor has many choices of cloth, construction, and shapes to choose from to optimize his sail inventory, the cruising sailor just wants sails that will fit his boat and let him enjoy sailing around the bay. Buying cruising sails should be easy and worry-free.

Many lofts now offer their own specialized line of sails made especially for the cruiser. Since these lofts specialize in racing sails, their cruising line is a spin-off of the development on the racing scene. Usually the sails are lower in price than the racing line because construction and materials are more basic, even though you get the benefit of racing developments.

Although it's easy to categorize the cruising sailor as anyone who doesn't race, it's not always easy to draw up a sail inventory for him because of the different kinds of sailing he may be doing. While one cruising sailor might be happy just sailing around the bay on weekends, another cruiser might be doing extended passages, or overnight sails in which he may be subjected to all types of weather. So in choosing your cruising sail inventory, talk to your sailmaker about the

type of sailing you'll be doing and get his recommendations.

The size of your inventory, in terms of how many sails to have, is another important decision. Although price is the most important overriding factor in building your inventory, the amount of manpower you have on board makes a big difference. Of course, you certainly don't need four jibs and a spinnaker if it's just you and your wife cruising around. You don't have to make many sail changes; you want to sit back and relax.

Because of this, multipurpose sails have grown in popularity among the cruising set. It's possible to buy a genoa with a reef installed so when the wind starts to blow, you can reef the sail down and get the benefits of two sails out of one. Although there is a small trade-off in performance, it's well worth the benefits.

Let's look at cruising inventories for different-size boats and break them down to find the options available in mains, jibs, and spinnakers. As you will see, it is possible to tailor the inventory specifically to your requirements.

Mainsails

The first matter to decide is the weight of the mainsail. Normally it should be at least one ounce heavier than what the sailmaker might recommend for a similar-size racing boat. Naturally, the bigger the boat, the heavier the main should be. A good guide to follow: boats up to 25 feet in length should have a main made of five-ounce cloth. Boats 25 to 33 feet should have a 6.5-ounce main, 35 to 40-foot boats should have 7.5 to 8-ounce mainsails, and 40 to 48-foot boats should have nine-ounce mains. Above that, consider either 10-ounce sails or a stronger two-ply five- or six-ounce main. Whatever the weight, make sure the cloth used is special cruising cloth that's soft and easy to handle and not stiff, resinated Dacron. Most cloth manufacturers make a special line of cruising cloths that are finished so they fold and stow easily. The soft cloth is especially nice when you get caught in a squall and are forced to reef in the sail. It's much easier to reef a softer sail than one that's hard and stiff.

The shape must be well built into the sail because you don't want to be troubled with contorting the sail to get the best shape to move the boat. Besides that, there aren't many cruising boats that have all the go-fast equipment on board. The sail designer should understand this and build the sail knowing the mast is set up to be straight without the ability to flatten the sail with mast bend. The sail should be designed knowing the only controls that will be used are the outhaul, halyard, and Cunningham.

The reefs should be spaced at generous intervals. When it starts to blow, you want to reduce sail fast to a comfortable setting and angle of heel. Most racing boats have their reefs spaced to allow for 15 percent area reductions. The cruising sailor should have his reefs spaced to allow at least 20 percent of area off at a time.

Recently, slab reefing has taken over from reefing as the most popular and cheapest way of getting sail area off in a hurry. Work with your sailmaker as he builds the sail so you know exactly where the reefs are placed so you can position the reefing blocks on your boom to match the sail. Also, you can get him to splice a messenger line through the reefs so you can rig your reef lines as you need them instead of having lines hanging on the leech. Remember, when you do reef, tie up the reefed sailcloth to the boom with plenty of sail ties. Not only is this proper seamanship, it also prevents the dangling sail from reducing visibility and getting caught on something.

If you limit your cruising to inland-waters, a simple off-the-shelf main should provide you with years of sailing fun without the need to have the sail checked over and repaired annually. But if you plan more adventurous sailing, there are a few things you can do for your mainsail to get more life out of it and keep your repair bills down. If you have slugs on the luff instead of bolt rope, have the slugs sewn on with webbing instead of just shackling them onto the sail. This is especially useful in light-air areas such as Chesapeake Bay, because when the wind does die and the main starts to slat, the sail won't chafe itself on the shackles. The webbing absorbs some of the shock of the sail banging against the mast. If you're going offshore, have the batten pockets reinforced with extra-heavy patches. A batten pocket failure can send the batten into the water, causing the leech to become unsupported and flutter itself to ribbons. An ounce of prevention is worth a pound of cure.

If you plan to do any long-passages and anticipate storm sailing conditions, have patches put over the main where it would press against the spreaders when sailing downwind. Simple spreader patch material used on genoas will do the job. Chafe is a sail's worst enemy—do everything possible to prevent it right from the start. The farther offshore you're going, the more you should look toward beefing up your sails. There are no sail-makers at sea!

Genoas

The same care in preventive mainte-nance should be taken for all the jibs on your boat. The genoa inventory for your cruising boat should be well thought out. Take into consideration the area you're sailing in, the size of your boat, and the size of your crew. Again, the best way to do this is to talk with your sailmaker and detail your requirements. Naturally, a Pearson 30 sailing in windy San Francisco Bay will have a different inventory than the same boat sailing in the light air of Tampa Bay. The heavy-air conditions will require smaller, heavier sails, while the light-air regions can use lighter, big-ger sails for better performance.

Here are recommendations for com-plete genoa inventories on boats under and over 35 feet in length. Both catego-ries are again broken down for light-air and heavy-air regions.

Under 35 LOA

	Light Air	Heavy Air
#1	160%	145%
#2	125%	115%
#3	95%	85%

LOA 35 or Over

	Light Air	Heavy Air
#1	165%	150%
#2	130%	130%
#3	100%	100%
#4	85%	85%

The thinking behind these inventories reflects a trade-off between performance and ease of handling. The smaller boat will have less crew and less stability, so it's important to keep the number of sails down. On the other hand, the larger boat will have more crew, more stability, and be more likely to make longer pas-sages, so its inventory can add another sail for more performance.

The 150 to 160 percent larger genoas should be built of a lighter cloth and cut full and powerful to get the boat moving. This sail will be the workhorse in all light to moderate conditions, so the sail should be capable of going up to 16 knots. Be sure to have adequate spreader patches put on so the sail doesn't catch and tear on the spreaders during a tack.

The midrange genoas of 115 to 130 percent will be the powerhouse sails to be used in moderate and heavy air. They should be designed to go from 14 to 24 knots of wind and be built of material at least as heavy as that of the mainsail. Depending on the stability of your particular boat and how much heel you can sail with without becoming uncomfortable, you may not use your #2 up to 24 knots, but it's good to have the sail built that strong. Everybody gets caught in a sudden line squall at least once in their sailing career, so it's good to have that safety margin.

The #2 is a good candidate for use as a multipurpose sail. Because of its smaller size, you could have a reef installed to cut the area by 35 to 40 percent and turn it into a #3. Although it won't perform as well as a true #3, you'll have a smaller sail to use when the wind blows up. Just be sure to tie up the reefed cloth below so it doesn't drag in the water and chafe against the lifelines. If you do go for this option, it might be wise to have the upper portion of the sail built out of a heavier material. Normally this weight increase means using a cloth that's an ounce heavier.

The #3 range jibs should be built so they don't overlap the mast. Normally the luff length is reduced by 10 percent to lower the center of effort and reduce the healing forces. The cloth should be at least an ounce heavier than the mainsail. Because this sail will be used in heavy wind and bigger waves, the clew should be higher than the other sails so any water that comes on board won't get caught up in the foot and add extra pressure to the sail as well as slow the boat down. Raising the clew also increases visibility to leeward under the jib when the boat heels.

The #4 or storm jib is for the serious offshore cruiser who will be making longer passages and might get caught in bad weather for a while. It's important that this sail be built extra strong, with triple-stitched seams and oversize patches. There should be a generous amount of leech hollow cut out so there's no chance of the leech flapping in the heavy air. An uncontrolled leech would soon flutter itself to ribbons, rendering the sail useless.

The International Offshore Rule sets requirements for the maximum size of the storm jib, and it is a good rule of thumb to use in determining the size for your boat. The IOR states that the area of the sail should not be greater than 5 percent of the "I" dimension ("I" is the maximum distance from the base of the mast to the intersection of the headstay and the mast) squared, and the luff length can be no longer than 65 percent of "I." So the storm jib for a C & C 35 with an "I" dimension of 44 feet would be 96.8 square feet and have a luff length of 28.6 feet.

Even though you may never use your storm jib except in the worst weather, it's a good safety precaution to own one. During light winds, get your crew used to how it's set and where the lead goes, so during heavier weather it can be set with a minimum of problems.

Having roller furling systems is a great alternative to having a multiple headsail inventory. Simply, the sail is set on a rotating luff headstay that rolls the sail up. In heavier air, the sail can be partially furled to any degree to reduce sail area. At the end of the day the sail can be fully rolled and stored on the stay in a furled position. The first roller furling systems were just heavy wire sewn into the luff that supported the sail. The wire is connected to a drum at its base, which contained a control line that turned the wire and furled the sail. The problem with this system was that the wire stretched a lot and created sag that was detrimental to the sail shape.

The advent of the solid rod grooved extrusion and extruded sections that fit over the headstay has solved the problem of luff sag and enabled roller furling systems to produce the same performance as a normal headstay. Not only do you get the full performance from the sail, but also these new systems are easier to rotate, so furling is done quicker and with less muscle.

There are many good and not so good furling systems on the market today, and they cover a wide price range. Here are some things you should look for when purchasing one. First, look for a system that is easy to install with a minimum amount of tools and time needed. The better units come from the manufacturer engineered so all the pieces fit together nicely. Length adjustment within the system is important also, because over time the wire headstay may stretch and sag when under load. If you have the capability of tightening the headstay, you can counter this.

The bearings in the roller drum and head swivel should be made of a material that requires little or no lubrication, because any oil or grease that's needed on the headstay will eventually end up on your sail. Some systems use a Teflon-impregnated roller bearing that reduces friction and needs no lubrication.

If you purchase a roller furling system for your boat, your sails can be easily converted for use on it. Bring it into your luff so the hanks are cut off and the proper-size luff tape can be sewn on to fit into the headstay groove. Sometimes the luff length has to be shortened to make room for the furling drum under the tack.

If you intend to store the sail on the furling system when at the mooring, it's wise to have a protective cover sewn onto the leech so ultraviolet rays won't deteriorate the sail. When the sail is furled, the protected leech covers the body of the sail. The only drawback to this is having a bulky two-ply area at the back of your sail. If you have a vertically cut sail, the last leech panel can be made of special sailcloth that has a UV coating on it. The sun cover then becomes an integral part of the sail with no loss of performance. Another advantage of the vertical sail is that the back two or three panels can be made of heavier cloth, so when the sail is partially furled in heavy air, the lighter cloth is rolled up while the heavier fabric is doing all the work.

10
MARINE ELECTRONICS

When we talk about sailing, we talk in terms of numbers. Our sailing conditions are defined by angle of heel, wind speed, apparent wind angles, distance to the mark, etc. We use these numbers to compare performance in different conditions. Are we going as fast now as we did in the same conditions last week when we won the race? Does our new jib make the boat point higher than our old #1?

Most of these numbers are generated from our performance instruments, and the instruments you need for your boat depend on the kind of sailing you do. Most cruising sailors are concerned with navigation more than performance, so their inventory might consist of a log, depth sounder, and knotmeter. But the racing sailor needs the performance instruments so he can better judge how his boat and sails are doing. With this information he can set standards and compare present situations with past ones.

You don't need instruments to sail or race a boat, though. Certainly, someone racing a Laser has no need for wind-speed information or calculated time to the layline, as he can evaluate his position on the course and his performance instantaneously by looking at his relative position in relation to the other boat and the next mark. His inputs are position in the fleet, position to the mark, puffs on the water, wave conditions, and so on.

But larger boats racing longer distances in unfamiliar waters and at night can use sailing instruments effectively as guides to sailing performance. Just as a Laser sailor uses his senses to help him, sailors on bigger boats use instruments as an extension of their senses. On bigger boats you sometimes lose the feel you have on a dinghy that flows through the tiller, mainsheet, and the seat of your pants. Instruments can help you get some of the feeling back. They won't take the place of your sailing ability, but they will supplement it by giving you more information about present conditions so you can make better and faster decisions.

The basic instrument package you should use on your boat gives the boat speed, wind speed, and wind angle. Knowing the boat speed will allow you to compare your present performance to times in the past when you know the boat was going at full speed. This is especially useful at night when you lose sight of your competition. Your speed is the only link to past performance when you lose the benefits of daylight. During the day, you can see the other boats, and you know right away if you're going faster or slower. Then you see your speed go down and performance dropping, you look around the boat and see that the genoa lead might have to be changed, or the main should be trimmed harder. But at night, your bench mark is gone. If you're sailing along at 5.8 knots and past experience tells you the boat should be going 6.2 knots, you retrim the sails to get the boat speed back up to maximum.

Wind speed and wind angle are used in determining the right sails to use at different times. If your sailmaker tells you the reacher is better when the wind angle is 50 degrees off the bow, you need to have an accurate instrument to judge this by. Also at night, you can use the apparent wind indicator to steer by. When it's dark you can't see the telltales on the genoa, but if you know the boat is in the groove when the wind angle is at 30 degrees, you can use your angle indicator in place of the telltales.

Knowing the wind speed is equally important in determining the proper sails to use. More and more specialty sails that have defined wind speeds and ranges they can be used in are appearing on the racing scene. Having accurate wind information will result in better use of these sails.

Judging wind speed without an anemometer can be hard because of different accompanying conditions. If you're about to start a race in a dying wind after a storm, there is usually leftover chop pres-

Ra Carat instruments: These instruments are bright and visible from anywhere aft of the mast. Not only are they in the helmsman's line of sight when he's watching the waves, but they also allow the crew to keep up to date on wind speed, angle, and boat speed. *Photograph by Mike Toppa*

ent that can fool you into thinking the wind speed is higher than it actually is. Also, a dense wind such as wind and fog or wind and rain can feel heavier than it is. When you feel this dense wind on your face, you might think it's blowing harder and set too small a jib.

Location of the instruments on the boat is vital to getting the most use out of them. The primary user will be the helmsman, so they should be mounted around the cockpit in such a way that they are unobstructed and easy to read. This is especially important when sailing upwind because the helmsman will use the instruments to confirm his feelings when he thinks the boat is in the groove or going slow.

Ideally, there should be separate sets of instruments on each side of the boat; they should be mounted as far outboard as possible so they will be in the helmsman's line of sight. His eyes can shift from the telltales to the waves in front of the boat and down to the speed or wind indicator. Having digital readouts helps tremendously because only one number will be displayed at a time. In the case of the knotmeter, which is the helmsman's primary tool, the boat speed is presented as a real number in tenths and hundredths of a knot, instead of an analog dial, where you have to follow a pointer. This makes the readout much more accurate. You'll see smaller fractions of speed change and get a better feel for how small trim adjustments affect speed.

The exception to digital readouts being easier to use might be the apparent wind angle indicator. Many a sailor prefers the analog dial with the outline of the boat superimposed on the face where the pointer shows the wind direction in relation to the boat.

Computer-Based Electronics

The biggest improvement in recent marine electronics is due to the explosion in computer technology. Until now we have read off our instruments information that gives relative or apparent numbers. Wind speed was really a combination of the true wind speed plus or minus the boat speed depending on whether you were going upwind or downwind. The sailing scientists have found that when given the inputs from the various sensors, such as wind speed and angle, and combining them with an electronic compass and even loran, they can produce powerful new outputs such as time and distance to the laylines; VMG (velocity made good upwind and downwind); and polar boat speed, which compares your present boat speed with the theoretical highest speed your boat should go under the present conditions.

It comes as no surprise that the explosion in computer-centered sailing instruments has found its way into competitive sailing. Sailing computers first came on the scene when *Southern Cross* came from Australia for the 1974 America's Cup match with her mysterious "black box." The challengers arrived with something that was to help them sail their boat more efficiently: a machine. Some call it an extra crewman. PROTEST!

Obviously, then, the sailing world was

not ready for such innovations in such a Corinthian sport. But now, through the sail aids of microprocessors, microcomputers, and the silicon chip, computer-technology-based marine instruments have increased in both popularity and capability.

All of the computed functions provided by the new instrument systems are not new to the sailing world. With patience and a calculator, you could figure out your time and distance to the layline, knowing the boat speed, heading, wind direction, current set, amount of leeway, etc. By the time you got an answer, the conditions would have changed and you'd have to start all over.

What the new systems have that we lack is a microprocessor that has these equations stored in memory and calculates the solutions up to four times a second. These little wonder chips are stored in the "brain" or central processing unit. The CPU is fed all the information necessary from the masthead wind sensors, boat speed, paddle wheels, and loran.

These new systems now give us more information about the wind and boat performance than we've ever had before. While they will never be capable of sailing a boat alone, their purpose is to give us a better understanding of the conditions around us and to better evaluate the way we're sailing the boat. The more accessible and accurate information we have, the faster we will be able to learn about the boat and the better our decisions will be on the racecourse.

Probably the most useful output is wind direction. This output is the actual direction the wind is coming from relative to magnetic north. What's useful about this display is that the wind direction is displayed throughout the race. Before the start you usually go head to wind to get the wind direction, and you use those headings as a basis throughout the race to tell if the wind is shifting. Having the direction displayed is like being able to go head to wind in the middle of the race! It also allows you to separate lifts and headers from puffs and lulls. If you're sailing upwind and there is a three-knot decrease in the wind speed, you have to bear off to keep the boat moving. You may mistake the lull for a header and tack only to find your mistake after it's too late. In this situation a quick look at the wind-direction display will confirm whether it's a lull or a header.

True wind speed is also valuable because it remains constant despite changes in boat speed and direction (See Figure

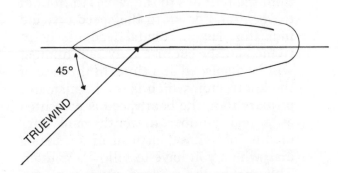

45°

TRUEWIND

Figure 44: "Apparent" wind is the combination of the true wind and the boat's forward motion. Until the advent of the C.P.U., instruments could only measure apparent wind as the boat sailed forward. Now, the C.P.U. can formulate the true wind speed and direction by plugging in the apparent wind speed, boat speed, and apparent wind direction into its internal formula to compute and display the true wind numbers.

44). Apparent wind speed can be confusing because it combines true wind speed and boat speed. As the boat slows down or bears off, the apparent wind will change radically, so it can be misleading. True wind, on the other hand, remains constant and can be used to determine wind conditions accurately on the next leg, especially when considering sail selection.

A good example of this was when Mike was racing a Serendipity 43 in the fall of 1982 that rated in the bottom of Class A. We had gotten a bad start, so we had to sail the first beat in the bad air of the bigger boats' wind shadows. As we got to the weather mark and had to decide which spinnaker to use, our apparent-wind-speed meter showed 14 knots, although the true wind speed showed only 10 knots. The wind had gone to the right during the beat, which means the first reach would become more of a run. Knowing the true wind speed to be 10 and that we would be running on the next leg, we figured the apparent wind speed to be only five knots on the reach, so we decided to set the .5-ounce chute instead of the .75 one. We went around the weather mark in last place, but the rest of the fleet set their .75-ounce spinnakers, which didn't fill in the lighter air. We set our .5-ounce one and passed everybody with it full and drawing by the time we got to the reach mark!

VMG is the speed at which the boat is traveling toward either the windward or leeward mark, and it is determined through boat speed, course, and direction of the wind. If your boat is going 6.3 knots and you're sailing 35 degrees off the wind, the speed directly toward upwind would be about 5.2 knots. VMG is an interesting readout because it tells you your actual progress toward the upwind or downwind mark. When sailing on a run, you can see your VMG increase or decrease as you head up to gain more speed. It will tell you if sailing a longer distance at higher speed is better than sailing a shorter distance at lower speed. The higher the VMG number, the better course you're sailing. With practice and experience, you can use VMG to determine how low to sail coming out of a tack in order to gain speed, and what your best angles are for jibing downwind.

VMG should be used cautiously, though; never sail the boat according to just that output. Say you're sailing upwind in the groove and the boat speed is maxed out at 6.5 knots, and the VMG at 5.3. If all of a sudden you were to point the boat 15 degrees higher, the VMG would shoot up because the boat is now sailing closer to the wind and the boat speed is the same. This would look good for the moment, but soon the boat's momentum will slow down and the VMG that once looked so good would be taking a fast dive. Use the VMG only for long-term evaluation.

Adding a loran interface with the CPU can produce even more useful navigational and tactical information. Most modern lorans can enter the position of the next mark or way point. Combining this information (where you are and where you want to go) with the boat speed (how fast you're going), compass (direction you're going in), and an internal clock, you can have outputs such as range and bearing to the next mark, and the time it will take to get there. Going one step further, the CPU can add this information to the wind direction and tacking angle data to construct laylines from the mark. On *Defender* we had a computer that took all these into account and gave us a simple readout of the time remaining to the port and starboard laylines. Calculating this would normally be a full-time job for the navigator. Add some famous Newport fog and a close race where we'd have 45 tacks on the first beat, and his job was made a lot tougher; he'd simply lose track of where we were. Knowing the time to the laylines was important tactically to the helmsman because when leading a race he knew how much time he could stretch a tack out to the closest layline. When behind, he knew how close to the layline he was and how much time he had to sail to get back into the center of the course.

Performance Prediction

As computers have enhanced sailmaking and performance instruments, they have also helped boat designers see how their new boats will perform before they ever hit the water. Until the use of a computer, the designer had only his experience to judge how fast the boat might sail. But now, by digitizing his hull lines and sail plan to number inputs, he can sail his boat through computerized seas to determine speed, stability, and rating. Once the proper trade-offs are made and the design is decided on, the boat is built.

The information used to design the boat can be used by the people who will sail her. We can use the designer's projections of predicted speeds in different conditions to learn about the new boat faster than without guidelines. Given a constant of true wind angle and speed, we will have a theoretical boat speed to shoot for. The numbers come in the form of polar diagrams that show which are plots illustrating potential speed, true wind angle, and true wind speed. Since each boat is different, there is a separate polar plot for each kind of boat.

There are a few new companies that make a business of generating these polar diagrams for boat owners and designers. They use sophisticated velocity prediction models, some of which are generated from the programs used for the MHS rating system.

Many new instrument systems can input these polar speed numbers into the memory where the CPU can compare actual to predicted boat speed under various conditions. Having this information displayed on deck can be valuable to the helmsman. If he sees that the boat speed is slower than predicted speed, he can head off to get the boat moving.

Of course, these theoretical numbers will never be 100 percent accurate, but they can be used effectively in achieving the maximum potential of the boat in the shortest period of time. At times you will never be able to reach the given projected top speed, and at other times you will go faster than the prediction. By using these numbers as standards, you will learn the boat quicker.

If you have a stock racer-cruiser, or you don't want to go through the expense of getting professional performance predictions, you may record your own sailing data to make observed performance charts. These can range from detailed notes taken during and after racing, to simple recordings of maximum boat speed for a given wind speed and condition. This kind of exercise can be not only fun, but it also can give you a better insight into your boat. Also, writing down your thoughts and observations forces you to think harder about the causes for the particular day's performance and implants those causes, positive or negative, to memory.

Start by recording your boat speed for every wind speed at two-knot increments. You can expand this to have two sets of numbers—one for rough water and another for smooth. Make copies of the charts and put them in waterproof plastic. Tape these charts near the knotmeter and at the sail trimming stations so the people there can tell if you're up to speed or not. In the exact sailing world of 12-Meter racing, each boat has its own set of numbers that trimmers use when racing. If the boat is going slower than it should, the trimmers ease the sail out, forcing the helmsman to bear off and gain speed. At times when the speed is above the numbers, the boat is actually going "too fast." Then the trimmers sheet the sails harder and the helmsman heads closer to the wind to burn off the extra speed and gain distance to windward.

After the race, go over the conditions and write how the boat reacted, what you could have done to make her go faster in hindsight, and how other boats seemed to go relative to yours. This kind of knowledge can be useful tactically. If someone lee-bows you, you'll know how

much speed you'll be able to generate and if you'll be able to roll him or will have to tack.

When collecting all your data and using them on the racecourse, remember that they are just numbers representing the conditions around you. Numbers don't lie, but there is always more to the big picture, so always allow room for your judgment to override the instruments' data. Nothing takes the place of pure seat-of-the-pants sailing, and the feel you obtain from the boat should always be the basic criterion for judging performance.

However much time you spend recording instrument readings and comparisons, spend twice that time just sailing without the instruments. Try to obtain the feel for going fast. Get out into open water and sail with your eyes closed. Without vision, your other senses will be more acute. You'll hear how the waves sound different and feel the small fluctuations of wind speed and direction on your face. You'll better feel the rhythm of the boat that you take for granted. It's hard to get used to at first, but this kind of steering practice will help you become a better sailor, letting you concentrate less on getting the boat going fast and more on pointing it in the right direction.

The way our sailing instruments perform depends largely on the information they get from the sensors. Wind speed is displayed by converting electric current generated by the spinning cups at the masthead unit to numbers in the system. The more current, the higher the number. Problems arise with the accuracy of the numbers when the masthead crane or the boat speed paddle wheels get canted off at an angle or the wires connecting the sensor with the readout are damaged. The results of these problems can mean erroneous readings or different readings from tack to tack. Careful inspection of the system every couple of months will prevent misleading numbers on the racecourse. In a recent survey done by *Practical Sailor*, it was found that 90 percent of instrument problems were due to improper installation and that 50 percent of the instruments were installed by the buyers themselves. Be careful.

The more sophisticated instrument packages that are interconnected through a CPU rely on the accuracy of each sensor so combined functions will be correct. When calculating time to port layline, the CPU needs boat speed, wind angle, electronic compass, and loran information as inputs. If one of these is off slightly, the computed solution will be way off, only causing confusion and mistrust on deck.

In the future, these problems may well be eliminated. Research is going on now to develop a system where information is sent from the sensor to the CPU, not through wire but via telemetry. Wind speed and direction reported at the masthead will be sent to the navigator's station through radio waves.

Accuracy of all instruments will be upgraded through compensation for upwash of wind from the sails for wind information differences in hull symmetry for boat speed sensors. The capacity of instruments to be calibrated for these influences will provide accurate information to the CPU so it can provide us with the reliable answers we need to sail well.

PART FOUR

Go-Fast Techniques

Probably the greatest thrill in the sport of sailing is steering the boat. The wind flows across the sails, and the boat responds in a complex pattern of changing loads. The stresses placed on the boat increase with the fickleness of the wind and the confusion of the sea. And through this conflux of air, water, and boat—and their sometimes erratic interactions—a helmsman is expected to guide either several tons of offshore racing yacht or a light dinghy at top speed.

One of the world's best helmsmen is Tom Blackaller. He has won the Star World Championships twice, the 6-Meter Worlds, and numerous offshore racing championships, including the Southern Ocean Racing Circuit, the Bermuda Race, and the Transpac. Blackaller has the unique experience of having competed as helmsman in both dinghy and offshore competition. We talked at length with Tom about his steering techniques.

He is quick to point out that even the best helmsman will steer efficiently for only an hour and a half. In the most severe conditions, twenty minutes is about the limit. On a boat steered with a tiller, Blackaller recommends using two

helmsmen who face each other while steering. In this manner, even in heavier sailing straight downwind, the pair will last for a good hour and a half. On a reach, it is best to have a second helmsman as an assistant. When steering with the wheel, however, it is difficult to coordinate two helmsmen simultaneously; therefore, your helmsmen should be rotated more often.

All sailboats have an optimum range between pinching and driving, within which the boat will sail upwind in a combination of maximum speed and maximum pointing (See Figure 45). Generally, the greater the width of this range, the faster the boat. For this reason, steering in heavier-displacement boats is crucial. While a catamaran might have an optimum steering range of as much as five degrees, a 12-Meter may have a groove of no more than one degree, and the modern IOR yacht about three degrees—certainly small margins on which to concentrate.

The problem with many modern ocean racing boats is there is no natural feel to the helm. Steering takes such great concentration that a second person, the tac-

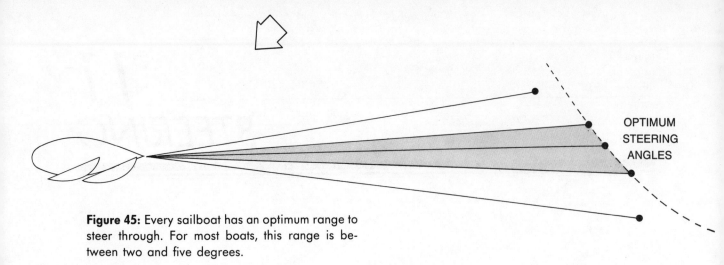

OPTIMUM
STEERING
ANGLES

Figure 45: Every sailboat has an optimum range to steer through. For most boats, this range is between two and five degrees.

tician, must do all the looking around and give feedback on performance. For this reason the role of the tactician on larger boats has increased in importance over the past few decades. One person cannot steer and concentrate on tactics simultaneously. Harold Vanderbilt in the 1930s first developed the team approach to sailing by delegating jobs: trimmers, navigator, helmsman, tactician, and grinders.

Fin keels used on modern ocean racers and centerboards used on dinghies have a much smaller groove than older designs, with keels running the length of the yacht, and require great concentration when steering.

To steer precisely through such a narrow groove, helmsmen must use every source of information available: the waves, the angle of heel of the boat, the wind on the water, the apparent wind direction and strength, and the masthead fly (See Figure 46). Most important is your performance relative to that of other boats.

In a fleet race your competition is your best bench mark for judging your per-

formance. Tom Blackaller tells us how he uses his mind as a computer to constantly update how his boat is performing compared to his opposition. It is up to the helmsman to determine why his boat is sailing slow. The reasons might be steering technique, sail trim, or sail selection. After getting an accurate reading on performance, the helmsman should call for the necessary changes.

To determine performance, telltales should be relied upon only sparingly, as they can distract you from the competition. The masthead fly can become more important, as the wind always changes at the top of the mast first, a good indication of whether you're being lifted. Most masthead flies have an angle index that can help you judge the boat's apparent wind angle (See Figure 47). If as you sail to windward, your apparent wind is generally 25 degrees off your course, spread your masthead fly angle index to 50 degrees so the fly is directly in line with the apparent wind angle index. At night use a good light on your masthead fly and telltales.

Your compass is also a helpful refer-

Figure 46: The most important factor when steering a boat to windward is concentrating on sailing with the correct angle of heel, which you have learned from experience. Helmsmen must use every source of information available.

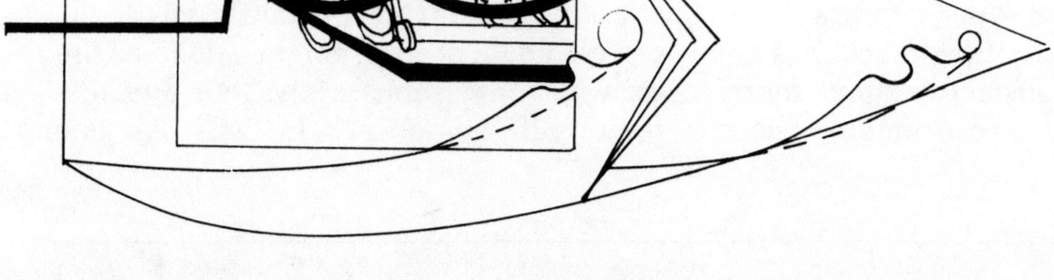

Part II: The helmsman must also stay organized in the boat by keeping the tiller, mainsheet, and his legs parallel.

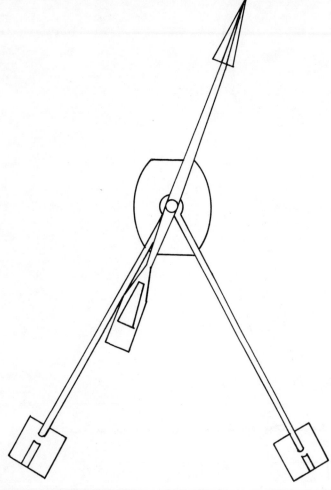

Figure 47: Use a masthead fly as an indicator for your apparent wind angle. In this illustration, the helmsman is steering slightly too high because the masthead fly is inside the apparent wind angle indicator. Your goal when sailing to windward is to keep the wind indicator in line with the angle indicator.

effect, steer as if the bow is an extension of yourself. With as little helm movement as possible, aim the bow so the waves push it slightly to windward. At the very least, avoid intersecting them at anything less than a 45-degree angle. It is better to foot the boat too much than to allow yourself to steer high and slow. The trick to steering in waves is to avoid them. Your goal is to keep your speed up.

Another obstacle can be weather helm. This should be reduced to keep rudder drag low. To do so, move the crew weight to windward or shorten sail, ease your traveler, ease your sheets, rake the mast forward, or flatten the mainsail.

The headsail and mainsail trimmers must coordinate with the helmsman to ensure that the boat is performing at top efficiency. The mainsail can be flattened or made fuller, the draft moved forward or aft, and the genoa coordinated through sheet tension or by changing the draft with headstay tension to suit wind and wave changes. You can also steer a course farther from the wind, but you should ease your sails when you do.

The toughest steering Tom Blackaller finds is in light winds sailing upwind or straight downwind at night. He uses the speedometer and his wind speed indicator as primary references.

He uses a number of references when he is steering, including the headstay sag and the angle of heel of his yacht. Many sailors believe the latter is the most important reference when steering. Blackaller, in an effort to constantly sail at the correct angle of heel, might ask an entire crew to move inboard one foot during a light puff. Sometimes he will ask one

ence point, but it can be difficult to read and still maintain a straight course. Sight a cloud or another boat periodically and steer by it, regularly updating your visual reference with your compass.

When a yacht sails upwind, it has to overcome several obstacles, none more difficult than waves. To overcome their crew member to move in six feet.

Good steering is using a balanced combination of weight, sail trim, and rudder. The helmsman must work with all three to avoid oversteering with the rudder. Anticipate puffs by moving crew and trimming sails. Coordination between the helm and trimmers extends to attaining an optimum angle of heel through sheeting and sail handling, which also will neutralize weather helm and rudder drag.

While most boats are designed to pick up waterline length and, theoretically, speed as they heel, too much heel can make the underwater foils less efficient, causing the boat to make more leeway. Excessive heel is sometimes difficult to recognize. Because you are forced to steer the boat into the wind to compensate for the boat being overpowered, your compass course is actually higher than your course steered. Your course-made-good, though, will show that you are losing ground.

Steering is often a combination of details that make the difference between winning and losing. Such seldom-considered items as posture and clothing can have significance on the outcome of a race.

During the infamous Fastnet storm while Gary was steering *Tenacious*, skipper Ted Turner appeared on deck and shouted, "Take your hat off, Jobson." He realized that *Tenacious* could not be steered efficiently if the helmsman did not use all his senses to steer the boat. The waves were building up over 30 feet, and the 60-knot winds were making it impossible to see. With a hat and a hood on, Gary could not really get a feel for the strong puffs, the big waves, or even the course of the boat.

It is crucial for the helmsman to tune up to maximum efficiency before the start of the race. It is best to do this when another boat of relatively the same size and speed is alongside.

Generally it takes five to 10 minutes for the helmsman to gain enough momentum for peak performance, and his most effective time at the helm can range from 20 to 90 minutes, depending on the conditions. A crucial consideration in helmsmanship is to know when to give the wheel to someone else. Follow the change by coaching the new helmsman back into the groove.

Staying calm in the heat of the battle is hard for many helmsmen, particularly the less experienced. In a dinghy, with two people, you might find it helpful for the helmsman to watch for boats to leeward, particularly at the start, while the person up forward watches the performance and the position of the boat to windward. In this case, four eyes are better than two.

On larger boats, the helmsman usually can see everything, although this is not always the case. In 6-Meter races, for example, the helmsman can see only half the racecourse because the boom is right down on the deck. Even windows in the sails don't seem to help the 6-Meter, which often sails at a 30-degree angle of heel. In this case the helmsman is at the mercy of the crew.

There is no substitute for helm time on the racecourse. As your level of confidence improves with experience, you will learn to keep cool and calm even during the toughest of situations.

Surfing, Planing, and Towing

When sailing downwind, you can gain valuable distance by getting your boat to plane, surf, surge (in the case of big boats), or catch a tow from another boat. These techniques can work well on all sailboats.

A boat planes when it breaks the water friction and rides on top of the water, sailing faster than hull speed. It is said to surf when a wave propels the boat past the point of friction into a plane. To bring the boat out of the water, you must accelerate—easy enough in high winds, but difficult otherwise.

For a boat to plane, it must first of all be in balance so that there is absolutely no pressure on the rudder. Have your sail trimmed and keep the boat flat; a sailboat will not plane if it is heeling. As a puff hits, hike the boat down, bear off slightly, move your weight aft to get the bow to ride up over the water, and accelerate by trimming your sails rapidly. Trim your vang so the boat is still under control but the top batten is about parallel to the boom. Ease your outhaul and Cunningham, and move your jib leads outboard. Trim both the guy and the sheet of the spinnaker at the same time to increase sail area. All this will give you forward momentum to start the boat planing or surfing. Also, the centerboard should be pulled up at least halfway to reduce lateral resistance.

For surfing, the course of your boat should be perpendicular to the waves passing under your bottom. Since waves crisscross each other on diagonals, watch for them 40 degrees on either side of

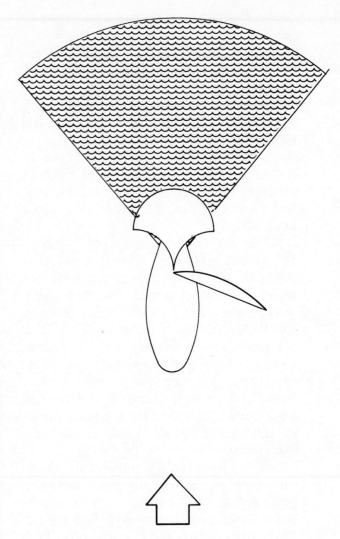

Figure 48: To get your boat surfing down a wave, watch the waves 40° on either side of your bow.

your bow (See Figure 48). Aim your bow into the deepest trough and toward the highest peak to catch as much of the wave as possible. As the wave passes under you, give the boat extra acceleration by trimming the sails rapidly or heeling the boat to windward suddenly—in effect, rocking it. This rocking creates wind in your sails, but more importantly, it breaks the friction underneath the hull so that the boat will start surfing with the wave and begin planing. Also, rapidly adjusting the helm helps to keep the boat perpendicular to the waves. Moving your weight forward will help accelerate the boat down the wave. Once you start surfing or planing, return your weight to the normal position, and at this point keep the boat flat.

In order not to plow into the wave ahead of you once you catch a wave, bear off, staying with the wave you are on just as a surfer would—by cutting across it on a diagonal. This way you make valuable distance to leeward, staying with your puff and wave for a long time. Keep watching the waves, and practice steering from one wave to the next as long as you can. With practice you will be able to sail 50 percent faster than the fleet every time you catch a wave, even though you are sailing by-the-lee as much as 20 or 30 degrees.

It is difficult to get larger boats to plane or surf, but you can get tremendous surges from them through a series of waves, which may lead to a surf. The problem is that the boat gets going so fast that its apparent wind dies and, without extra acceleration, it cannot maintain the ride. However, boats such as Solings or larger keelboats—one-tonners, for example—do surge down waves and actually start surfing. On *Courageous* we did 14.6 knots surfing down an eight-foot wave off Breton Reef. That was our fastest. However, one-tonners can hit speeds of 15 or 16 knots at times while surfing.

Approaching the finishing line in the 1983 St. Petersburg to Ft. Lauderdale race was a thrill we will never forget. On *Boomerang*, Gary steered the 65-foot yacht in 20-foot swells, obtaining speeds of 20 knots. During the infamous Fastnet race of 1979, the 78-foot *Condor* surfed down one wave at a staggering 29 knots. The boat got going so fast that it spun out of control and ended up heading straight downwind. The spinnaker plastered itself against the shrouds, and the boat started sailing in reverse at five knots. The helmsman reacted by reversing the wheel, and the boat got itself out of this situation. The spinnaker popped with great force, and *Condor* continued on her way to set the Fastnet race record that stands to this day. In larger boats you can catch a tow from boats bigger than yours simply by riding their waves. It is conceivable, if the wind conditions are right, for a one-tonner to be towed across the ocean by a 12-Meter. In some races one can find as many as five boats following one another, each riding the waves of the boat ahead. Making it possible for smaller boats to sail as fast as larger ones, towing can effectively wipe out handicaps.

Towing works when the apparent wind is between 70 and 120 degrees and when the backwind of a lead boat is not sufficient to hurt the boat behind (See Figure 49). This is when keelboats are moving the fastest and also making the biggest waves. Towing works because you sail in the dead water of the boat ahead while not being blanketed with bad air. You can catch a tow of a boat that rates two to four feet higher than you in rating, but it is difficult to catch a tow of a boat much larger.

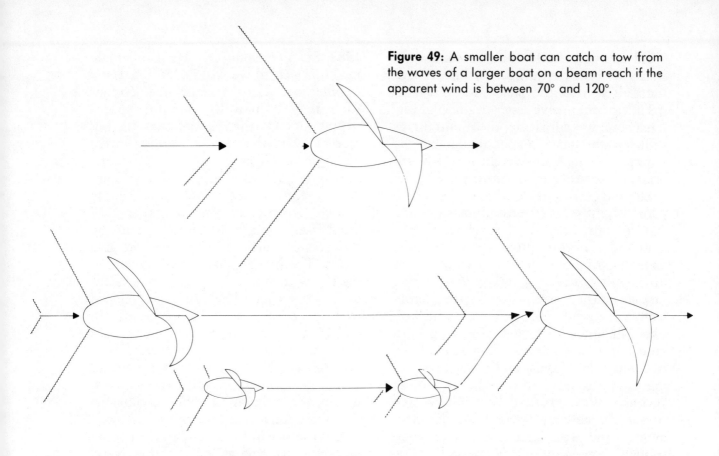

To catch a tow, position your boat so it is within one boat length astern of a boat ahead of you. This is done by heading up and going right for the stern of another boat as it passes you—normally to windward, though preferably (for you) to leeward. (By intimidating a larger boat with a luff, you may force it to pass to leeward.) Once you are in position behind the bigger boat, your boat will be towed along at the speed of the boat ahead. The defense against a tow is to bear off sharply or come up hard so that the boat behind has to get off the wave to avoid hitting your stern.

In a race several years ago on *Tenacious*, to Key West from Fort Lauderdale, we had an all-day battle with *Running Tide*. After several hours, the 12-Meter *Heritage* passed close to leeward of *Tenacious*, and we were able to grab a tow for about two hours. This enabled us to gain about three miles on *Running Tide*, and we won the race!

Sailing by the Lee

Contrary to traditional racing tactics, sailing by the lee can occasionally be advantageous in certain wind conditions. You are sailing by the lee when the wind is hitting your sails over the leeward quarter while sailing downwind. There are many tactical situations where it could be useful, such as sailing by the lee for a short distance to avoid a time- and distance-consuming jibe.

Sailing by the lee should be done with considerable caution; it works best in light-to-moderate air. Boats become unstable when sailing by the lee in heavier winds, and sailing by the lee for sustained periods is risky.

Yacht designer Ron Holland speaks of "taking bites to leeward." The best time to take a bite is when the boat is sailing its fastest. Normally when sailing downwind, a helmsman will steer the boat to leeward in the puffs, and reach up to gain speed as puffs dissipate. A helmsman can take a "bite" (an alteration of course) to leeward in a puff or breeze, or when surfing down a wave (See Figure 50). When using waves for acceleration, watch for the deepest trough and head the bow into it, steering the boat at a 90-degree angle to the wave. Just before the wave passes under your hull, accelerate your boat by trimming sails, keeping the boat on an even keel with no pressure on the rudder either way.

Beware, however, when your boat begins to slow down. It is important to act quickly by heading up to keep the boat under control. In slower board boats, a skipper can easily be lulled into sailing by the lee puff and end up capsizing to windward as the apparent wind comes aft with the slower speed.

Keep aware of your masthead fly; avoid sailing more than 20 degrees by the lee. If the boat feels out of control because the underwater surfaces are taking over and beginning to steer for you, simply experiment with all angles of heel. When sailing by the lee, this will

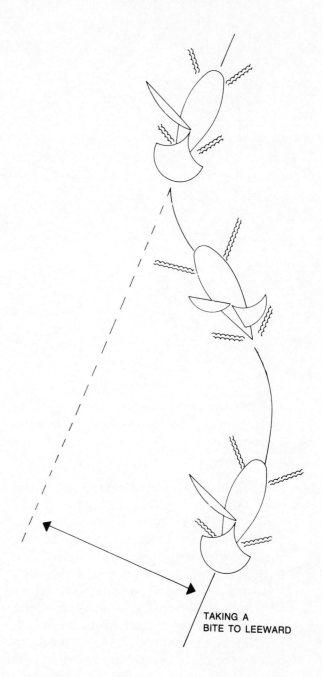

TAKING A
BITE TO LEEWARD

Figure 50: Downwind you can gain valuable distance and cut down on the number of jibes you have to make by sailing by the lee in strong puffs.

AVOID

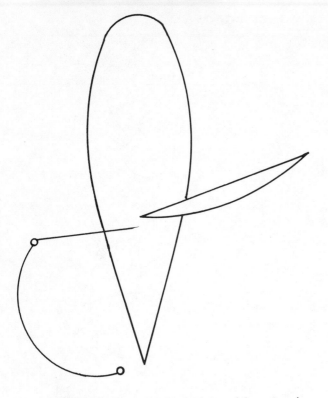

Figure 51: Sailing with both clews of the spinnaker on the same side of the headstay creates an unstable condition.

normally be about a 10-degree windward heel. When sailing with a chute, stability for sailing by the lee may be enhanced by choking the sail down. Overtrim the sail, making sure you place equal tension on both sheet and guy so the clews stay on opposite sides of the headstay (See figure 51). Both clews on the same side of the boat will induce rolling and instability.

After making a jibe and continuing to sail by the lee, trim the spinnaker so it is in clear air, not blanketed behind the mainsail. It's possible to sail too far by the lee, causing the chute to collapse due to this shadowing effect.

If the boat gets out of control, over-trimming will help in trying to stabilize it. Be careful here. Overtrimming can cause an unscheduled jibe unless a preventer has been rigged at the boom to restrict it (See Figure 52). A wild-flying boom is dangerous on any boat, particularly on boats with hydraulic boom vangs. A preventer rigged to a block led forward is the solution.

When sailing with the jib winged out to weather, either by hand or by using a whisker pole, ease the sail forward until it starts to become blanketed by the mainsail (See Figure 53). A jib is flatter than a chute and therefore can collapse easier, another way to keep the boat from becoming overpowered.

Figure 52: A preventer is essential in heavy winds to restrict the boom from flying inboard, causing an unscheduled jibe.

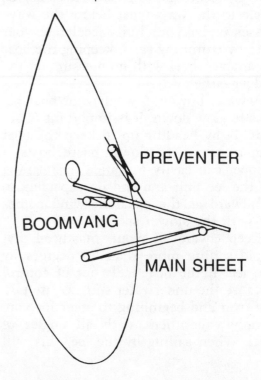

PREVENTER

BOOMVANG

MAIN SHEET

150° APPARENT WIND

Boom Vangs

The boom vang is a helpful piece of equipment on sailboats. It helps keep the boom under control and gives the sail better shape. It also projects more sail area to the wind by preventing the boom from riding up the mast in choppy waves. The boom vang also helps to stabilize the rolling of a boat. It should not be confused with a preventer, which is a line used to secure the boom from swinging inboard during an "unscheduled jibe" or violent roll.

The boom vang has been in existence for at least half a century and is also known as a boom jack, kicking strap, or boom downhaul. In earlier days, crew

Figure 53: You can effectively wing your jib to windward when the apparent wind is aft of 150°.

Tactically, sailing by the lee can help you in a variety of situations. When rounding marks, for instance, you can sail by the lee either to break or to gain an overlap. Simply accelerate as previously described, using waves and pumping the sails aft as the apparent wind moves forward.

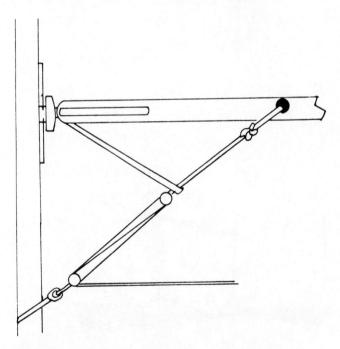

Figure 54: The boom vang must be secured at the base of the mast directly over the gooseneck of the boom.

members sat on the boom to keep it from bouncing in waves.

A boom vang should be very strong. It is generally a block-and-tackle arrangement attached to the boom approximately 25 percent aft of the mast and attached with a swivel to the base of the mast, either at the maststep or at the deck mast partner (See Figure 54). It is important that the swivel be directly below the gooseneck so the boom vang can swing smoothly.

The block and tackle usually has a mechanical advantage as small as 2:1, or as much as 64:1 in high-powered racing boats. The line runs through a series of blocks and exits at a cleat or cam cleat, which is preferred since it is safer and faster to remove. On powerful ocean racers the boom vang is now a hydraulic ram, which is controlled from the cockpit. The boom, where the vang is attached, should be reinforced, since a great deal of pressure is exerted here.

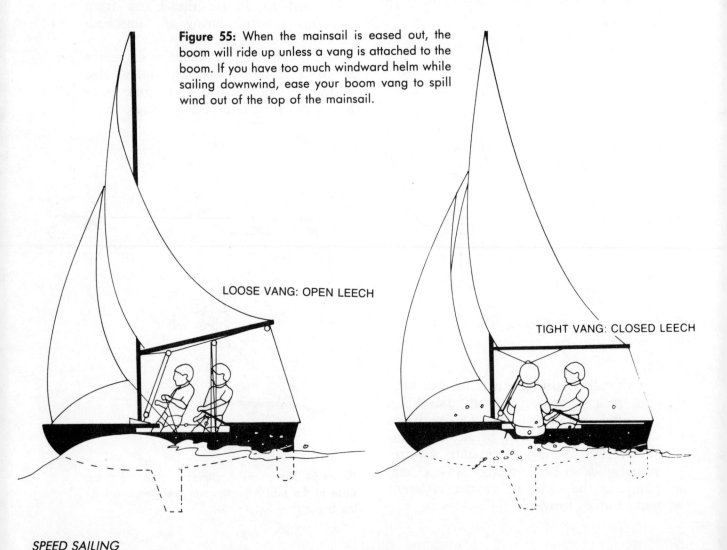

Figure 55: When the mainsail is eased out, the boom will ride up unless a vang is attached to the boom. If you have too much windward helm while sailing downwind, ease your boom vang to spill wind out of the top of the mainsail.

LOOSE VANG: OPEN LEECH

TIGHT VANG: CLOSED LEECH

The boom vang also helps to act as a traveler. When a mainsail is eased out, a boom will ride up unless a vang is attached to the boom, restricting it (See Figure 55). Therefore, when the vang is tight, the boom will not ride up in the air, spilling wind when the sail is eased out. In smaller boats this technique has become known as "vang sheeting" and has proven to be very fast.

When the wind is aft of beam the boom vang helps to create more sail area. By keeping the leech tight, the sail takes a better shape, with the maximum amounts of draft in the middle of the sail. As a rule, you can tell if you have the proper amount of boom vang by comparing the boom to the top batten of the sail. They should be parallel to each other.

In moderate breezes, if your boat starts rolling, the boom vang will help to keep the boat under control since there is less give in the sail. The boom vang has safety value because it is easy to uncleat during a broach. If the boat is wildly out of control in heavy breezes, it is important to ease the vang to spill wind out of the top of the sail.

Be extra careful with hydrologic boom vangs because there is little give in the system. On *Defender* we attached the boom vang to a "breakaway" line to the track so this line would break before the boom. In windy conditions it might be necessary to have one crew member standing by the hydrologic valve or the cleat to be ready to ease off if the boom starts dragging in the water. This puts the most stress on the boom.

Normally, the boom vang is not used when sailing on the wind or in very light wind, since the weight of the boom and the mainsheet keep the sail light. The exception to this is in grand prix racing boats, where the boom vang is used to fine-tune the shape of a sail in any kind of breeze.

If the boom vang is not being used, a shock cord attached to the gooseneck in the middle of the boom will help pull it forward and therefore out of the way of the crew when one crosses from one side of the boat to the other.

Using a tight boom vang upwind will help flatten the main by bending the mast.

12
MANEUVERING

The faster you maneuver a boat, the faster it loses speed, so to keep up momentum, move the rudder slowly and use your weight to help steer (See Figure 56). A sailboat will usually turn a complete circle in about a one-boat-length radius. Turning any faster will kill speed. Whenever you are maneuvering a sailboat, whether to accelerate, tack, jibe, head up, or bear off, the most important thing is to have as much speed as possible going into the maneuver.

The heavier the boat, the longer it takes to get it moving. To get a 12-Meter up to full speed from a dead stop takes about a minute (See Figure 57). In a Laser, on the other hand, you can go from a dead stop to full speed in about 15 or 20 seconds (See Figure 58). The great J-boats that raced for the America's Cup in the 1930s took over five minutes to obtain full speed after a tack was completed.

No boat will maneuver until it starts to move. Trim your sails in and pull your tiller in the opposite direction so that the two forces help the boat start moving forward. But try to use as little helm as possible so the rudder does not

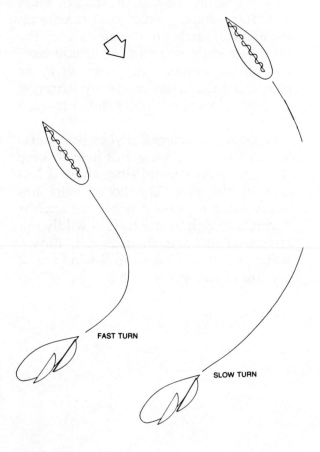

FAST TURN

SLOW TURN

Figure 56: The faster you turn a boat, the faster it will stop. If you want to keep momentum, turn the boat slowly.

Figure 57: To accelerate for speed in a keel boat, you will have to sail at least 10° low for three to four boat lengths.

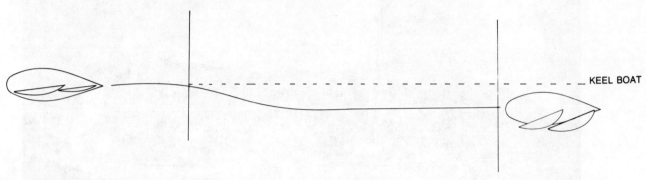

KEEL BOAT

Figure 58: A dinghy will accelerate to full speed in two to three boat lengths but will have to sail at least 15° low of close-hauled to attain full speed.

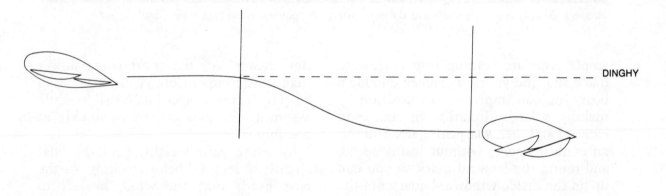

DINGHY

break the boat's forward momentum. Continue to adjust the sails to complement the motion and movement of the boat, depending on the course you intend to take. If the boat starts rounding up too quickly, ease the sails to bear off. Keep the boat on its best sailing lines. A boat that is heeling too much is out of balance and will be slow to move. If it is a boat that should be sailed flat, keep it flat or heeled slightly to leeward so that the sail takes shape. Never let a boat heel to windward when you are trying to accelerate.

As the boat starts moving, sail in a straight line for a distance of one to three boat lengths before starting to bear off to attain full speed. Once the boat is up to full speed, you can begin to maneuver.

Many sailors concentrate so much on speed that they have a hard time learning to slow down when they have to. A good way to do it is not by slowing down but by adding more distance. If, for ex-

Virago's (31424) crew takes a wave during starting maneuvers. *Photograph by Carol Singer*

ample, you are coming into a leeward mark and find yourself trapped outside a boat, you can improve your position by making a large alteration in course to leeward and then sharpening up. You sail an extra distance, without losing speed, and round the leeward mark so you end up on the inside windward quarter of the boat ahead after the rounding.

Tacking

Generally it takes between one and three boat lengths to tack in winds stronger than five knots, and as much as five to seven boat lengths in winds less than five knots. For this reason, tack only if you are up to full speed, or at least are going as fast as your competi-

tion. Never tack if you are going slower than the competition. Your aim is to keep up as much speed as possible while assuming the new course as quickly as possible.

By using your weight, heel the boat slightly to leeward before tacking. As the boat heads into the wind, heel it to windward hard, rolling the boat through the tack. To maintain your speed, use as little helm as you can. As you head into the wind, trim your sails in, keeping them full. In a sloop, you should trim both the main and the jib at the same time. Several years ago, this "roll tacking" was used only in dinghies. Today, it works in almost all boats, even in Solings or one-tonners (See Figure 59, A, B, C). It's easy and fun and it helps to get the boat up to full speed quickly.

Whenever you tack a lot, put more

Figure 59: Roll tack.

Part A: The boat is heeled to leeward at least 15°. The crew rocks the boat to windward as the helm goes over and the sails are trimmed.

Part C: The boat is flattened out, creating wind in the sail in light air or getting the keel to work in heavy air. The sails are eased to accelerate for full speed. The trick to good tacking is using your rudder, weight, and sails together.

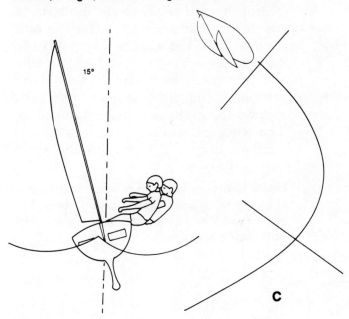

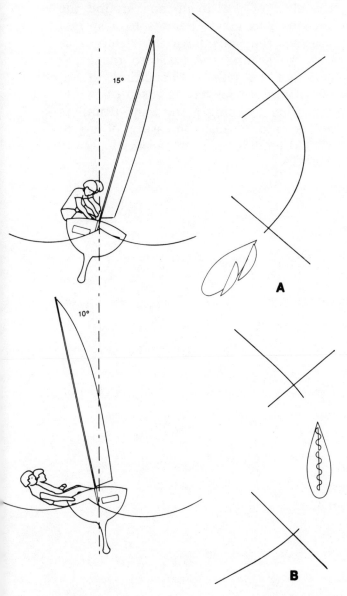

Part B: As the boat passes head to wind, the crew shifts sides of the boat.

power into your sails so that you increase speed sooner. It may help to head down slightly after a tack, close-reaching to accelerate, and then, as your speed increases, to head up to your normal course, all the time playing your sails for maximum speed (See Figure 60, A, B).

Here is a brief description of what happens on board a 12-Meter during a tack:

First the tactician passes the word to the helmsman and counts down the distance in boat length: "Stand by for a tack in two and a half boat lengths . . . two boat lengths . . ." and so on. When it comes time to tack, the helmsman calls "hard-a-lee," giving good warning to the crew that the boat is beginning to turn. At this time the jib is being trimmed in to keep the sail full and help the boat round up into the wind. At the same time, the main traveler is pulled to windward, also helping the boat head up.

As the boat rounds into the wind, the helm is turned faster to get the boat on the new course sooner. The boat is now rounding into the wind more quickly. To bag the main as the sails begin to luff, the permanent backstay is eased off to straighten the mast, and the hydraulic ram on the outhaul is being pumped in. The genoa halyard is moved forward and outward during a tack, and the main Cunningham is eased off so that the sails will become fuller when the boat is on its new course.

A tacking line in the middle of the foot of the jib makes it easier to bring the clew of the jib up and around the shrouds and mast. Thanks to a special coating, the sails have less friction as they go around the mast to the other side. As the sails are beginning to fill, one running backstay is eased off while the other is being ground up. (Runners are wound to exert pressure of up to 17,000 pounds on the headstay.)

Figure 60A: Only begin your tack if your boat is sailing at full speed. After the tack is completed, you will have to sail for at least three to seven boat lengths to accelerate to full speed.

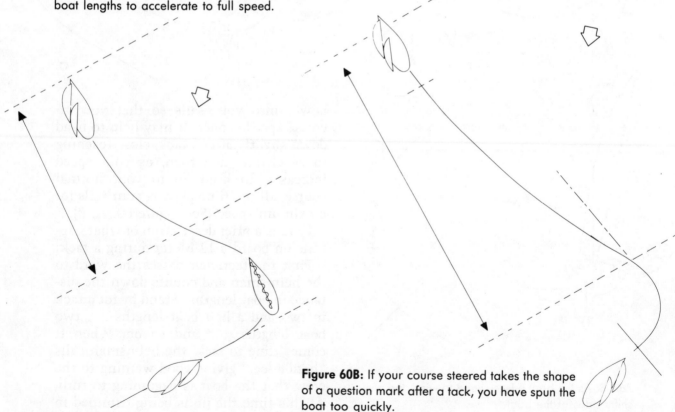

Figure 60B: If your course steered takes the shape of a question mark after a tack, you have spun the boat too quickly.

Courageous and *Clipper* cross tacks during the America's Cup trials of 1980. *Photograph by Carol Singer*

At this time, speed begins to increase, and the traveler is reset to its normal position, lead aft and inboard, the jib halyard is put back up, and the main Cunningham goes down. The hydraulic ram on the outhaul goes back out as the permanent backstay comes down to bend the mast once again. Then we are up to full speed and it's time to stand by for a tack once again.

Jibing

The time to jibe is when you are moving the fastest, because it's easier to keep wind in your sails and you will lose the least distance. In a dinghy the best time to jibe is when you are surfing down a wave with maximum speed, since you

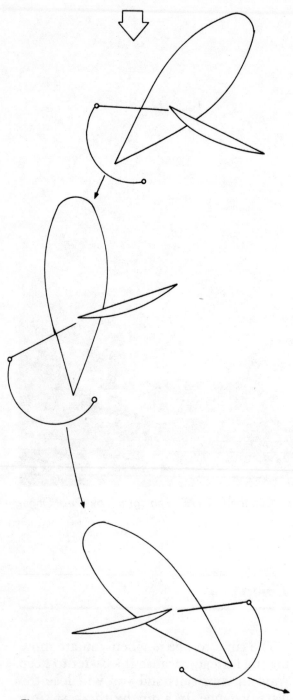

Figure 61: The trick to good jibes with a spinnaker is to get the spinnaker as far away from the boat as you can before jibing.

have less power in the sails (apparent wind is less) and therefore are stable. Always keep the boat flat. The centerboard should be down about one third of the way for control, but too much centerboard will cause the boat to flip over.

Use all your crew, stationing everyone at a different part of the boat. And use marks to indicate how much to ease or trim your guys and sheets. Marks can also tell you how far to dip your spinnaker pole when passing it underneath the forestay.

In jibing with the spinnaker, the trick is to get the spinnaker away from the boat as far as you can before jibing. Before swinging the pole over, trim it all the way aft so that it is perpendicular to the mast (See Figure 61). In this manner you will be able to change course quickly on the new jibe and the spinnaker will not collapse, since it is already on the leeward side of the boat. As the pole comes aft on the new side, the spinnaker will follow automatically.

Try not to jibe the main over until the wind is just passing straight aft of the boat. Jibing too early will collapse the spinnaker. On the other hand, if you are in a circling maneuver at the start, no matter what the boat, throwing the mainsail over early (prejibing) will cause the boat to jibe sooner and will round it into the wind, helping you to make a circle quicker (See Figure 62).

Many sailors lose as much as two boat lengths unnecessarily when jibing, especially in light air, because they make too great a change of course. In winds of five to 10 knots, you need to change course only about 30 or 40 degrees to jibe. In heavier winds you need to change course only some 20 degrees (See Figure 63).

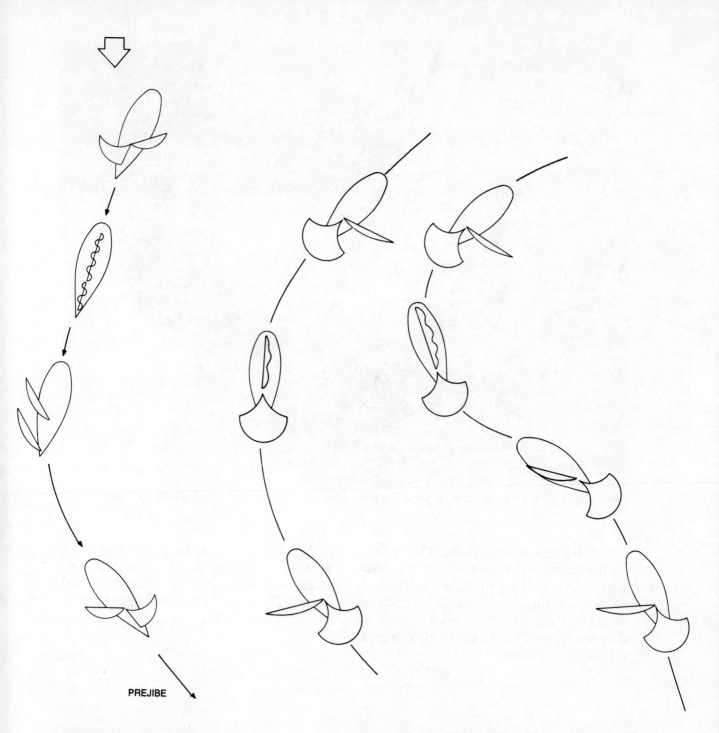

PREJIBE

Figure 62: Prejibing helps to get you up on the wind earlier by switching the main across the boat before the wind passes astern.

Figure 63: When jibing, change course as little as possible to cut down on the loss of distance.

The skipper of this Penguin should hand the mainsheet over to her crew. *Photograph by Carol Singer*

Roll jibing will help prevent too great a course change. It works well in dinghies, particularly in light air. First heel the boat to leeward, then heel it hard to windward so that the main changes sides quickly. In this way you will not have to make a great alteration of course.

Another common error in jibing is forgetting to change hands in holding the sheet and tiller, putting yourself off balance. To avoid this, it may help to switch hands before you jibe.

13

SPEED AROUND THE MARKS

We finally saw the perfect mark rounding. Gary was running a sailing clinic in Long Beach, California, when one young Laser sailor came into a leeward mark on a full out plane and rounded it in one swift motion. He maintained the boat at a perfect 10 degrees of heel the whole time. The sail came in smoothly, angled for optimum power at every degree of course change. The maneuver was flawless.

Perfection is a difficult goal to achieve, but considerable distance can be gained on your competitors by rounding marks efficiently. You can go into a mark behind and end up ahead by planning your rounding in advance. There are several things you must do.

First, learn the optimum turning radius of your boat when bearing off, jibing, tacking, and heading up. The more gradually you can make your turn and the less rudder (with its braking effect) you use to make it, the better. In most boats any maneuver requiring a 90-degree course change or more will take at least two boat lengths. In heavier air you are moving faster, so the same maneuver will take even more space.

Almost as important as your turning radius is your angle of heel. Sailboats have the least resistance to turning when they are on a relatively even keel. At a leeward mark you should ease the burden on the rudder and help the boat steer herself to weather by carrying a slight (about 10 degrees) leeward heel. At the windward mark as you bear off, try to keep the boat as flat as possible. Learn the correct angle of heel, ideal turning radius, and proper sail trim for maximum boat speed by practicing mark roundings on your own.

We have found it very helpful to be clear about our own priorities in mark rounding. While the emphasis we put on them changes at the three different types of marks (windward, leeward, and reaching) rounded in most races, the order remains pretty much the same. The first priority is boat speed. Try to maintain the maximum velocity while covering the shortest possible distance. Next comes your position relative to the competition. The third priority is setting new sails, and fourth is the host of minor adjustments necessary when you go from one point of sailing to another (Cunningham, vang, traveler, outhaul, center-

Courageous and *Clipper* jockey for position on the starting line. The foredeck man must have good judgment in this situation. *Photograph by Carol Singer*

board, and so on). Each of the marks presents a different set of problems, but we have found that these priorities hold up well all around the course.

Your approach to the windward mark is critical. Most sailors are so anxious to get there that they tack short of the layline and wind up pinching their way to the pin. When you think of the boat speed lost this way and how easily it is to make up any extra distance traveled in overstanding by the speed you can gain footing off, it makes little or no sense to gamble by tacking too soon.

Use a tacking line to gauge the layline. It should be a line on board placed where you can sight along it easily. It should run at 90 degrees to the centerline of the boat (See Figure 64). A line taped or painted on the deck can give you a concrete reference point that should prove a big help in backing up your hunches about whether you've "got it made." Not all boats tack in 90 degrees. In light air your tacking angle probably will be wider than 90 degrees, and in heavy air and seas it also will be a bit wider than it will be in smooth water with moderate

Figure 64: Use a tacking line to judge when you are on the layline for a mark. In the illustration, the tacking line is drawn perpendicular to the center line of the boat and works if the boat is tacking through 90°.

WINDWARD MARK

Figure 65: It is a good practice when making your final approach to the windward mark to overshoot it by half a boat length to allow for misjudgment or a bad tack.

WINDWARD MARK

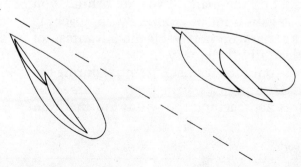

air. If you sight the tacking line a few times before the start of a race, you'll have a good handle on what it means in the conditions that you're sailing in. If you use it consistently, it will improve your accuracy in judging the layline no matter what the conditions.

When you overstand you avoid the consequences of a misjudgment, a bad tack, an unexpected current, an unfavorable chop, or another boat tacking on your wind. Even if you tack exactly on the layline, a header or any of the possibilities listed above could cause you not to fetch the mark. Also, the air on and to leeward of the starboard tack layline tends to be chopped up by the boats ahead of you. If you go a length or two beyond the layline you should have clear air (See Figure 65).

If you see a long line of starboard tack boats parading down the layline, don't tack in it or below it. Look for a hole and duck through it. Make certain to sail well above any of your competitors to assure yourself of clear air and maneuverability.

Avoid tacking right at the windward mark. If you are coming in on port tack and you must tack to starboard to round the mark, it is best to make your approach five boat lengths low to allow time to set up for the rounding. There will be times, however, when this is impossible and you will have to come in right on the mark. If you are behind, you can gain a lot of ground by approaching the mark on port with the advantage of clear air all the way in.

In one race against *Enterprise* during the 1977 America's Cup trials, *Courageous* was approaching the windward mark on port at a full 8.3 knots. *Enterprise*, approaching on starboard tack, appeared to be fetching the mark easily. If all went well we would be able to cross just ahead of *Enterprise*, tack around the mark, and be on our way. But as we approached the mark, it became apparent that this particular crossing and tack would be closer than we had hoped. Should we dip, or should we go for it? It was an all-or-nothing race, so we went for it. Skipper Ted Turner asked, "How high should I sail?" Gary answered, "As high as you can." "If I go any higher," Turner protested, "we'll sail to windward of the mark." The second our bow got to the mark, Turner spun the wheel, and we rounded half a boat length in front of *Enterprise*. It is these exceptions to our rules that keep tacticians' lives interesting.

You can help your boat speed by making only a single tack on your final approach to the mark. Repeated tacks slow you down at the best of times; in the troubled air and water to leeward of the weather mark they are really costly. If you find that you are not fetching the mark, it is better to tack early in wide-open water than to take your chance with the crowd that collects at the mark.

Make your final approach to the windward mark on the lifted tack. Avoid tacking in the vicinity of the mark because you won't have a good chance to prepare for the rounding.

If you are trapped to leeward of several boats, the only recourse is to wait to tack. Never make unnecessary tacks—they lead to trouble.

If you must approach a (starboard) windward mark on port tack, overshoot it to allow for starboard tack boats.

The priorities at windward marks are boat speed first, position and other adjustments second. *Photograph by Carol Singer*

Don't let them tack in front of you. You can discourage a boat from tacking in front of you by heading directly toward her. Also, a hail helps discourage a starboard-tack boat. If he doesn't tack, chase his stern and round behind him. If you have given yourself room you will still make the mark.

If you are barely fetching the mark, stop by luffing up and let the starboard tack boat round ahead of you. Avoid tacking again because it means a tremendous loss in speed along with the possibility of fouling out.

Boats are in close quarters at marks, tempers tend to flare, and fouls tend to occur. Try to avoid fouls at all costs. To help in that regard, make sure you understand the complete Rule 42.1

When yachts are about to round or pass a mark, other than the starting mark, surrounded by navigable water, on the same required side . . .
(a) an outside yacht shall give each yacht overlapping her on the inside room to round or pass the mark. . . . Room includes room for an overlapping yacht to tack or jibe when either is an integral part of the rounding or passing maneuver.

The modifications, qualifications, and exceptions to the basic rule are many, and you should study the complete rule until you understand them all. At the weather mark, though, Rule 42.1 (c) is crucial:

When boats are beating, the basic starboard over port right-of-way rule takes precedence.

SPEED AROUND THE MARKS

At the mark, if you are on port tack and in-side a starboard-tack boat you may not tack so close as to make her alter her course.

Another important rule here is 42.3, "Limitations on establishing and maintaining an overlap in the vicinity of marks and obstructions":

When a yacht is clear astern and establishes an inside overlap, she shall be entitled to

room under Rule 42.1 (a), only when the yacht clear ahead: (i) is able to give the required room and (ii) is outside two of her overall lengths of the mark or obstruction, except when one of the yachts has completed a tack within two overall lengths of the mark (See Figure 66).

This means that if one boat has tacked within two boat lengths of the mark, the two-length rule for determining room

Figure 66: Boat A is entitled to room because she has tacked within two boat lengths of the mark according to rule 42.1 and rule 42.3.

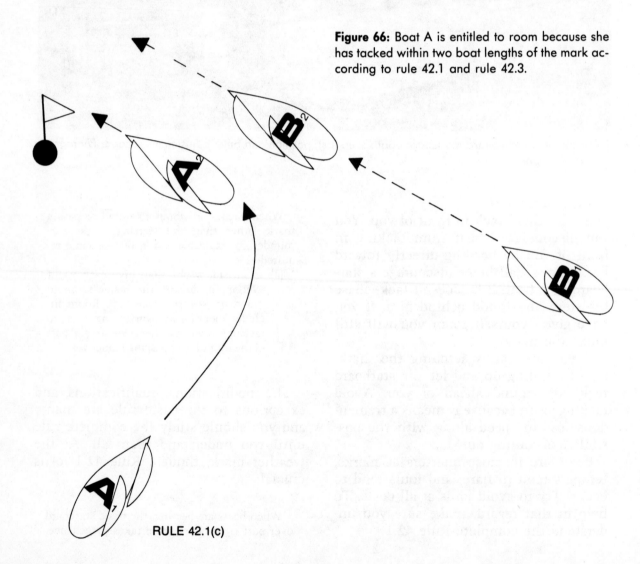

RULE 42.1(c)

does not apply. Therefore, a boat clear astern can establish an overlap and be entitled to room if the yacht clear ahead is able to give it.

The boat handling required for smooth mark roundings does not come easily. Make sure your boat is set up properly for the approach by assuring that all lines are free to run as needed. A piece of shock cord across the jaws of cam cleats is excellent insurance against lines getting jammed when you can least afford it. Sheets should be hand held, if possible, during the approach to the mark to make certain you can ease them instantly as you bear off. Crew motions should be as economical as possible. Strive for simple athwartships movement by crewmen in their regular stations. Running forward or aft disturbs both the trim and the momentum of the boat.

Before you round the weather mark you should know what your next course will be. Pick a prominent landmark or steer by the compass to make sure you're headed for the next mark. Don't follow the leader! Make sure you know where you're headed. Often the leaders don't.

Once you have made your approach, start rounding by keeping the boat flat. One rule of thumb is "keep the boat under the mast." This allows you to bear off fast and keeps your boat under control while you increase speed and lose little distance. To keep the boat "under the mast," dump the main out fast and ease the jib out while rounding. An overtrimmed jib will prevent your boat from bearing off. And if you let the boat heel, the centerboard will begin to cavitate and your rudder will become ineffective,

forcing your boat off balance (See Figure 67).

In two-man boats one member of the crew must keep hiking and watching the boat. If both crew members have their heads wrapped in halyards and adjustments, they are potentially in for trouble.

Any mark rounding is easier and faster with as little course change as possible. The greater the change in course the faster your boat will slow down. One way to avoid making major course changes when rounding the windward mark is to slack off before rounding is begun.

Once the windward mark is rounded, don't delay in making a fast getaway. At this point you head in the direction you wish to sail, haul up the spinnaker, adjust your sails, and settle in for pure speed. Often sailors arrive at the windward mark only to relax downwind. This is the opportunity, however, really to get tough and make as much ground as possible. Your getaway sets the stage for your approach to the next mark.

There are two basic legs after a windward mark: the reach and the run. As a general rule, if on a reach, pass boats to windward at the beginning of a leg and pass boats to leeward at the end of a leg. Always work toward finishing up on the inside at the reach mark. If you elect to stay outside, be sure you can break the overlap; otherwise, go inside so you have that overlap.

If an adverse current is running that sets your boat away from the desired course, the rule is to fight the current early in the leg so you have it in your favor at the end, when you make your

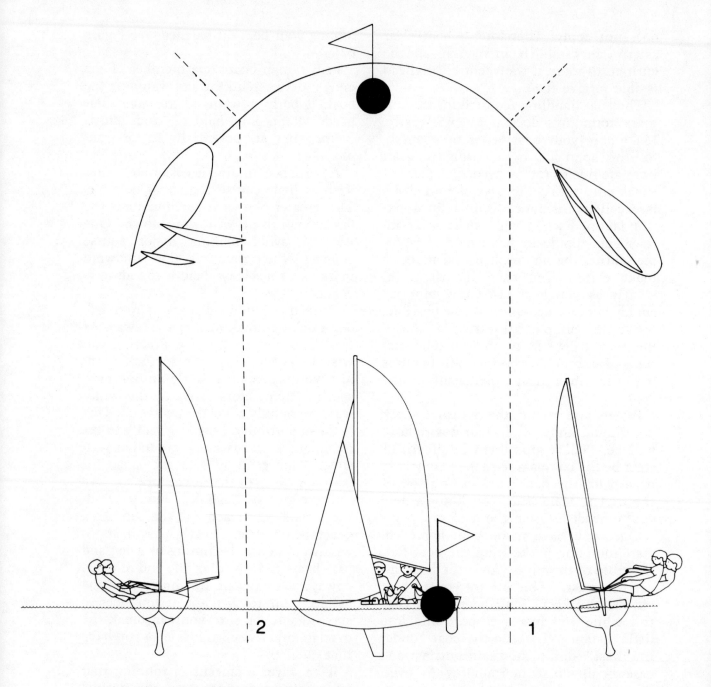

Figure 67: Keep the boat flat when rounding the windward mark and dump the mainsail out and ease the jib as fast as you can while making your rounding.

final approach and need the extra speed.

While making a rounding, concentrate on nothing else and you will stay out of trouble.

Many helmsmen forget where the mark is and follow the boats ahead. Look for the next mark before you make your rounding so you know where to head. When boats ahead of you get into a luffing match, dive low to get clear air with a better angle coming into the next mark.

Marks drift and sometimes are reset by the race committee. Never assume you know the location of a mark. Look for it and check it often so there will be no mistake.

If starting on a run, it might be advantageous to jibe early to get clear air. Later in the leg this maneuver will give you an advantage when covering the fleet— namely, a starboard advantage, leeward boat, or the inside at the mark.

Use your starboard advantage to force boats to the outside. If a boat jibes to stay clear of you, jibe back to escape his bad air and maintain your starboard advantage. Using starboard tack is the most powerful technique for controlling other boats.

Keep your wind clear of the boats rounding with you or behind you. If your masthead fly is pointing at another boat, you are in danger of being blanketed. Off the wind, a wind shadow will extend eight to 10 mast lengths to leeward (See Figure 68). Keep your boat moving fast by steering for clear air. Although it is desirable to be the inside boat at the reach mark, if you aren't you still can salvage an opportunity for your approach to the all-important leeward mark.

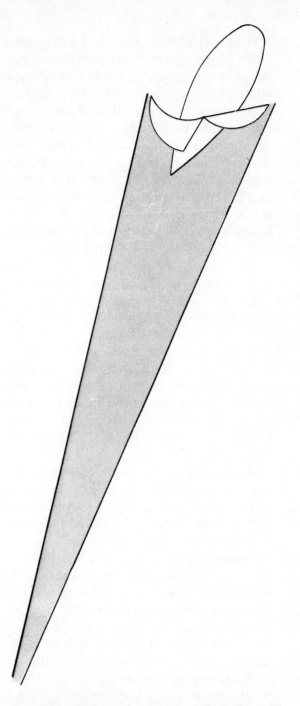

Figure 68: Downwind a boat's wind shadow will extend at least eight to ten mast lengths to leeward.

When ready to round, hail outside boats for room early so there is no doubt as to your position, and give outside boats plenty of opportunity to stay clear. This resolves any question of overlaps. If the outside boat hails "no room," then do not take room; your only recourse is to stay outside and protest. A witness will help clear up any arguments arising in a hearing, so be sure to have a witness at the time of the incident. An inside boat must prove that she did indeed have an overlap. Rule 42.2 (d) (ii) states:

> A yacht which claims an inside overlap has the onus of satisfying the race committee that the overlap was established in time.

Racing rules are made to avoid collisions. It is a myth that you can prove your overlap by tapping the outside boat. Establishing room at the mark is a judgment call, and the outside boat is privileged, under the rules, to make the judgment.

Wait to haul the spinnaker up until the apparent wind direction is 70 degrees or farther aft. In light winds avoid setting the spinnaker until your speed stabilizes. It is best to sit in a puff.

On spinnaker boats you will set the chute at the weather mark more often than not. If there is a question of whether you can carry a spinnaker on the next leg, sail conservatively. Round the mark and see for yourself. You'll lose much less by setting late than you will by setting and then having to douse. On big boats and small, the key to a good spinnaker set is preparation. If sheet, guy, and halyard are led properly, it's a mechanical proposition to haul the chute up. If not, it's a nightmare. Presquaring the pole and pre-trimming the chute to settings approximately right for your point of sail help the chute "pop out" quickly.

If you will be sailing on a dead down-wind leg after rounding the windward mark, you may need to jibe immediately after the rounding. If you are setting a spinnaker in this case, a bear-away maneuver is always preferred if it is unclear which jibe you will be sailing on. However, if the opposite jibe is favored by 20 degrees or more, it may be useful to do a jibe set. A jibe set requires considerable loss in boat speed and loses valuable time (See Figure 69).

The jibe mark can be the most exciting of all. In 1972, Laser sailor Craig Thomas approached a jibe mark on the Berkeley Circle in San Francisco Bay in last place but picked up every competitor on the course who had already capsized. Fourteen of America's best single-handed sailors, all capsized around the reach mark, sat in the water watching Thomas come in. As he went into the jibe, he yelled "watch this, I'll show you how!"

He certainly did! He did a full pitch-pole that flung his body headfirst over the bow of his boat in grand style. Needless to say, his performance aroused enthusiastic cheers as he swam toward the capsized boat.

Jibing is easiest when your boat is moving fast because you have less apparent wind in your sails. Allow a minimum of two to three boat lengths to make your jibe; it certainly can't be made on a dime, especially if you are flying a spinnaker. Jibing the chute can be tricky even when you can pick your spot. Jibing around a mark is tougher, but the same rules followed for a good jibe help make for a good rounding. Square the pole completely as you bear away. If you trip the pole early and fail to continue trimming on the old guy, the chute will be undertrimmed and unstable. If the helmsman thinks of directing the masthead fly into the chute as he turns, and the trimmers are briefed to swing the chute as he swings the boat, you can jibe without breaking the sail. Never allow both spinnaker clews to be on the same side of the headstay. That invites a collapse (See Figure 61).

When sailing dinghies, it helps to pre-jibe the main. Throw it from one side to the other before the wind has passed dead astern. This not only lets you complete the maneuver quicker and thus be free to concentrate on steering around the mark, it also provides (via the wind pressure on the sail) some turning force of its own that helps you use less rudder (See Figure 62). Finally, it can often be an advantage to jibe onto starboard tack ahead of your competition.

In heavy air, trim the main to the center line prior to a jibe to help your control. If the boat begins to yaw, head up 10 or 20 degrees. This puts the waterflow on one side of the keel or centerboard and should make steering easier.

You can increase stability by "depowering" the swing of the main in heavy air. The S-jibe is used to keep your boat under control when jibing in heavy wind. In heavy-air jibing, the main boom comes over with such force that it goes too far out on the new side and the boat begins to round into the wind. At its worst this loss of control can capsize

Figure 69: In this case, if the opposite jibe is favored by at least 20°, a jibe set may be preferred. When in doubt, always use a bear-away set.

dinghies or broach larger-keel boats. To stay upright, keep the boat under the mast and the boat in balance. An S-jibe can accomplish this.

As you go into an S-jibe, bear off and keep the boat sailing slightly by the lee. Keep the main overtrimmed at this time, or if you are sailing with a spinnaker, choke it down slightly by overtrimming the guy and sheet. Then as the mainsail is coming across the boat, steer back in the direction in which the main is going.

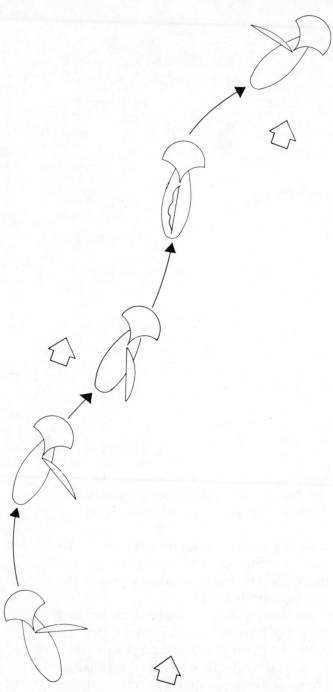

This change of course reduces the power in the sail and doesn't allow the boat to round into the wind. As the main fills on the new side, keep it overtrimmed and resume course, having completed your jibe. Don't begin to head up until the boat is under control. Needless to say, you need more water for an S-jibe than for a conventional jibe (See Figure 70).

Your rounding of the jibe mark depends upon what your new course will be. If it will be a close reach, steer wide on your approach and round tight to the mark on your turn. This puts you on the weather side of the track to the next mark, free to sail the shortest, fastest reach you can. If you are jibing onto a broad reach, be somewhat wide of the pin so you will have a sharper (faster) sailing angle for the next mark. Remember also to keep your wind clear after you jibe. Heading sharply up or down to avoid being blanketed is well worth it.

Overtrimming the main during a jibe also helps keep a boat under control. This technique works best in cat-rigged boats such as the Finn, Force 5, and Laser.

Once you complete your jibe, start your getaway by planning your approach to the leeward mark. If the fleet is heading very high, sail below their course. If you are one of the first boats around the mark, you can discourage other skippers from going high by making a sharp luff and then coming off to your proper course before another boat has the chance to sail over you. This will enable the competition to sail low, yet they won't be able to break your inside overlap since they must sail through your lee.

Figure 70: The S-jibe. the trick to making an S-jibe is steering back in the direction the boom is swinging to help de-power the force of the mainsail.

The crew of number 3 should ease the mainsail faster to bear off and move the weight aft. *Photograph by Carol Singer*

It is bad practice to make a reaching leg a continual luffing match. If a boat tries to go over you, give her one sharp luff. The rules allow this because it is the only protection a leeward boat has against boats sailing over the top. One sharp luff is infinitely better than a series of short and continuous luffs. A windward boat will get the message that you mean business and will stay low.

The leeward mark presents perhaps the biggest challenge of all. Because there is so much going on, sailors often lose sight of keeping their boat moving at maximum speed. One thought is to approach the mark on as much of a reach as possible to maximize your speed. Also remember that any distance sailed to leeward of the mark is distance sailed away from the weather mark. Therefore, stay wide (about two boat lengths) of your approach so you can round up right at the mark as you make your turn.

Keep your boat heeled slightly to leeward (about 10 degrees) to induce weather helm that will make turning to weather easier. If you heel your boat too much, it will cause her to slip sideways. This leeway widens your turning circle and slows your turn.

At the Canadian Olympic Regatta for Training at Kingston, Ontario (CORK) in 1971, Gary was approaching a leeward mark with 20 boats in a line. Realizing that these boats would make a wide pinwheel around the mark, and being stuck in the middle, Gary trimmed his mainsail at midships and slowed down on the

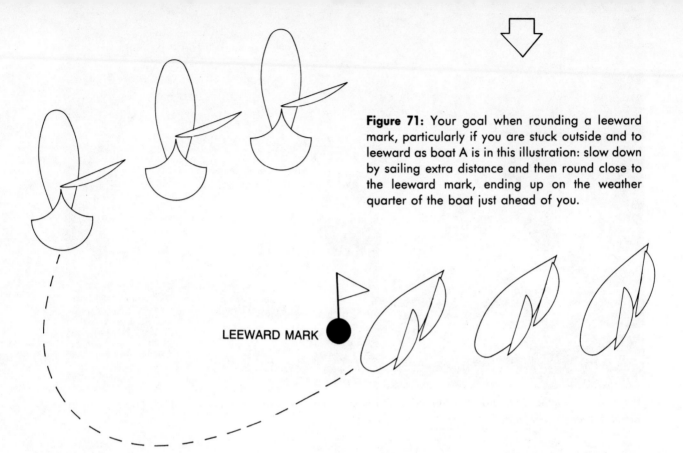

Figure 71: Your goal when rounding a leeward mark, particularly if you are stuck outside and to leeward as boat A is in this illustration: slow down by sailing extra distance and then round close to the leeward mark, ending up on the weather quarter of the boat just ahead of you.

LEEWARD MARK

final approach to the mark. Sure enough, the intense battle to gain the inside position caused the inside helmsman to forget to put his centerboard down. His fin slipped sideways, banging into every boat. Gary simply rounded several boat lengths later, but he was instantly 20 boats farther ahead.

One midshipman at the U.S. Naval Academy got so excited in a close race deciding who would go to the National Championships that year that he forgot to head up after rounding the leeward mark. Keeping your eyes outside the boat helps remind you where you are.

At the leeward mark, always remember your position relative to the rest of the fleet. If you round a position where you are to leeward of your competitors, you will be blanketed and forced either to slow down or to tack. Your goal is to round into a spot on the weather quarter of the boat or boats just ahead of you (See Figure 71). Here you will receive some backwind, but you will not be blanketed. Thus you will be sailing fast enough to pick the side of the course you choose rather than being forced to one side to get out of dirty air.

While having an overlapping inside position at the mark is desirable, don't sacrifice your overall position to get it. If you go for an overlap and don't get it, you will be high on the mark, which forces you to make a wide turn, which then puts you to leeward of the boats ahead. If you delay reefing to establish an overlap going to leeward, the time you lose on the fleet reefing while going to weather could cost you more than the place you picked up by having the overlap. I find it wise to try to put myself in position to pass people after a mark rounding rather than gambling on passing them during a mark rounding. This holds true for carrying the chute until the bitter end. It is better to take the spinnaker down a little early rather than a little late. Don't give anything away, but you can hurt yourself a lot more than you can help by taking foolish chances.

Plan your mark rounding in the relative calm of the open water leading up to it. Once you've decided not to sprint for inside position, give yourself room to make the rounding that will put you in command once you've passed the mark.

Even if you are trapped outside three or four other boats, plan early to assure yourself a wide approach and tight rounding. Even if you must slow down by sailing a greater distance than the boats inside of you, gauge your turn so you can round sharply onto or above the weather quarter of the boat just ahead.

Don't tack right at the leeward mark if you can avoid it. Get the boat up to speed before you come about (See Figure 72). Avoid sailing over your own wake or the wakes of the boats still coming downwind. Avoid their wind shadows, too.

The tactical possibilities involved in mark rounding are many, and sometimes lots of places can be yours by playing

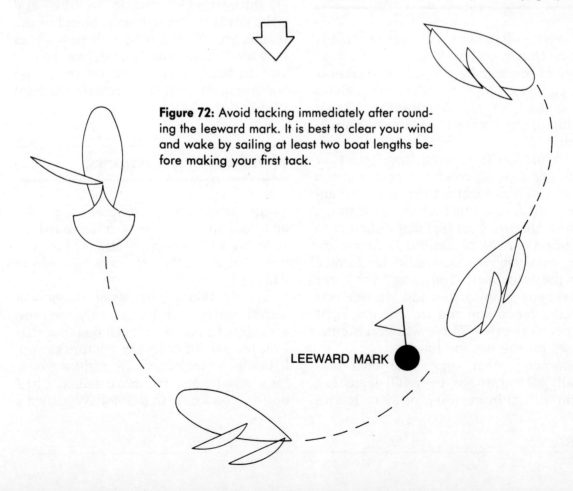

Figure 72: Avoid tacking immediately after rounding the leeward mark. It is best to clear your wind and wake by sailing at least two boat lengths before making your first tack.

LEEWARD MARK

your cards right. More often, though, sailors tend to focus on winning the battle at the mark and wind up losing the war at the finish line. Take the tactical advantages when they present themselves, but don't forget that keeping your boat moving fast all around the course and around all the marks is the best way to place well.

Practice mark roundings on your own by setting up a short three-buoy course and sailing it often and hard. Practice may well make perfect. After all, in all our years of sailing, we have seen only one perfect mark rounding.

Tacking Lines

Every sailboat can use a set of tacking lines. Drawn on the deck, these lines are easy to mark and are valuable references when you are sighting other boats, ahead or behind, or are determining who is going to cross whom in a crossing situation.

To mark the tacking lines, start by running a string down the center of the boat. Use a protractor to measure the angle, then draw a line perpendicular to the string, then another line perpendicular to the first one. Next, mark a 45-degree angle, bisecting the perpendicular formed by the two lines. You now have three lines: one running fore and aft, one perpendicular to fore and aft, and one right between the two. These will become the bases for the tacking lines.

Knowing what angle your boat normally tacks through, be it 100 degrees in light air, 90 in medium, or 80 or less in

higher winds and flat water, draw your tacking lines accordingly. For example, on *Defender* we set up three tacking lines, at 90, 80, and 70 degrees. If the boat was tacking through 70 degrees, we knew we were on the layline when the mark lined up on the 70-degree tacking line.

For determining whether a boat to leeward is ahead of or behind you as you are about to tack across it, you need another set of lines, half the angle of the first set—or in our case, 45, 40, and 35 degrees. Likewise, to determine whether a boat to windward is ahead of or behind you, you need an identical set of lines on the other side. Using the lines, you simply choose the appropriate half of the angle through which you are tacking—and sight down it. If the boat is ahead of the line as you extend it, it will pass ahead of you; behind, and it will pass behind you. In both cases we are assuming that the speeds of both boats remain constant (See Figure 73A).

Hand-Bearing Compass

The hand-bearing compass is a valuable tool in determining how your boat is faring in relation to others. You can use it in a number of ways (See Figure 73B).

First, by taking bearings on the bow of a rival boat at intervals of, say, one minute, you can see how much distance that boat has gained or lost in relation to you. If one boat length equals eight degrees, for example, and you have gained a half degree, you know that you have gained a sixteenth of a boat length. Such a small change is often difficult to discern with the naked eye.

Second, a hand bearing compass can determine whether you are gaining windward or leeward distance on a rival boat, provided the boats do not alter course. Let's say that sighting through the compass you find it is six degrees from the bow to the stern of a boat to leeward. After sailing for two minutes, you take another reading, and the boat to leeward now bears 5.5 degrees, while the bearing on the bow has remained constant. The explanation is that the boats have moved farther apart laterally. A hand-bearing compass can be used as a range finder. Turn the compass

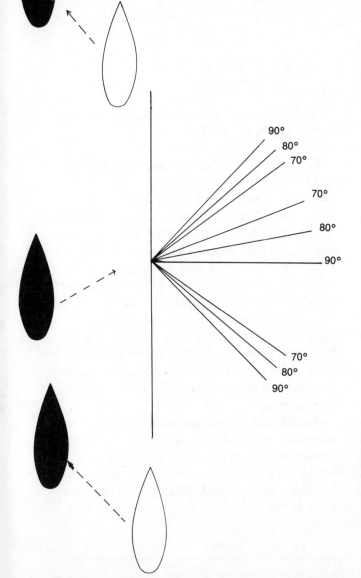

Figure 73A: Tacking lines are an important reference to tell whether you will cross a boat to windward and behind, or a boat to leeward and ahead will cross you, or whether you are on the layline for the windward mark.

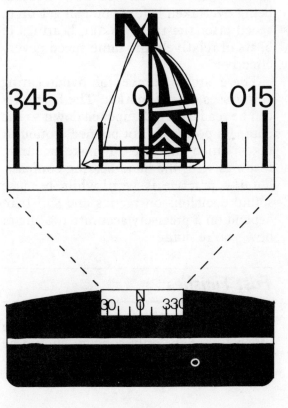

Figure 73B: By using a hand-bearing compass you can observe whether you are getting closer or farther away from another boat by counting the number of degrees to a boat length. If a boat length equals more degrees on the second bearing than the first, you are getting closer together.

on its side and note the height of the mast or the distance from the spreader to the water in degrees. You can see a change in distance by noting the change in degrees of the height you have observed.

The hand-bearing compass also comes in handy in crossing situations, for determining whether you can get away with a tack on the leeward bow of a converging boat. Check its bearing every 15 or 30 seconds. If the boat is gaining bearing on you, it will cross ahead of you. If you are gaining bearing on it, you will cross ahead. If the bearing stays constant, you'll have to maneuver to stay clear of each other.

If you find that you can cross the boat by a half boat length, then you also have room to tack on its lee bow without being overtaken before you can get up to speed after the tack. Taking bearings of boats of relatively the same speed is very effective.

There are a number of hand-bearing compasses on the market. The best ones can be read easily, dampened down so the compass points do not bounce around. It takes much practice to make accurate readings with the hand-bearing compass, but the practice is worthwhile because sound decisions on tactics and sail trim depend on a precisely accurate reading of how you're doing.

Fast Finishes

When making the final sprint to the finish line, your only concern should be to get the bow across the line as quickly as possible.

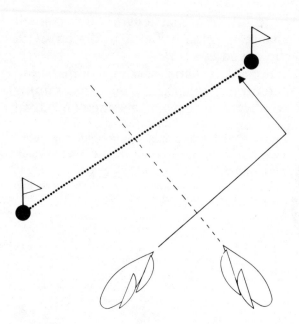

Figure 74: Always cross the finishing line as close to right angles as possible.

Set yourself up so you are approaching the line on the favored tack, which is the tack most nearly to right angles to the finish line (See Figure 74). Take a bearing of the finish line and head for the end that seems to be closer to you. It is better to finish at one end of the line or the other because you have a better reference of where the line actually is. In addition, the race committee official calling the line will have either end obscured from his view and will tend to notice your boat earlier than another boat that might be crossing simultaneously in the middle of the line.

Avoid tacking in the middle of the line because this tends to lose distance. Shooting the line, however, closes the angle from your bow quickly and should be done when your boat is within one boat length of the line (See Figure 75A,

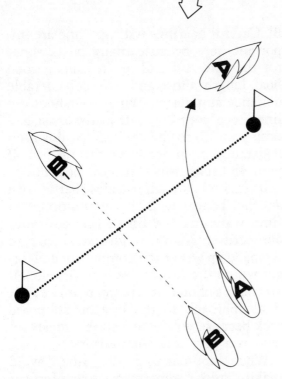

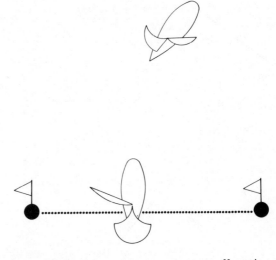

Figure 75A: If you plan to shoot the line, be sure your bow closes with the line at the same time it opens with your competitor to leeward. After your bow crosses the line, it is important to completely clear the finishing area.

Figure 75B: When running, square off and sail perpendicular to the line when you are within two boat lengths of the finishing line.

Courageous rounds the leeward mark just ahead of *Freedom* in a tight race. It is better to take the spinnaker down early rather than late. *Photograph by Carol Singer*

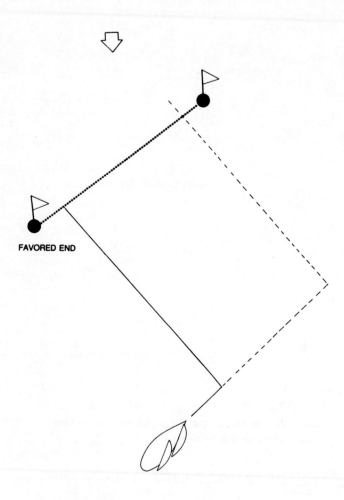

FAVORED END

Figure 76: By sailing for the favored end of the finishing line, you will sail less distance on the last leg.

B). Careful bearings with the line are important here because many boats shoot for the line and end up in irons a good boat length short and lose considerable distance and places. When you shoot the line, keep your crew aft of the mast and drop your jib to the deck to cut down on resistance or at least let the jib luff. If your jib backs, this slows the boat down.

If you find yourself in a close battle with another boat, spend an equal amount of time watching the finish line and your competitor. Many sailors tend to get wrapped up with their competitor and forget where the finish line is positioned. If you have a choice, it is better to make your final approach to the line on starboard tack because you have a starboard advantage over port tack competitors.

When approaching the line, avoid making minor adjustments to equipment such as Cunninghams or hiking straps. Be ready to trim your sails and balance your weight for the final shot across the line.

Once your bow has crossed the line you are considered finished, but you should continue sailing until your boat is well clear of the line and away from other competitors.

Always head for the favored end of the finishing line so you sail the least distance from the leeward mark (See Figure 76).

14

PREDICTING WIND SHIFTS

Predicting the wind is a vital element in sailboat racing. You will sail better by being ready for changes in wind direction and wind velocity. Anticipating shifts lets you cut down the distance you sail on the course by sailing at a closer angle toward the next mark, both upwind and downwind. It also permits you to use wind shifts to escape from competitors when you are sailing in blanketed wind. If you know that the next puff is going to be a header, you can foot off and gain speed to take the best advantage of it. If it is going to be a lift, you can gain distance by pinching up. Predicting the shifts also helps you choose the favored side of a course. By studying what the wind does on the water, you can gain a valuable competitive edge.

Circumstances vary from race to race, so concentrate on being in phase with every shift as it comes along. Still, some general principles help you anticipate what the wind will do, and you are most effective at predicting shifts if you can fit your minute-by-minute observations into a big picture.

Wind is a result of variations in atmospheric pressure or in thermal activity, or both. The National Weather Service issues a considerable amount of information to help forecast the wind. For some regattas, such as the Southern Ocean Racing Circuit, the Bermuda Race, the Transpac, and even the America's Cup trials, we have used private weather consulting firms to our advantage. Quite a number of consulting firms in the United States belong to the American Meteorological Society, based in Boston. In Newport, during the 1983 America's Cup trials, both *Defender* and *Courageous* were able to receive updated weather forecasts, maps, and analysis over a teletype. This information, along with our local forecasting, gave us accurate weather information right up to the minute throughout the Cup summer.

The National Hurricane Center in Miami, Florida, will provide information on weather patterns and Gulf Stream position and strength.

Most forecasts start with a description of present conditions (temperature, barometer reading, visibility, cloudiness, wind direction and strength, and precipitation) and follow with a prediction of the expected changes, usually through the next hours. Despite the fact that the conditions experienced on the course

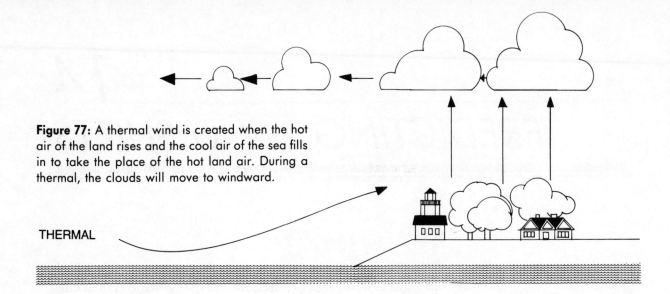

Figure 77: A thermal wind is created when the hot air of the land rises and the cool air of the sea fills in to take the place of the hot land air. During a thermal, the clouds will move to windward.

THERMAL

may be somewhat different from those described in the forecast, when you start to notice any of the predicted changes taking place, you can begin to look for a change in your wind.

For example, if the conditions on the course are partly sunny skies with winds out of the northeast at 10 to 15 knots and the forecast is for increasing cloudiness with winds shifting into the west and increasing to 20 to 25 knots, keep your eye on the cloud cover. If the sky clouds over, chances are that the forecast was accurate and the wind will shift.

Thermals occur when heated air (such as that over land in the summer) rises and cold air (such as that over water) flows in to take its place. Normal thermal winds will shift in the direction that the sun is moving as the day wears on. As a thermal wind is building, thermal clouds will appear. They are scattered and puffy and look like doughballs. They work in the opposite direction of the breeze. They will float seaward, for instance, during an onshore breeze. The faster they move, the stronger the air cir-

culations, so if they move fast they indicate that the breeze soon will get stronger (See Figure 77).

Sailmaker Robbie Doyle taught us in Newport, Rhode Island, on a clear, sunny morning, that the amount of dew on the grass will tell you how much of a thermal you have that day. The more dew on the grass, the harder the wind will blow.

The wind behaves in somewhat predictable ways in most sailing areas. For instance, the prevailing conditions off Newport, Rhode Island, on a typical summer day will have the breeze filling in from the south (180 degrees). As the day goes by, the wind direction will follow the sun and bend to the west, ending up at approximately 235 degrees. It might fill from 180, shift to 195, swing back to 185, and oscillate back and forth with progressive westward movement through most of the day. Still, it's risky to rely on any predetermined pattern for predicting shifts.

There are times, though, when local conditions or objects on or near the course will cause definitely predictable winds. For example, when sailing off the Merchant Marine Academy at Kings Point, New York, it pays 90 percent of the time to take the left side of the course no matter which way the wind is blowing, largely because a large hill with buildings on it disrupts wind near one portion of the shoreline. Gary coached the sailing team at Kings Point for many regattas before the "go left" revelation struck him, but it certainly made coaching easier from then on.

Talk with local sailors. While coaching the U.S.-Finn team at the pre-Olympics in Tallinn, Estonia, in 1978, Gary learned much valuable information from the local sailors, which he in turn passed on to the Finn team. It was interesting that even though the Estonians who were helping out were under Soviet rule, they wanted someone other than the Russians to win.

Avoid sailing near anchored boats or close to shore. The wind bends around and rises over objects in its path, which makes it lighter in these areas. The wind starts to bend at a distance equal to roughly twice the height of the object in its path. Therefore, if a ship is 40 feet high, it affects the wind at least 80 feet to windward of it (See Figure 78). This is called the "snow fence" effect. If there are a large number of spectator fleets in the area of the starting line, favor the end away from the spectator boats (See Figure 79). During the America's Cup trials, many spectator yachts would crowd just to starboard of the committee boat and motor forward to get a glimpse of the 12-Meters as they sailed off the starting line. The first 12 to tack to the right and sail close to the "snow fence" was

affected dramatically. The second 12 on the port side but to windward and clear of the "snow fence" of the spectator fleet gained at least one boat length ahead and one boat length to windward while sailing away from the "snow fence." During the 1983 trials, the America's Cup committee observing the races on a large yacht with a high tower would often come in close to get a good view of the 12's, sometimes even forward of the beam and within a boat length. The effect would slow a 12-Meter down by a tenth of a knot while the other 12 would gain valuable ground.

The shape of an object affects how the wind bends around it, but normally it bends equally around both sides. Objects also create a blanket zone to leeward that is from five to 10 times their height. The air to leeward of a 40-foot-high ship, then, could be disturbed for as much as 400 feet.

If you get a good weather forecast, keep an eye on the clouds, know local conditions, and avoid objects that will disturb your air, you'll certainly still be in the race. But to be in the thick of it competitively, you should also have a good sense of what each wind puff is going to do to you. Many sailors feel that timing the shifts can be effective in calculating their impact. These sailors spend prerace time recording the time interval between shifts and the variance in degrees and use that information to anticipate shifts during a race.

The wind usually behaves with regularity, and although some successful sailors swear by timing shifts, we believe that the wind's regularity isn't dependable enough, however, to make the sys-

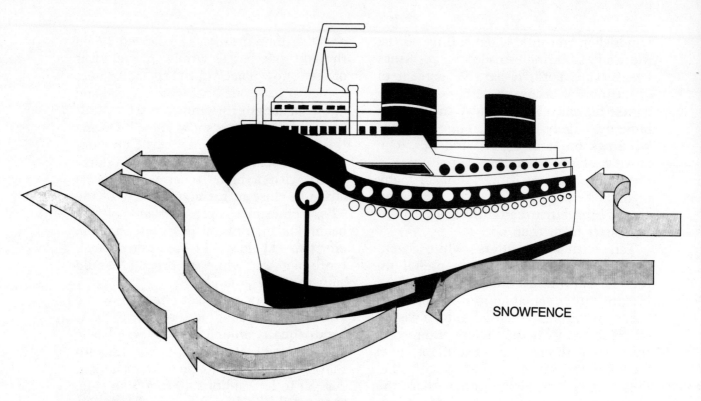

SNOWFENCE

Figure 78: The snow-fence effect is created by a stationary object such as an anchored ship. The breeze is affected at least three times the height of the ship to windward of a ship.

Figure 79: A large spectator fleet can also cause a snow-fence effect to occur. Avoid sailing in this area.

AVOID

SNOWFENCE

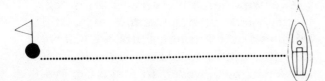

tem dependable. Also, it's difficult in short-course racing to know precisely where you are in relation to the phases of the wind. When you come around the leeward mark, for instance, it's very hard to know how soon to expect the next wind shift.

We believe that the safest and most effective way to be on top of wind shifts is to try to predict the direction and strength of the next puff as it approaches by using the signals available on the water. The ripples the wind creates on the surface are good indications of what the wind is doing (See Figure 80). By looking closely at the water ahead and to weather, you can often tell how the new wind differs from the wind you are in. We check an area four or five boat lengths ahead and to weather (going to windward) every five seconds or so. By checking our observations along with our sails and masthead fly, we can develop a sense of what a lift or a header looks like as it approaches. We also note the feel of the wind on our neck, face, and ears, and we keep an eye out for flags on boats or buoys that can help. The wind changes at the top of your mast be-

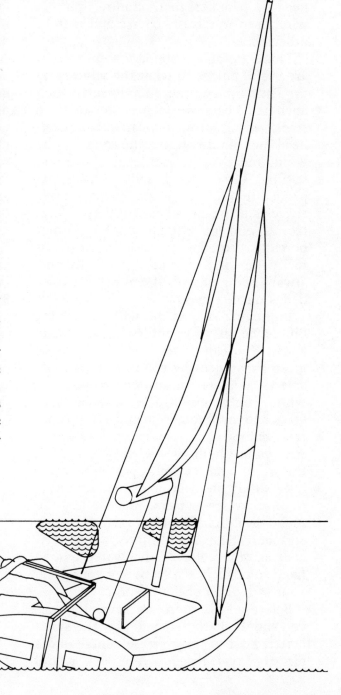

Figure 80: Closely observe the water in front of your bow and continuously try to predict how the next puff of wind will affect your boat.

fore it does on the water. You can anticipate wind shifts by watching the change in the wind as indicated on your masthead fly. The best method in reading the wind is to watch the course and trim of other boats.

There are also secondary sources that are useful guides to what the wind is up to. They include the direction in which anchored boats are facing, smoke from stacks ashore or boats nearby, the masthead flies of other boats, the sound of the wind, and the direction that clouds are taking. Some gifted sailors have expanded this list of signals. Buddy Melges suggests using cows because they always face aft end into the breeze. Ted Turner notes that to take off, ducks must fly directly upwind. Simple as it sounds, always being observant can pay big dividends on the racecourse.

Improving your vision will make a big difference in your ability to see wind shifts. You can "train" your eyes to see greater distances by trying to read roadside signs as far in advance as you can while you're driving. Wear good sunglasses for eye protection and to help contrast colors when you're on the water. Always use both eyes when you look at the water, and let your eyes blink naturally. Study one section of the horizon at a time to see patterns developing. To make the different colors of wind changes and puffs stand out more completely, contrast the color of the water with a fixed color such as a section of your deck, your sail, or an object onshore.

Before a race there are several things you should do to help you play the shifts better. First, using a grease pencil, and a piece of Mylar taped to your deck, record your course on both tacks, upwind and down, prior to the start. If you have a chance to record a high and a low for each tack, so much the better. This will help you tell at any point upwind or downwind whether the course you are sailing is a lift or a header.

To choose a favored end of the line, begin by coming head to wind in the middle of the line. Whichever end your bow points closer to is the favored end. To choose the favored side of the course, team up with another boat. First, equalize boat speed by sailing together. Next, sail off on opposite tacks from the center of the starting line. After two minutes,

Figure 81: Boat A sails to the left side of the course while boat B sails to the right. Since boat B crosses ahead, one can assume that the right side of the course is favored.

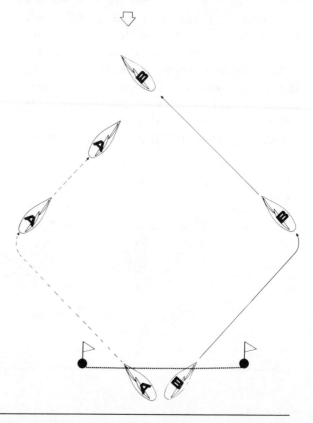

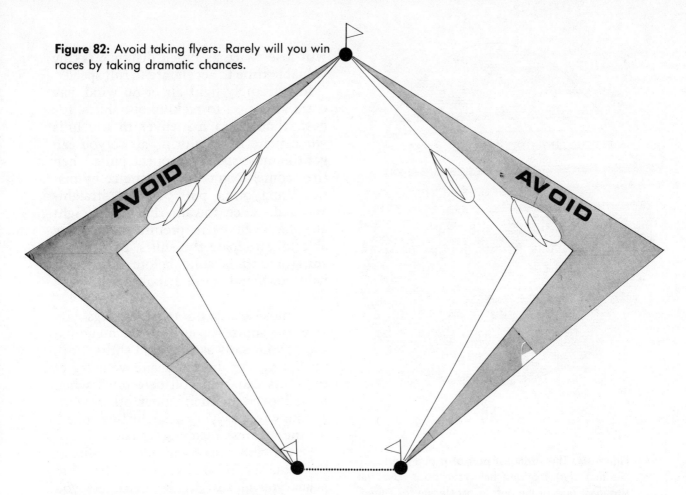

Figure 82: Avoid taking flyers. Rarely will you win races by taking dramatic chances.

tack, so both boats are sailing toward one another. The boat that crosses the other has sailed to the favored side (See Figure 81).

Before the start, observe the course. Stand up to get the height of eye you'll need to see as much as you can. Study the sectors of the horizon one at a time to see if you can tell what wind patterns are developing. Which side of the course seems to have more wind? Are boats on one side heeling more than those on the other? Use any and all of the signals you can to get as clear a picture as possible of the wind on the course.

Predicting shifts is useful only if you can do something based on your prediction. Therefore, avoid sailing out to the layline early in a leg, because you are limited then to a single tack. Also avoid taking fliers (leaving the rest of the fleet and sailing well to the opposite side of the course). Once or twice a season a flier will make you look like a hero, but most of the time the majority of the boats are sailing the favored side of the course and you will go down in flames (See Figure 82).

The strongest part of a puff usually is the part just behind the first wind ripples on the water. Use the strongest part of the puff to accelerate for speed (See Fig-

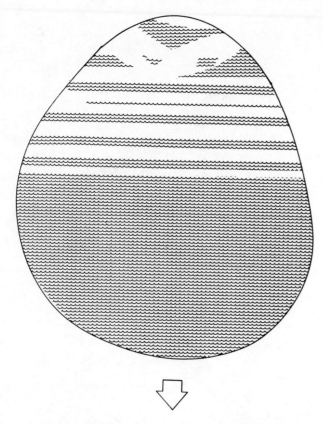

Figure 83: The strongest part of a puff is usually the first part that reaches your boat. Use the strongest part of the puff to accelerate for speed.

ure 83). Sail two to three boat lengths into a puff before you tack. This helps you make the best use of the strongest air and also will help you avoid a false header. This happens when you tack on what you think is a header and immediately find yourself being headed again on the new tack. Always use the wind shift that gets you into the lead the earliest.

In all winds, particularly lighter breezes, it is important to tack or jib only during the strongest part of the puff because it is easier to accelerate just as you complete your maneuver. If you tack in a light spot you will lose twice as much distance taking valuable time to accelerate to full speed.

In extremely light air or no wind, pay extra attention to picking out shifts. It's best, though, to maneuver in the lulls when there is little or no air so you can get the most speed out of the puffs when they come. Don't waste distance by maneuvering on a puff. Go for straight-ahead distance toward the mark. Light air places an extra premium on being able to anticipate the shifts. Be sure the shift or puff is solid before tacking. It helps to stand up and look at the cat's paw.

In most cases on reaching legs you steer the shortest course to the mark and adjust your sails as the wind shifts. Still, predicting the direction and velocity of the puffs can help you determine when to sail over or duck under other boats and how to vary your straight-line course for the greatest reaching speed.

Downwind your basic rule is to jibe in the lifts. Try to sail away on the jibe that heads you closest to the mark. As you get lifted, you will have to sail lower (in relation to the wind) and therefore slower to maintain the same course. It is exactly the opposite of upwind sailing; while on a leeward leg sailing with the wind you want to jibe on the lifts. It is really a case of simple math—sail on the closest course to the next mark.

Wind shear can be upsetting and confusing. It happens when the wind at the top of the sail is different from that at the bottom. Wind shear occurs most often in a new breeze or in a dying breeze when the wind is light (See Figure 84). Be patient; don't let the conflicting signs from aloft and below confuse you. You can get the most out of the troubled

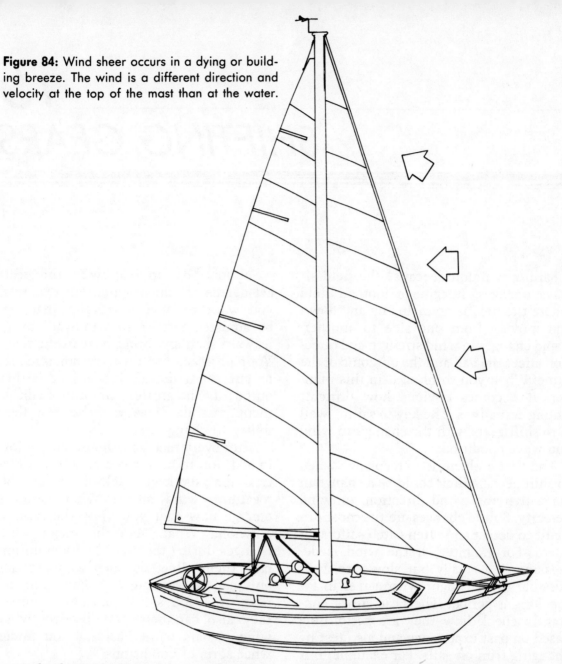

Figure 84: Wind sheer occurs in a dying or building breeze. The wind is a different direction and velocity at the top of the mast than at the water.

period of wind shear by trimming the largest part of your sail for the strongest part of the breeze.

You can check for wind shear by observing the direction in which telltales are blowing from the top of your mast to your lower shrouds. On a 12-Meter we often found the wind strength to be as much as three knots greater at the top of the mast and the wind direction to be as much as 15 degrees different than on the water. This sometimes meant that the jib lead would be farther forward on one tack and farther aft on the other to allow for the difference in one strength and direction.

15
SHIFTING GEARS

Sailing is unique because the field always changes. Imagine a football field where the field is bouncing up and down and moving from one side to another. Rapid changes in wind strength and direction affect the ball and the outcome of the game. When you think of it in this manner, it becomes obvious how difficult sailing actually is. The key to sailing well is to shift gears with the changes in wind and wave conditions.

The first problem is to recognize when to shift gears, which could be a change in wave patterns, wind direction, or wind velocity. Subtle changes are the most difficult to detect and often catch sailors off guard. For example, if the wind is decreasing at a steady but slow rate, it is possible to be caught with a reef in for too long a period. The best crews constantly check how they are performing based on past experience and also test by changing trim on sails. For example, if it is not clear whether the #2 or #3 is the best sail, perhaps it's best simply to change sails and observe your performance with either one. Observation—comparing your boat's performance to that of a competitor—is the best testing you can do.

Set your boat up to allow for the greatest degree of adjustments. For example, you want to have a traveler that can be adjusted farther to windward or to leeward than any other boat in the fleet. Your jib leads should have adjustments to put them farther inboard or farther outboard. The greatest amount of adjustment possible gives you the best flexibility to change gears.

After every race you should keep a log. In addition to boat-speed details and tactical analysis, keep track of information regarding wind shifts. What patterns emerge now that you view the race as a whole? What were the major wind changes during the race? Did you anticipate them? Records such as these not only can be valuable in helping you the next time you sail a particular course, they also can help you discover what wind signals work best for you under what sorts of conditions.

If you wait for the speed to change before you react to a puff, the wind will be long gone and you will react to puffs that have happened boat lengths earlier.

You can sail faster and more efficiently both upwind and downwind by using air speed (apparent wind speed, that is) as a reference instead of boat speed (velocity through the water). Boat speed on offshore boats is reported by a knotmeter in most cases, while one-design sailors must rely on performance vs. competition, or simply "feel," to judge speed. Although wind strength changes rapidly at times, a boat will respond slowly as it accelerates or decelerates. Therefore, changes in boat speed resulting from puffs are monitored late on all the "gauges" you have at your disposal.

The direct-drive speedometers that the America's Cup contenders all used in 1983 are the best on the market because they have a constant rate of acceleration. It is important to calibrate your speed-ometers and your anemometer to get an accurate reading at all times, which is helpful in determining your sail selection and steering.

To counteract this and to stay up with the puffs, be constantly aware of your boat's changing acceleration. This information will help you decide when to change gears—sail trim, steering, sail selection, angle of heel—as the wind changes. The relative color of the water tells you the strength of the puff. Sailing by air speed and becoming more sensitive to the puffs and lulls will improve your boat speed by helping you anticipate needed changes.

Your goal is to sail as close to straight

K 879 bears off for speed after a sharp luff hits rival number 2. *Photograph by Daniel Forster*

downwind without losing speed and changing course as possible. In lighter airs it is better to err by sailing too high, while in heavy breezes it is better to err by sailing too low.

Feeling out the puffs is really the easy part; reacting to them according to the sometimes drastic changes in the apparent wind speed and direction is something else. As a refresher, apparent wind speed is the true wind speed in combination with the additional wind created by the boat moving through the water. On upwind legs aboard offshore boats, sails are selected by air speed over the deck. On most boats, a change of six knots will mean a change of headsails. Helmsmen and sheet trimmers should realize that a boat's movement through the water will also change the direction of the wind, drawing it farther forward as the wind increases, moving it aft as the wind diminishes.

The critical time for shifting gears is during marginal situations when the boat is just beginning to get over- or underpowered. A major question may be: Is it time to reef or change to a smaller headsail? First, try all the possible combinations during any marginal situation. Note your air speed when you find the best combination, and use it as your reference for gear changing in the future.

Use all your senses to detect changes in air speed. You can feel the air-speed changes on the back of your neck or by more or less tension on the sheets. When sailing downwind, do not allow any crew member to stand behind you so you can feel what the wind is doing on the back of your neck. A wet finger is sensitive to the wind. In light air, the best telltales

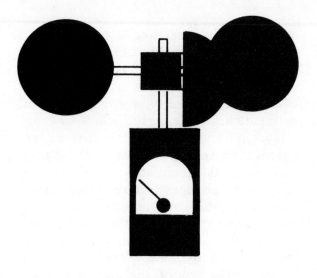

ANEMOMETER

Figure 85: The anemometer is used to detect apparent wind speed.

for air-speed changes are long, thin strips of tissue paper taped to the shrouds. Remember, with most changes in air speed, there is also a corresponding change in direction.

Mechanically, the anemometer can be useful in detecting changes in air speed (See Figure 85). Also, make notes of readings on your anemometer during a race so you know what pattern the wind is developing. By taking measurements at certain time intervals, you may be able to detect the phase of the shifts of a particular leg. There is also an unexpected premium to using the anemometer in detecting air-speed changes: The wind usually changes at the top of the mast a few seconds earlier than it does across the deck, allowing you to anticipate needed steering and trimming changes.

You can gain several boat lengths on

downwind legs by sailing by air speed instead of boat speed. In heavier air this means sailing almost straight downwind. In lighter air, boats usually perform better if they are sailed more and more on a reach. Additionally, the higher the performance peculiar to a particular class, the more downwind reaching you will have to perform. To make the best of the wind on a leeward leg, you must steer the closest course to the next mark without losing speed. Your optimum boat speed is based on experience and by observing your performance compared with that of other boats around you. Once you have determined this speed, you now use the air speed to make more sensitive changes.

The rule of thumb downwind is to sail down or bear away in the puffs, luffing up toward the wind in the lighter spots. If you feel a puff hitting your boat, or if

Collegiate sailors jockey for position on the starting line. The key to a good start is never to sail slower than your competition on your final approach. *Photograph by Carol Singer*

The key to sailing well is to shift gears with the changes in wind and wave conditions. On this ocean racer, a small headsail and a deep-reefed main have been set, both of which seem appropriate for the conditions. However, if the wind is decreasing at a steady rate, the crew should be prepared to set more sail. *Photograph by Daniel Forster.*

you see the wind speed climb on your anemometer, you can immediately begin to bear away.

Try to anticipate the puff by looking behind for new wind. Anticipate changes in the wind so you'll know to change course as the new puff hits your sails.

The spinnaker trimmer is a key person for sensing air-speed changes while sailing downwind. A puff fills the spinnaker and increases tension on the sheet. Therefore, the trimmer should call for the helmsman to bear off several degrees. The trimmer and the helmsman can work well together here, using the air speed as a reference for determining when to bear off and when to sail up. Use as light a spinnaker sheet as possible.

The more accurate information you use when sailing, the faster your boat will go. Your air speed is your most accurate source.

Reading the wind takes practice. The more experience you have at interpreting the wind's signals, the more accurate you will be. Still, keeping a weather eye open and concentrating on anticipating what the wind will do will help you use wind shifts to your advantage.

16

SAILING IN NO WIND

For us, sailing in no wind is the most frustrating and physically exhausting kind of sailing. You must work hard for every inch gained on the racecourse. It takes hours to make the slightest gain, and yet this gain can be wiped out with one sudden gust of wind from the wrong direction. When there is no wind you might be better off not sailing at all. But in the middle of a race, before the time limit has run out, you usually will be working to catch every puff of wind.

Racing in no wind, you need patience while you pace yourself. Many sailors get burned out by trying too hard in the early part of a calm. When you are well behind in a fleet, sailing "no wind" is a great opportunity because it gives you a new opportunity to break the race wide open. Unfortunately, when you have a big lead, the world can cave in on you when there is no wind.

In 1981 Gary was racing as watch captain on the maxi yacht *Condor* in the Fastnet Race. Both *Condor* and rival maxi *Kialoa* had been racing neck and neck. Fifty miles from the finish line, the breeze stopped completely. The two great yachts anchored and stopped for 48

hours; then they hauled the anchors off the bottom to drift with the tide as it flowed toward the finish at Plymouth, England. Later they reanchored when the tide turned foul. After 48 hours the rest of the 237 boats in the fleet surrounded *Kialoa* and *Condor*, who ended up last and next to last, respectively, in the fleet on corrected time. Sometimes the breaks just don't go your way.

There are some things you can do to maintain headway as the wind drops off to almost nothing. The first is to force the boat to heel (See Figure 86). This keeps the rig out over the side of the boat, which helps maintain some sort of feel or weather helm. Because the center of effort of the sail is to leeward of the center of resistance of the hull, the resulting force attempts to turn the boat to windward, causing the helmsman to pull the tiller to weather (weather helm) to keep the boat tracking straight ahead.

Heeling also causes the sail to be acted on by gravity, which helps the draft stay in position in the sail and avoids shape disruption by wave action. But the stray puff that hopefully will come along will give the boat motion instead of its pre-

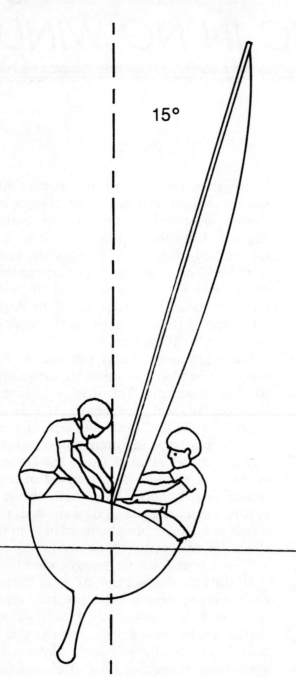

Figure 86: When sailing in no wind, maintaining a 15° leeward heel will help your sails keep their shape and also induce some windward helm.

15°

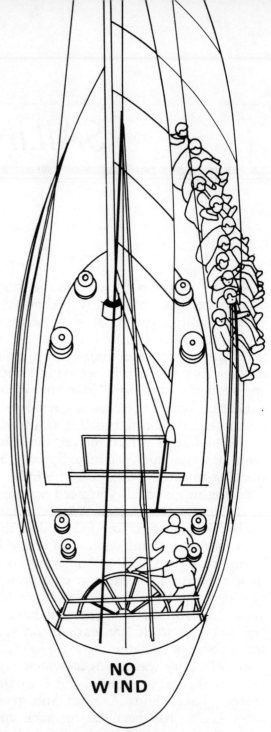

NO WIND

Figure 87: In no wind, reduce your wetted surface by moving your crew weight to leeward and forward.

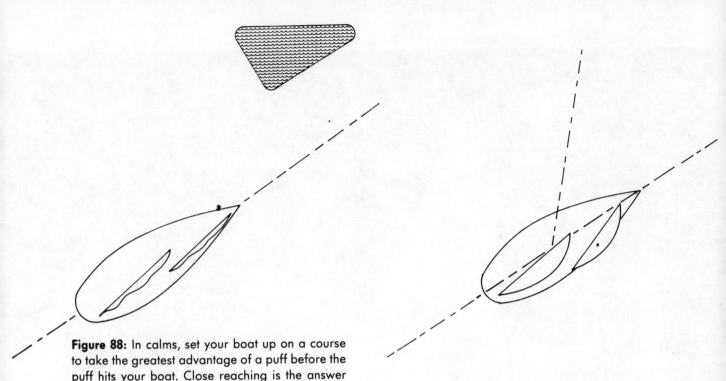

Figure 88: In calms, set your boat up on a course to take the greatest advantage of a puff before the puff hits your boat. Close reaching is the answer to accelerating for speed.

cious tiny amount of energy being used to create an airfoil shape in the sail.

It is imperative to reduce your wetted surface and therefore friction with the water. This can be done in no wind by moving the crew weight as far forward as possible to get the stern of the boat out of the water (See Figure 87).

As the breeze gets lighter and lighter you probably have "powered up" the rig and the sails. This means making things fuller so the boat can overcome the waves. You probably have loosened the backstay, the vang, and perhaps even the rig to reduce hobbyhorsing and to allow the sails to "twist" off up high. As the wind drops further, however, flatten the sails and move them outboard with the traveler and barber hauler to a close-reaching position. The theory here is

that the wind is so light that fullness is not the answer. The small amount of energy in the wind can be extracted by a small amount of camber, but to maintain any chance of headway, the boat now must be sailed on a reach around the course because sailing close-hauled is impossible. Reaching also means that hopefully the action of the waves on the boat will be reduced and therefore the sail's shape will remain aerodynamic (See Figure 88).

Also remember to have the crew sit very, very still. You must have the boat heeled well over, everybody quiet and conscientious of not losing any momentum, or any breeze out of the sails. When someone has to move, he should glide like a cat to accomplish the job. One exception to sitting to leeward may be to

These dinghy sailors must concentrate in light air. They heel the boats to leeward to help shape the main-sail and reduce wetted surface. *Photograph by Carol Singer*

have the helmsman to windward, where he may have a better "feel" for the boat and the waves, or to have someone looking toward the horizon for the new breeze. In no wind, it isn't who goes the fastest who wins but rather who gets the new breeze first. Anything you can do (which won't be much) to position yourself toward the side of the course that will have the new breeze will help you win the race.

Anticipating and predicting the new breeze is both an art and a science. You should know what the official forecast is, but this information is often misleading. North America in the summer is a light wind area, and consequently many races turn into the proverbial "crap shoot." Local knowledge is mainly an awareness of the tendencies of the present breeze, the dying breeze, and the new breeze. You would do very well to have a notebook of local knowledge where you record your and other sailors' experiences (particularly the winners' experiences) so you can build up a bank of information in this area. Additionally, you can improve in predicting weather and wind shifts by studying weather forecasting.

To anchor in light air is an effective tool, as we found on *Condor* in the 1981 Fastnet race. Keep taking bearings on navigation aids or landmarks, and when you discover you are being set back, gently slip an anchor over the side near the shrouds, where it will not be visible to the competition. Usually people are sitting to leeward, and the anchor can be handed up on deck unnoticed and set over the side without loud command. The trick here is to be sneaky.

The boat gives the illusion of sailing, although you are anchored to the bottom. Everyone else is slipping back while you maintain your distance to the mark, so you actually increase your lead over the other boats. It will appear to the other boats that you are sailing directly upcurrent. They, of course, are being sent directly downcurrent.

If you can anticipate the need to anchor, it is best to sail into shallower water, where it is easier to anchor. If you predict the time of sunset (it usually happens about the same time from day to day) and a drop in the wind, you can tack or reach up to position yourself onshore at that time.

When in a calm situation, have an awareness of the physical condition of your crew. It is often very hot, and the crew should be adequately protected from the sun. Dehydration is a serious problem. The crew should be encouraged to drink lots of water.

The crew's mental condition is very important so they are ready to continue racing when the wind does come back. It might be good to take a lunch break, or even have a swim call. You might also send some people below to nap.

Sailing in no wind is tough stuff. It may be best either to head for the beach and stop sailing, or pace yourself with patience, realizing that anything can happen, so it is best to enjoy the experience.

17

SAILING AT NIGHT

Graham Hall is generally considered one of America's top sailors and coaches. He is a wizard at night sailing. We talked at length with Graham and prepared the following approach to this mysterious topic.

The main problem with sailing at night is that the physical senses are dull—particularly the sense of sight. So much of our ability to sail fast effectively is based on sight—sailing by the telltales; observing the depth and location of sail draft; seeing snarled lines or crossed halyards. Some people can tell that boat speed is down by the appearance of water going by the hull. Try sailing with your eyes closed for one minute and notice how your performance changes.

When sailing at night, much of the information formed during daylight is not quickly or automatically available. One major solution to the problem is the flashlight. This sounds simple, but it is surprisingly often overlooked. There never seem to be enough powerful flashlights or enough spare batteries on board.

The current technology of flashlights is quite adequate to light up the scene on a sailboat moving at night. Disposable lights are quite good, and each crewperson should have one packed in his pocket. They can shine up at a sail, or be handy to spot potential problems. Another reason to have one in your pocket is in case you go overboard. In fact, as a crew member on a night sail you should bring your own small but powerful pocket flashlight with you. If you do go over the side, the ability to shine a light toward your potential rescuers could save your life.

There should be one very powerful spotlight on board that plugs into the boat's power supply—probably 12 volts DC. The light can shine down through the water or out across the night. It can be used to find unlighted buoys or in emergency situations. However, these lights are too bright to use for sail trim or depth perception because they blind the skipper and crew.

The best invention is a simple plastic universal joint that clamps a small flashlight to one of the forward stanchions angled at the sails. After tacking to windward, the flashlight can be redirected up and forward onto the jib telltales. When sailing on the wind at night this device is extremely effective in helping the helmsman keep the boat "in the groove." The telltales should be different colors and different heights on both sides of the jib. Telltale windows are commonly used; however, you may have to order these installed in the sail. There are usually two or three windows spread the length of the jib luff.

The second part of solving the lack of sight problem at night is having good instrumentation. Besides the obvious big three (speed, compass, and depth sounder), which should be on any offshore boat, there are several other important instruments.

The wind speed over the deck is very important for sail selection, sail trim, and as a check against potential top speed through the water. This will usually be measured as apparent wind, but some systems can read true wind.

Velocity made good (VMG) to windward is quite valuable when sailing on the wind. This is the ultimate answer to the age-old sailing question of whether you should "point" the boat up close to the wind or "foot" the vessel for faster speed through the water. The right answer is whatever gives you the greatest "VMG."

VMG on some instruments can also be set for downwind sailing. If you have the instrument tell you VMG downwind, remember that it may not necessarily be your VMG directly downline. In big boats you rarely sail a true downwind course. Here again the performance prediction tables for your boat are extremely important. Should you sail the rhumb line with the breeze at 170 de-

grees apparent? Or should you reach up to 160 degrees or 150 degrees apparent with a dramatic increase in speed?

During the day you can have a good seat-of-the-pants feel for these different sailing angles. By watching the competition you can determine your correct angle.

At night you don't have this advantage. You are in the dark. But there is a right solution. There is one optimum course and speed downwind that will get you to the next mark in the minimum amount of time. By using a programmable calculator that will give you your polar plots or even several trial-and-error vector plots, you can find the right answer.

As we said, you don't have visual track of your competition at night. Attempt visual tracks on the other boats for as long as possible after it gets dark. At dusk take bearings on your close competitors, and keep a bearing log of their lights through the night. Perhaps their lights are distinguishable—very bright or dim, etc. Of course, your own lights should be as nondescript as possible. This is difficult but very worthwhile to the successful night fighter.

The apparent-wind-angle instrument, along with the compass, are the two most *over*used instruments by the novice helmsman. Neither of these instruments will react quickly enough to allow championship helmsmanship. They should be used only as secondary information sources.

First choices at night are stationary lights ahead, low stars on the horizon, or even the horizon illuminated by moonlight. These objects are most useful when a wave pushes the bow off course. You can observe this immediately if you are looking ahead through the rigging. These changes are slow to show up on the compass or the apparent-wind indicator. If the night is particularly black, with no reference light or stars and other considerations neutral, you probably should tack just behind and to windward of a competitor who might cross a little ahead of you. By heading to leeward you now can see a stern light just behind your genoa and thereby maintain a more perfect course. If you had chosen instead to tack a minute earlier, you would be abeam to windward but in no position to see the opponent's light. If it is a dark night with no horizon, use an inclinometer to measure the angle of heel (See Figure 89). The key to good steering at night is a reliable reference.

So far we have talked about attempting to make the night more like the day—flashlight and instrumentation

INCLINOMETER

Figure 89: The inclinometer is a valuable reference to tell you how much you are heeling, particularly at night when you cannot see the horizon.

helping to remove the visual handicap of darkness. There are several other areas of discussion to be considered, not the least of which is safety. The key consideration is to be aware of the problems and then realize that when sailing at night all normal hazards are increased. Remember that objects and waves look bigger at night, and the sensation of speed then is greater.

Most importantly, the need to take responsibility for safety on board remains with the skipper, but one strong suggestion would be to name a safety officer. This may indeed be the skipper, or someone else with safety experience and knowledge. It is most helpful when one person is thinking about safety and is conscious of when to recommend putting on life jackets, or safety harnesses, or lessening sail.

If you sail on a boat as a crew member and there apparently is no positive consideration being given to safety except for an "every man for himself" attitude, volunteer to act as a safety officer. There is no excuse for accidents. Safety on a boat at night is simply a good, solid dose of common sense, awareness, anticipation, and prevention.

Another key item to sailing at night is the watch system. The simplest is the "full-court press"—nobody sleeps; everybody works. Sometimes this "watch system" can win a race—particularly a short one with a lot of sail changes, spinnaker reaching with staysails, or varying conditions. Obviously it is not so good for the longer races or for cruising. Our biggest mistake in distance races over the years has been "burnout" by staying up all night.

The standard watch system of four on and four off is common, as is the slight variation of three on and three off. There are "Swedish" or "Norwegian" systems that use four-, five-, and six-hour periods to divide up the twenty-four hours in a day, with the shorter time being used in early-morning hours when it is supposedly harder to stay awake. Most of these have an odd number of periods so that on long passages of several days or a week or more, each person changes his routine in a three-day cycle.

Friendly competition between the two watches—such as which had the higher boat speed—also boosts morale and makes races more interesting. It seems as if races always are lost on "the other watch." The "other watch" always steers an unsteady course, rips the sails, runs out of wind, has the wrong sail up.

Plan to be on deck at least five minutes prior to your watch to get acclimated to conditions and to discuss the boat's situation with the person you are relieving. Look carefully at the nautical chart before coming on deck and decide upon your objective during your spell. It is important that the logbook be kept up to date and that weather forecasts are listened to regularly. All watch members should have a function and be made to feel that they are part of the action.

You should be aware also of the three-section system. (All of the above are two-section systems—port and starboard watches). Here two sections are on deck at one time, while the third is below, asleep. If each watch was a two-hour trick you would stand four hours on deck and two below. Halfway through your period on deck, the section you

started with would be replaced by the section below. This system gives you more people on deck and cuts down on sleeping time. You will have to judge whether this gives you an advantage depending on the length and style of the race.

Finally, there are the systems that segregate the afterguard (helmsman, tactician, navigator, owner, etc.) from the deck crew. Maybe the crew will stand four on and four off while the helm is rotated among several of the best helmsmen aboard. Perhaps a four-hour trick is too long for a helmsman even if he feels comfortable. A pair of helmmates might go for an hour or two by relieving each other periodically, and then they would be relieved for the next couple of hours by another pair. The answer lies in what will get the most out of the crew in the time needed to complete the race successfully. You may want to combine two of these watch systems in one race. Often a standard watch system is sandwiched between two periods of "full-court press" at the start and the finish of a long race.

There are two reasons why most boats go slower at night. The first is that practice (if any) is not always conducted with the entire crew. The second is that practice always is conducted during the day, when everything is easily seen. To solve this problem the first suggestion is to practice with the entire crew. Probably you don't practice, either as a crew or as a boat owner—there isn't enough time, you can't get all the people together at once, there is work to be done on the boat instead. The second suggestion is to break the crew into watch sections and practice as small teams. The things that need work are reefing, changing sails, tacking, setting the spinnaker, jibing, and taking down sail. The third suggestion is to try to get out at night for some serious work in the above categories. You will be way ahead of your competition because few others do these things.

Finally, there is a category of information about racing at night that can be called "common sense"—such things as keeping warm, preventing seasickness, staying awake, etc. It is important to realize that most people underestimate the magnitude of change when the sun goes down on the sea. Even in the middle of the summer it can get cold racing a sailboat at night. If you have a novice crew coming aboard, be sure they bring lots of warm clothes and good foul-weather gear. People susceptible to seasickness should take active measures against the problem. There should be hot drinks and snacks available to the crew on deck through the night. The watch captain should make provision for these.

A skipper and his boat are only as good as the crew. A successful night-racing skipper realizes that darkness poses some special problems, particularly in the area of crew performance. He realizes that the boat can't be sailed as fine or in as narrow a groove as during the day; he realizes that his people aren't going to be as sharp, as awake, or as competent as during a nice, peaceful day race. He will be demanding, but he will allow a wider latitude and sail more conservatively and safely at night. These attitudes will allow the boat to reach a higher potential during the dark portions of the race.

18

THE PASSING LANE

Sailboats need a booster knob. Wouldn't it be great to have this booster knob so you could hit it and your boat would instantly accelerate around a competitor? Maybe in every race each boat gets two boosts just in case. Unfortunately, this fantasy exists only in videogames. Somehow it seems easy to catch up distance during a race but difficult to make that final maneuver around a competitor. This is particularly true on 12-Meters, which are far and away the slowest-accelerating boats we have ever sailed. In fact, the crews on *Defender* and *Courageous* referred to these "lead-bottom money-gobblers" as "empire walkers" from the movie *Star Wars* because 12's take so long to gain speed.

The most exciting time during any race is when your boat is in a position to pass another boat. At this time tensions mount and concentration peaks. If you are sailing faster, there is no reason why you should not be able to sail around your opponent. But there are many special cases you will need to keep in mind to pass another boat or to keep a boat from passing you.

There is great psychological value to be gained when passing a competitor. The frustration you can bestow by holding a faster boat back can psychologically damage a foe for an entire series. Passing another boat is the toughest move in yacht racing. It takes a combination of smarts and extra speed when you need it.

Without a booster knob how do you get extra speed? When sailing on the wind you can get extra speed by bearing off two to five degrees at the same time you ease your sheets out. Keep in mind that sailboats increase speed only when they bear off if the sails are eased out. If you are planning a special maneuver, plan it well in advance so you can concentrate on boat speed. It is critical to watch waves very carefully so you do not slam into one, stopping your boat at an inopportune time. Plan your passing maneuvers in smooth water or during a lifting puff where the breeze swings aft and you can use the lift for acceleration.

Downwind, you can gain speed by heading up at least five degrees to a better reaching angle and using puffs and waves for acceleration. The key to getting a boat surfing down a wave (even the smallest waves help) is to line the boat up perpendicular to the direction the wave is moving, trimming your sail rapidly at the instant the wave begins to lift the stern out of the water and keeping the boat on an even keel with no helm pressure.

Sailing is often a game not of brilliance but of elimination of errors. Most skippers are passed not because competitors have pulled brilliant maneuvers but because they let their rivals off the hook by failing to cover or stay in phase with the wind shifts, or they lose concentration and hence boat speed. When you are behind, try to get your competition ahead to make extra maneuvers. Boats that maneuver less generally gain distance on the racecourse.

In the 1984 Miami–Nassau race on *Jubilation*, we were dueling upwind with *Golden Eagle*. *Golden Eagle* gained substantially by tacking inshore along the Bahamian banks. It became our job to encourage *Golden Eagle* to sail offshore while we headed inshore. We accomplished this by tacking inshore; as expected, *Golden Eagle* tacked to cover. We immediately tacked back and *Golden Eagle* tacked once again, now heading offshore. On *Jubilation* we tacked a third time, which was simply too often for *Golden Eagle* to keep up with. They held on starboard tack for a considerable period with us heading inshore. When both boats tacked again on a converging course several minutes later, *Jubilation* had taken the lead. By making three simultaneous tacks, we were able to get *Golden Eagle* off our wind and heading in the wrong direction.

The "half tack" is a very effective maneuver we learned by watching Dennis Connor racing *Liberty* against *Courageous*. We encourage sailors to take a day out of their racing schedule to spend on a powerboat observing competitors (See Figure 90). We have learned a lot by watching our rivals from the shore or from a powerboat, as opposed to actually being on the racecourse. The "half tack" is used to escape a tight cover from one competitor or a group of competitors. A "half tack" works like this:

Let's say you have just completed rounding the leeward mark with another boat directly ahead. Your first reaction is to immediately tack away into clear air. If the boat ahead is concerned with covering, he will immediately tack and actually drive down, sailing a lower course than you to try to force you into a second tack or at least keeping you under control with a blanketing cover. You can anticipate this maneuver with a "half tack." If the leeward mark has been rounded to port and you are tacking onto starboard, just as your jib fills and you notice that the boat ahead is tacking on you, immediately start tacking back onto port. The boat ahead will rarely make a double tack to stay in phase with you, and you are now free. The trick here is to come out on starboard tack on as high a course as you can and still fill the jib. The more you bear off on starboard, the greater distance you will lose in trying to get back onto port tack. In a match race, the "half tack" can turn into a "triple half tack" and you will be able to get out of phase of your opponent in a short period without losing a lot of distance. But the "half tack" can be used anywhere on the racecourse.

Downwind you can use the "half jibe." Instead of swinging the boat all the way up onto your new course or higher to accelerate for speed, the second your spinnaker pole is made or the mainsail

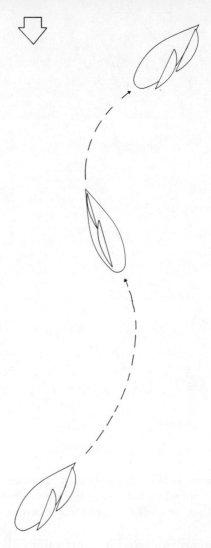

Figure 90: The half tack. The half tack is effective in shaking off a covering competitor. As soon as your sails fill, you immediately begin tacking back to your original course.

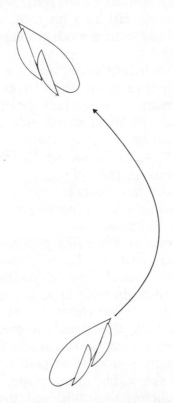

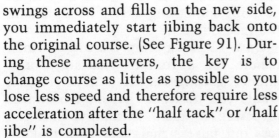

swings across and fills on the new side, you immediately start jibing back onto the original course. (See Figure 91). During these maneuvers, the key is to change course as little as possible so you lose less speed and therefore require less acceleration after the "half tack" or "half jibe" is completed.

A second trick we watched Connor use successfully when behind is to force a competitor ahead to make a double tack. In heavier-displacement boats, double tacks are disastrous because you lose twice the normal distance following the second tack (See Figure 92). If a boat ahead tacked on Connor, he would simply continue sailing on the same tack and coast up into the backwind and blanketing zone of the boat ahead. Connor would not tack away until the boat ahead was nearly up to full speed, and then he would tack himself. If the boat ahead immediately followed tacking before full speed was attained, Connor would recognize this and follow with a "half tack." This would afford him the advantage of making 1½ tacks to three tacks by his competitor. During this ma-

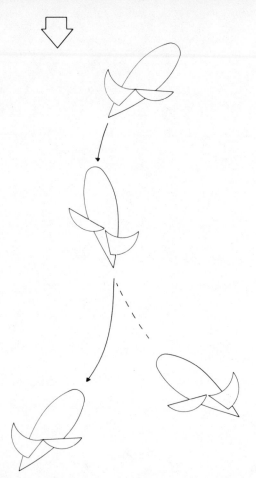

Figure 91: The half jibe is used to escape a covering boat which cuts down the alteration of course that you will need to make for a second jibe.

neuver, the wind in your sails will not be affected because the blanketing zone is not created until a boat sails through the turbulent wind. Therefore, you are not affected by a boat ahead until you begin sailing through the same water and the same wind.

The "half tack," or coasting into another boat's breeze, should be distinguished from a false tack. In heavy-displacement boats false tacks rarely work, but if you are caught reacting to a false tack of a boat behind you, it is better to follow through than to try to make

a second tack. In lighter-displacement boats that maneuver quickly, false tacks are very effective because the skipper of the lead boat simply has to glance away for two seconds, overreact to your tack (by spinning too fast), and you immediately fall back on your original course. Bingo! You are out of phase and in clear air.

It is best to set up for a false tack or a "half tack" or jibe so you end up on the favored or lifted tack, or the tack heading toward the favored side of the course, leaving your competitor confused and sailing in the wrong direction. These maneuvers take planning, and it is important not to fake out your own crew. Subtle signals are imperative here.

Anytime you plan to tack or jibe, avoid telegraphing your intentions to the competition. Keep yourself and your crew steady and in position even when you begin your tack. If your crew stands up, or if you shout that you are preparing to tack, this signals to competitors what you are up to. The automatic response of many sailors is to tack with you if you make a big commotion, because their subconscious will tell them they must be doing something wrong. Be sneaky on the racecourse.

On a 12-Meter simply lifting a winch handle for a running backstay, or a grinder getting set in a new position would tell me that the other boat was preparing to tack. Naturally, you can toss out false signals and even make a quick maneuver (the head fake) to try to get the boat ahead overanticipating your maneuver and tacking away at the slightest change in your course.

Although it is difficult to pass a large

number of boats at one time, it is possible to pass several boats if they are closely bunched. At all costs, avoid sailing near large packs of boats. This only spells trouble and cuts down your maneuverability and your options. Use other boats on the racecourse as blockers. Anytime you are planning to tack, wait until a boat has crossed either just ahead or just behind. Continue sailing for at least five boat lengths before making your tack. Following your tack, the boats to leeward and ahead will act as blockers, converging on the opposite tack, out of your way before they reach you. This allows you to sail in clear winds and smoother water for longer periods and reduces the number of tacks you must make.

Perhaps the single most offensive move you can make in sailing is to be on starboard tack. Use your starboard tack to your advantage, particularly at the final approach to marks or the finish line. Always be the last boat tacking onto starboard. Make your competitors maneuver around you.

On the windward leg, if you are continually gaining on your opponent each time you cross tacks, you will eventually converge. In such a situation, you may be forced to dip under the stern of the other boat if you are on port and your competitor is on starboard. Dipping another boat is a tough maneuver to do well so you lose only a small amount of distance. If when you are on port tack there is no chance of crossing the starboard tacker and you are afraid to tack to leeward because you might get rolled, it is best to dip. If you noticed during the converging of the two boats that your

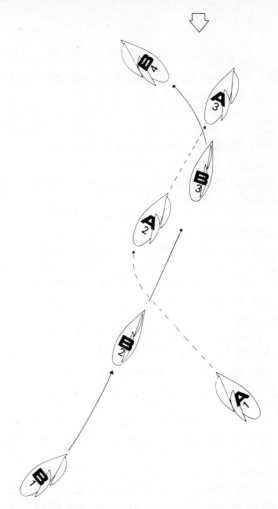

Figure 92: Boat B in this illustration can potentially force A into making a double tack by sailing up into A's backwind but tacking away before A has gained full speed. In heavy displacement boats, double tacks are costly.

bow is well ahead of the bow of the other boat, you will need to start your dip earlier. If the starboard tacker is ahead of you, you can hold off dipping until the last moment. The key to a good dip is to change course as little as possible. When your bow reaches the transom of your opponent, you want to be sailing close-hauled and on the wind at a greater speed, anticipating the lift you will receive from the starboard tacker's sails. Be prepared to take a bite to windward as you dip astern.

If you are on starboard tack during a dip and you notice a port tacker dipping you, pick a course while you are converging that is especially fast (five degrees lower will do) and also makes you converge faster and earlier, therefore causing the port tack boat to make a greater course change. Under the rules you are not allowed to obstruct another boat from keeping clear, but it is permissible to settle on one course when you are at least two boat lengths from engaging.

During a crossing situation, take continual bearings either with a hand bearing compass; a compass mounted in your boat; or by simple observations, lining up your target with objects onshore to see if you are gaining or losing. When you are gaining bearing, you know that you will cross ahead, but when you are losing bearing, you will cross behind. When the bearing stays constant, a collision is imminent. Offwind, we find that observing the mainsail of a converging boat gives us a helpful clue to who's ahead and who's gaining. If you can see the forward part of another boat's mainsail, then you can assume you are ahead. If the position of the mainsail changes so you begin seeing the forward part of the leech and the afterpart of the luff simultaneously, the boats are even. If you begin seeing the afterpart of a mainsail, the other boat is now ahead of you. This trick, we find, works whether you are on the same tack or the opposite tack.

Opportunities for passing do not exist at all times on the racecourse. On board *Condor* during the 1981 Fastnet race, Gary was intrigued by how patient Dennis Conner was following one mile astern of *Kialoa* on a reach, hour after hour. It seemed as if he should try to do something to pass the other boat, but the time simply wasn't right. Several hundred miles later in the race, the wind died, and at this point Conner made his move to sail around *Kialoa*. Sailboat races are won by fighting it out in the trenches and staying with your opponents. Being greedy can cost you dearly.

During the 1984 Miami–Nassau race on *Jubilation*, we were consistently covering the boats behind by jibing with the wind shifts. A major change in the breeze seemed imminent since we were experiencing calms, rain squalls, and rapidly shifting breezes. If the wind shifted to the forecasted northwest, or in about a 60-degree wind zone, we were in position to make a major gain if we split with the fleet. In reality, the wind was so unsettled that there was a possibility the new breeze could come from anywhere, but we took the gamble, which actually was a six-to-one shot, since there are 360 degrees to the compass. As luck would have it, six-to-one odds rarely work, and in this case they didn't work either. We sat in a hole for two hours while the majority of class B sailed away and beat us to the finish line at Nassau by two hours. A potential 10-minute gain turned into a two-hour route. Stay with the fleet until you get a real opportunity. In our minds a real opportunity is when you have at least a 50–50 chance of passing and never less.

A good time to pass an opponent ahead is when that boat is preoccupied with another boat. Stay away from boats that are in a luffing match, tacking duel, jibing duel, or are close in points to each other in a series. At these times be sure to stay in phase with the wind shifts, keep your own wind clear, and avoid sailing near packs of boats.

The "slam dunk" can be a very effective maneuver to trap a boat on your leeward side (See Figure 93). The "slam dunk" works best in winds of at least 10 knots. When you are crossing another boat and you are on starboard tack and want to tack yourself to port, you are in a good position to make a "slam dunk." Although this maneuver works best in keel boats, it is useful on boats of any displacement. Just as the boat's bow you are crossing crosses beneath your stern, you immediately start making your tack.

Figure 93: You can capture an opponent in your wind by using an aggressive maneuver called the slam dunk.

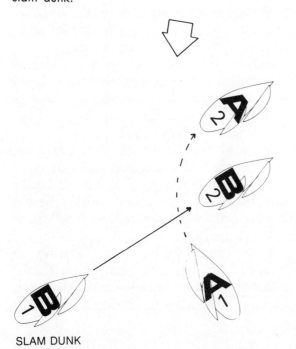

SLAM DUNK

If you are able to get on your new tack and start accelerating before the bow of the now leeward boat lines up with the bow of your boat, you have "slamdunked" your competitor because now you are sailing on his breeze, and yet he cannot tack away until his bow can clear your stern.

The defense for the "slam dunk" is to tack away immediately if you are dipping just a small amount (10 to 20 degrees). Be sure your bow clears the other boat's stern. Although under Rule 41.4 anytime two yachts are tacking simultaneously the one on the other's port side shall keep clear, in this case it would be the boat tacking from starboard onto port that is obligated to stay clear (See Figure 94).

If you are making a substantial dip of at least 20 degrees or more, work hard to get your boat sailing as fast as possible by easing your sails out and accelerating. If the starboard tack boat begins tacking on top of you, immediately harden up to a close-hauled course or even higher and you should be able to shoot through to leeward. If your bow ends up ahead of the bow of the windward boat, the windward boat will never have the opportunity to bear off and accelerate for speed coming out of the tack. The "slam dunk" has been thwarted here by a luff on the part of the leeward boat. The temptation to most sailors in this case is to keep sailing on a low course to gain speed after a dip has been made. Unfortunately, this only opens the door for the windward boat to steer a lower course and accelerate to full speed.

On the wind, if you are a windward boat, taking a dive at the right oppor-

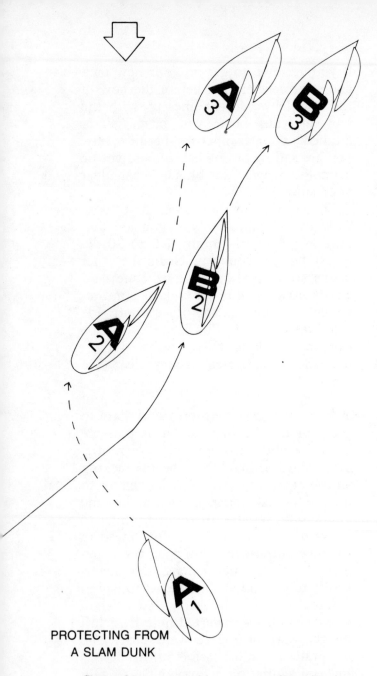

PROTECTING FROM
A SLAM DUNK

Figure 94: It is possible to protect from the slam dunk if you are dipping the boat that is tacking on your wind. Usually this works in ten knots of breeze or more. As soon as boat A begins tacking on you, immediately luff 20° until your bow has gone ahead of A's bow putting A in the backwind of boat B.

tunity will help you sail over the top of a leeward boat. The natural tendency when you are to windward is to sail a continuously high course to stay away from your competitors' backwind. Do not be afraid of backwind because if you get in trouble you always have the opportunity to tack away. We like to bear off for speed and try to sail over the top of a leeward boat during a smooth spot in the water just as a puff is getting to our bow. This new puff will often force the leeward boat to round up into the wind and simultaneously slow down. With your greater speed, thanks to your acceleration by bearing off, you may be able to ride over the top of the leeward boat. It may take several puffs before this opportunity develops, but angling down on a lower course usually works. Keep in mind that you should keep at least half a boat length distance from the leeward boat because the rules are not kind to boats on the windward side.

Deciding when to tack or jibe to cover is really the golden opportunity for passing another boat. When sailing on the wind, we watch the course being steered relative to the course of the other boats very carefully. For example, if a boat is sailing to windward and behind, we prefer to wait to tack until the bow of the windward boat is lower than our bow. This is the golden opportunity to tack. You will not be closer or have a better opportunity to go ahead than when a boat to windward and behind is sailing at a lower angle.

It is important to avoid getting so wrapped up with one competitor that a number of other competitors pass you. This is most obvious during a continual luffing match where one boat will luff another. If you find that you are close to a pest, jibe away early or stay high if you plan to pass to windward, but avoid getting close to boats prone to perpetual luffing matches. It is important to know your competition on the water.

Perhaps the best place to get the jump on the fleet is right at the start. There are numerous starting techniques you can use to get your boat off the line consistently ahead with clear air and with the option of tacking at will. There are several general rules of thumb we try to follow religiously to get consistently good starts.

First, we always keep our boat moving on the starting line at least as fast as or faster than other boats around us so we have more maneuverability and more options open to us. Second, when you make your final approach to the starting line, never sail slower than the competitors around you. Third, sail on the course you will be sailing as you approach the line. Avoid luffing head to wind within one minute of the start because it is hard to accelerate for speed. To help accelerate, heel your boat to leeward so your waterline is longer and your sails take shape and you accelerate faster.

If there is a boat to windward of you, squeeze up to this boat, putting your windward quarter on her bow, not allowing the windward boat to accelerate for speed. On the other hand, if you are the windward boat, stay bow to bow with boats to leeward of you and open up as much distance as you can. When it is time to go for the start and everyone starts trimming in for speed, always be

the first in the fleet to accelerate for speed. If there is a boat luffing to leeward of you, bear off and head down at this boat so while she is slowing and luffing you are bearing off and accelerating for speed, coming up to your close-hauled course prior to the gun. Your starting line should be an imaginary line two boat lengths to leeward of the starting line, and at this point you want to be at full speed.

Prior to the start, ask yourself specifically which side of the course is favored, and make a judgment based on actual upwind testing and observation; then, once the race begins, immediately start analyzing if you are gaining or losing by sailing on the side of the course you are on. If you are gaining, keep going. But if you are losing distance, perhaps it is time to tack. When you tack, make one tack, and make it count by setting up a blocker (as discussed earlier), a boat that ends up being to leeward and ahead to block the competition away from you, allowing you to sail in clear winds and smoother waters for longer periods. The name of the game when coming off the starting line is to make as few tacks as possible.

At the windward mark, we often find that many sailors tend to undershoot the mark. The belief that a boat must stay within the laylines actually hurts many sailors, because they end up tacking short and pinching for the mark. When you pinch you make leeway. In our minds, as a general rule it is best to overshoot the windward mark by at least half a boat length when making your final approach. This means that when you are within 10 to 15 boat lengths of the windward mark, give yourself extra room to allow for misjudgment, a poor tack, a bad set of waves, unfavorable current, another boat tacking on your breeze, or an extra-long anchor line attached to the mark.

After the leeward mark, it is important to get away from other boats so you can sail at full speed. Most sailors tend to pinch in the vicinity of other boats. If you find you are not doing well sailing around other boats, it is probably best to jibe or tack away even for 10 to 15 boat lengths of distance and then come back again and try to pass. Don't try to win a battle that is a continually losing effort.

At times it pays to gamble, and perhaps there is no greater gamble than sailing in shallow water. The penalty, unfortunately, is running aground and losing the race entirely. But there have been many races won by boats willing to hug the shore. It is important to know what the tidal situation is to the half hour when racing. For example, if it is three hours before low tide, the mean low tide is five feet, and the rise and fall of tide are four feet, you will know that there is seven feet of water under your keel at this time, and since you draw six feet, it's safe at least for a few more minutes.

Getting out of an unfavorable tide produces great rewards. A classic area is along the coast of Florida between Ft. Lauderdale and Miami. There is almost always a countercurrent along the coast, but yachts must be willing to sail in 15 feet of water to catch a favorable current. The differential is nearly two knots between 15 feet of water and 100 feet of water.

In heavier breezes, you can often beat many boats or pass boats that are ahead by being a little bit more conservative. Breakdowns tend to be common in a fleet in heavy breezes. It is tough to win a regatta when you break down and miss the finishing line in one race. Also in heavy conditions we find it is best to maneuver as little as possible. Many breakdowns tend to occur while maneuvering.

When sailing downwind, with two boats on port, we often find if we are the windward boat that we can get a quick jump on a competitor by suddenly jibing to starboard and forcing the port tack boat to jibe with haste. Once this boat has completed its jibe, we simply follow through and jibe back, giving us more room.

We find there are bad eddies coming off spinnakers and mainsails (See Figure 95). If you are on the leeward quarter of another boat sailing downwind, you are probably getting affected and will not be able to gain. It is best to sail high or jibe away.

Also downwind, you need to watch the apparent wind of other boats, realizing that blanketed breezes extend at least seven mast lengths away.

One way to pass is to sail to leeward of a windward boat as far as you can and just as your breeze falls into the blanketing wind shadow of the windward boat, harden up a good 20 degrees, pushing your apparent wind well forward so that your masthead fly is pointing well ahead of the bow of the windward boat. In this manner you will be able to shoot through to leeward. The biggest mistake by boats trying to pass to leeward is stay-

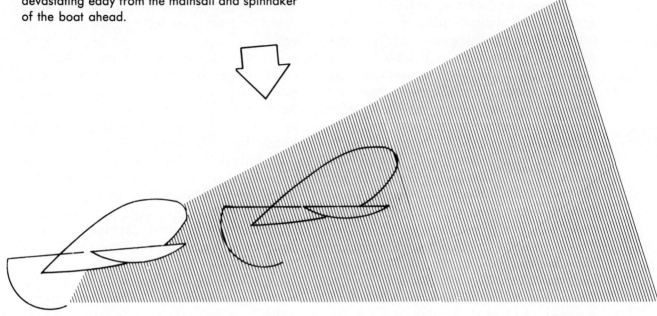

Figure 95: Avoid sailing within one boat length of another boat's leeward quarter. Although you will not be backwinded here, you will get an extremely devastating eddy from the mainsail and spinnaker of the boat ahead.

ing on a low course for too long and not angling up hard enough to break through the wind shadow. If after several attempts you are unable to break through, make two jibes to clear your air completely.

In planing dinghies you have a good opportunity to pass on a reach. If you plan to pass another boat on the windward side, be sure to give yourself plenty of distance to windward (at least four boat lengths) so you have room to bear off, ride a wave, and sail over the top. Make your move to pass when your competitor has just completed riding a wave, is heading into some bad slop created from a powerboat, or is not watching you. If you are sailing in surfing conditions, be careful that the wave you

catch doesn't put you way off course. Although you might be sailing fast and enjoying the ride, it does you no good if you are heading away from the mark you are sailing for.

There are hundreds of cases where leading boats have lost regattas by heading for the wrong mark. You and your crew *must* continually update where you are in relation to the next mark. Observation is the key. Know what your marks look like, particularly on bodies of water where more than one fleet is racing at a time. Marks often look the same from a distance, but subtle differences in marks can give you a clue to which one is yours.

It is a tricky balance of when to split with the fleet and when to hang tough. If

THE PASSING LANE

you are behind, the only way you can get a boat to tack is to keep splitting tacks. It is dangerous to allow a competitor to sit on your windward quarter for long periods. If the wind heads you, you will gain. If the wind lifts you, however, you will lose considerable distance. It is worth it to make a covering tack from time to time, pushing your competitor closer and closer to the layline to take away the room he has to pass you.

If you find yourself behind and hopelessly out of the race, this is the time to go for the gold, to go for greatness and try something bizarre, something weird. One never knows what bizarre moves could make a difference.

In the 1982 *Yacht Racing/Cruising Hall of Fame* regatta, Buddy Melges and Gary found themselves last and next to last, respectively, around the final leeward mark of race three. With a 1½-mile beat to the finish, it looked dismal, particularly since we were standing first and second, respectively, in the regatta at that point. Melges saw a new breeze all the way on the right side of the course, and Gary saw a breeze all the way on the left. They hit the corners of the course while the fleet stopped in the middle. As it turned out, Gary ended up crossing Melges by one boat length, and the two finished third and fourth, respectively. When you are way back, don't be afraid to try bizarre maneuvers.

If you do have good maneuvers that work when passing a boat, don't waste your best tricks when sailing in tune-up races. Make them count when you need them to count.

When sailing boats of different handicaps, don't stubbornly irritate larger boats. Eventually they will get by, and they will make you pay heavily if you have cost them considerable distance. Remember, when you are slowing a boat down you are also losing distance yourself.

Do not allow yourself to be intimidated by another competitor yelling and screaming at you. On the other hand, never verbalize that you are bothered. You don't want your competition to know that you are upset.

Although most of us are used to covering when we are ahead, you also can cover from behind. By staying close to your competitors, you can force the boat ahead into mistakes. Remember, trophies are awarded for regattas and not for individual races.

In our sailing careers, we have seen the most amazing things happen right at the finish line. No matter how hopeless you think the race is or how secure you feel your finish is, don't give up until you cross the line. This is a lesson we learn the hard way every year. In the 1984 St. Petersburg–Ft. Lauderdale race on *Jubilation*, everything was golden until three miles from the finish. The wind dropped completely and the fleet came zooming up from astern. In fact, one boat, *Morning Star*, did an end-around and beat us to the line even though we rated 2½ feet higher.

The easiest way to pass another boat is with a change in the wind direction or velocity or with greater speed. To pass a boat that is sailing faster takes great skill or luck. Some say they would rather be lucky than good, but some of these techniques will help you to pass your competitors when the time is right.

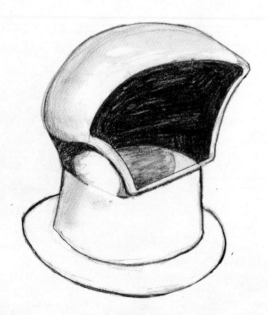

19
PRACTICING ALONE

What does it take to become a winner in yacht racing? Talent and natural ability certainly help, but for most people only practice brings success. Since yachts usually race in fleets, is practicing alone beneficial? The answer is yes. Through discipline and desire a sailor can organize his own practice sessions.

Getting the time to sail alone is easy because you can sail at your own convenience. Typical practices should last from one to three hours in the evening, on an afternoon off from work or school, or even early in the morning.

Some of the best practicing can be done at night, in calms, or in a real blow. Don't let the weather stop you. Regattas are set up by dates and not weather conditions. Regattas are held in storms, calms, and cold weather, and your practice sessions should follow suit.

First, set goals for yourself. Write them on a card and post it on your desk at work, on your refrigerator door, on top of the television set, in your wallet or purse, over your bed, or on your bathroom mirror. Let the card remind you what you plan to achieve.

Set high but realistic goals, both short- and long-range.

Examples of short-range goals might be:

1. Make no errors on the course.
2. Never give in, no matter what my position is.
3. Qualify for the Nationals in the Districts.
4. Place in the top three in the XYZ Invitational.
5. Stay calm in the boat.

Your long-range goals might look like these:

1. Be the most improved 470 on the sound.
2. Place in the 470 Nationals.
3. Win a berth on a 12-Meter.
4. Qualify for, and win, a gold medal in the Olympics.

Although these examples might seem remote, someone will win, so why not you? The late Vince Lombardi figured that if he worked his Green Bay Packers harder than any football team, he would

win, and he was right. An unprepared underdog may win a race, but rarely a series, and never a championship. There is no magic to winning. It is a matter of practice and preparation.

Now that you have set your goals and made up a practice schedule, the next question is: "How do I practice?" If there are no other boats to compete with you, race against the steadiest of all competitors, time.

Race from buoy A to buoy B and clock the time it takes. Resail the course, trying to beat the record. The wind, of course, will vary, but make the best of it. Look for two channel markers to use as a windward–leeward course (the shorter the course, the better). Sail between the two marks, each time trying to get around faster.

If a cruising boat or an outboard goes by, try to keep up with it. You can simulate racing against all kinds of craft.

There are many techniques and drills you can use to practice maneuvers, mechanics, and seamanship. Execute these drills as though the Olympics depended on them. Be serious and concentrate on every move you make in the boat.

A good first drill is a "spinner." A spinner is a continuous set of 720's (See Figure 96). Sail in a small circle as fast as you can four times in one direction, and then reverse your direction, spinning four times in the opposite direction without losing speed. This will improve your seamanship and boat handling.

To begin a spinner, sail to windward and then make a fast tack. When you tack, keep in mind that the faster you push the tiller, the faster you will stop. Your tiller action (to quote an old friend) should be "logarithmic (first slowly, then faster)"—that is, slowly increase the rate of your tiller movement as you tack. In a sloop-rigged boat, ease the main slightly, but trim the jib as you begin to tack. At the same time, push your tiller over slowly at first until the boat is head to wind, and then speed up the tiller to get the boat on the new tack faster. Your speed is lost while heading into the wind, not when bearing away.

Once your tack is completed, put the tiller all the way to windward while dumping the main out as fast as possible. At the same time, it is extremely important to keep the boat flat, or you will have trouble bearing away quickly. Don't jibe the sail until the wind is dead aft. When you do jibe, trim the sail rapidly, which will help you round up into the wind faster for your next spin. A series of roll tacks and roll jibes is the key to making good spinners.

Continue spinning four times until you are just about to get dizzy, then reverse your spinning in the opposite direction. Spinners don't take much time, yet they give you a lot of practice. They take a lot of physical work, but they will keep you and your crew in good shape.

Other than bad wind shifts and slow speed on a windward leg, more ground is lost while tacking than during any other maneuver. Naturally, it is important to practice. The 12-Meter crews tack for hours, repeating their finest motions until they reach perfection.

When you practice tacks, do them in a series of six or more, never spending more than a few seconds between each tack. After each set, take a short breather and think about what slowed you down.

The biggest problem for the skipper is coordinating weight balance with sheet tension and tiller action. This action, of course, varies from boat to boat. To roll tack, first heel the boat to windward slightly while trimming slowly on the sheet before you move the tiller. The crew should get ample warning so they can adjust weight and sheets quickly. Once the boat begins to round into the wind, start your tiller action. Then as the boat comes up, heel it farther to windward, then pop through and flatten the boat on the other tack as the wind fills the sail. This motion will accelerate your boat immediately after a tack. As you improve your acceleration after each tack, you can spin the boat around faster. Be careful not to bear too far off course. You may find it necessary to do this, however, to regain your speed (all sailboats gain speed when bearing off if the sails are eased out).

If it is blowing, don't let a centerboard boat heel after tacking because the board will cavitate when air gets under the hull, and the boat will stall and go sideways before it starts to go forward. There are two ways to keep a boat from heeling after a tack: (1) Keep the boat up into the wind slightly. Don't bear off until you are ready to hike. (2) Ease the main somewhat to spill the wind before the boat is blown over on its ear.

For the next drill find two pilings or buoys that are close together. If there is none, anchor two life jackets about two boat lengths apart. Start a series of figure eights around the marks. This will improve your control of mark roundings followed by tacks and jibes. Go through the two marks one complete time, then

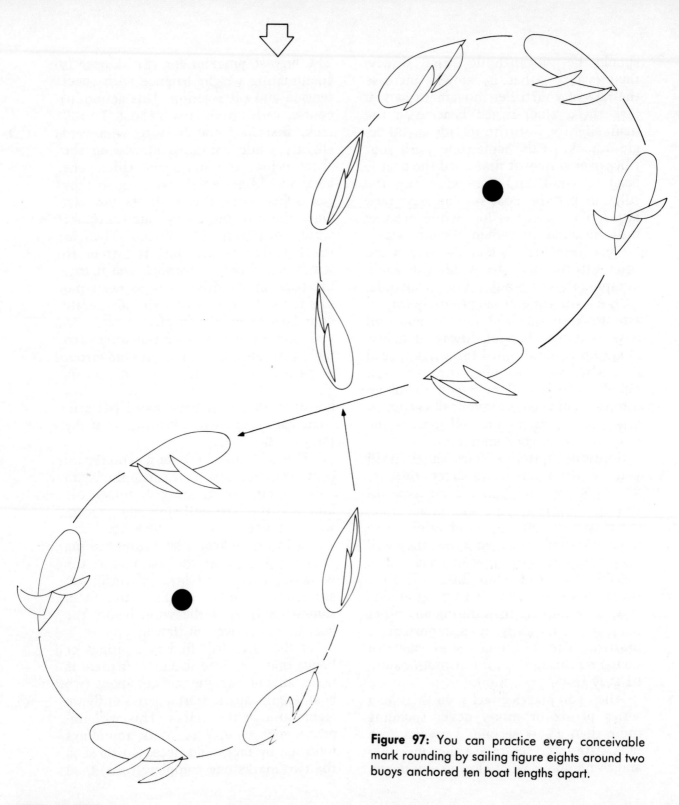

Figure 97: You can practice every conceivable mark rounding by sailing figure eights around two buoys anchored ten boat lengths apart.

approach them from the opposite direction (See Figure 97).

Everyone needs practice sailing with and into waves. If a motorboat approaches, stop what you are doing and set yourself up so that you will be in a position to surf the waves. Try to stay on each wave as long as you can, pumping your sails to promote surfing and adjusting your weight to keep you on each wave.

Normally in a race you will try to avoid a bad set of waves, but when practicing you should head right into the worst part and try to keep the boat going. Each wave is different, so practice steering up and sliding down the back of or blasting through them. You won't know the best way to sail through waves until you practice many different approaches.

You can work on balancing your boat by letting the tiller go and adjusting your sheets and weight to keep your boat on course. If the boat begins to fall off, trim your sails a little or heel to leeward and it will head back up. If the boat begins to head up, flatten it and ease the main.

A fun trick to practice in a dinghy is to take the rudder off completely and try to maneuver without it, using weight and sheet tension. Someday you might be forced to finish a race with a broken rudder, and you'll be prepared for it.

Another exercise is to sail backward by holding your main out. This will teach you how a boat responds when traveling backward. If you get into irons or want to escape from a foe in a match race, this drill will come in handy.

A single buoy or mark can be used as a starting pin, a windward mark, a reach mark, a leeward mark, a reference point for your tacking radius, or a point to judge the set and drift of the current.

To use a mark as one end of the starting line, make a series of timed runs. To make a timed run for one minute, begin by running away from the mark at one minute on a broad reach in the opposite direction than you would be sailing to windward toward the mark. After 25 seconds, tack for the mark, thus allowing 10 seconds to tack and to regain speed. If you hit the line early, try adjusting your run so you tack after sailing 30 seconds. If you find that you are reaching back to the mark, adjust your run on the way down by heading on a broader reach. The theory behind the timed-run technique is that a sailboat travels the same speed on a broad reach as it does going to windward.

To use a buoy as a windward mark, approach it by judging your layline. As you bear off, ease your sails and keep the boat flat. Practice this by taking the mark both to port and to starboard. Approach on both starboard and port tacks bearing away and also bearing away and jibing.

To use the pin as a reach mark, jibe in both directions. This is especially useful when sailing a boat with a spinnaker up.

Practice making a tactical rounding when using the buoy as a leeward mark. Stay wide as you approach the mark, and stay close to the other side as you round up. Judge the wind direction before you make the rounding so you have a good idea of the course you will be on. Thinking ahead will keep you from stalling out by heading too high or losing ground by falling off too much. Keep the boat flat when you round up so you won't go side-

This Laser shows good form in a heavy air reach. Strong vang tension keeps the leech tight and powerful. *Photograph by Phil Uhl*

ways, and trim the sails as you round.

When you trim your sheets, grab the line right at the block, making a long pull with your arm extended as far away from the block as possible before grabbing the line for a second trim.

By watching the mark as you sail toward or away from it relative to a reference point onshore, or another mark, you can determine the set and drift of the current.

Keep a record of your sailing by starting a logbook. Every time you go sailing, whether in a regatta or for practice, record what you did, mistakes you made, where you won or lost, weather and wind conditions, crew, results, date, drills you ran through, notes on different sailing areas, and any additional information and comments you come up with. In a short time you will have a valuable reference to turn to.

With the aid of a logbook you will be able to put everything you learn together in one handy source. When the time comes to sail in a regatta, look over your logbook to see what areas you should work on. There is nothing like local knowledge in a regatta, so phone to find out what an unknown body of water is like. This type of information can also be found in race circulars, class newsletters, magazines, and regatta reports from previous years—"boat Y passed 10 boats on the last beat by picking a port lift up off Stony Point in the gusty southerly." You can also pick up a lot of information through informal conversations prior to a meet. After an event, however, winners will talk more, so write down anything you learn from them.

Before each regatta, write an outline on the place where you will be racing. This will develop into a super list of information and will give you confidence when you show up for the first time. By preparing mentally and physically, you will rid yourself of any fear of losing and will gain confidence that you are ready to race.

Before every practice session, list what you intend to go over, then follow your plan. In a short time you will work to the top of the fleet, make fewer errors and faster spinnaker sets as well as smoother tacks, and reach most of your goals.

Don't try to practice everything in one session. Combine your practices with something you have been working on with something new.

Getting to the top of the fleet is one thing, but staying there is another. Many champions fall because they stop practicing and lose their desire to win. To win, every sailor must practice. Sailors who work hardest and make the most of their practice sessions will almost always come out on top.

Practice Session Sample

Note: crew, purpose, goals, date, time waters.

Drills

1. Four sets of six tacks

2. Two spinners

3. Figure eights through piles (two in each direction)

4. Four leeward mark roundings, followed by tack

5. Four sets of six jibes

6. Four spinnaker sets

7. Run four time runs

8. Surf in waves if chance comes

9. Look at mast rake (two minutes)

This Laser skipper is preoccupied with too many adjustments at one time. He holds the mainsheet with his teeth and the centerboard with his knee while he adjusts the downhaul with his right hand. He should concentrate on where he is going and make one adjustment at a time. *Photograph by Carol Singer*

10. Try sailing backward

11. Four windward mark roundings

12. Sail to windward balancing helm

Comments: Note time taken for each drill.

Systematic work on weak points and accurate practice records are essential to success.

20

PRACTICING IN PAIRS

Testing your boat speed against that of your competition during nonracing time will give you quick and accurate information on your performance. The difference between champions and middle-of-the-fleet competitors is often an exact function of how much speed testing sailors do. Champion helmsman Tom Blackaller will often spend as much as a week testing and refining one mainsail for his star boat. Dennis Conner, the speed-testing king of the universe, will spend thousands of hours testing hulls, sails, and crew. Often he finds very small improvements, but when added up, these will spell the difference between victory and defeat.

Some sailors have tried to speed-test using instruments and computers, but the most reliable method is to sail alongside another boat with relatively equal performance and sailing ability.

It is important to communicate thoroughly the objectives for your test with your partner. You may want to test-sail trim, hull speed, your crew, or the tune of the rig. Testing boats is considerably different from testing sails. When testing sails your trim changes often. When test-ing boats you switch your people and try to sail with identical sails at the same settings. During your actual test it is helpful to use a radio to talk back and forth to compare your results.

A speed test should last from five to 10 minutes, which is often the maximum amount of time a sailor can concentrate at a very high level. Use a hand bearing compass and/or a statometer to keep track of your performance. When you start a test, note the course you are steering and write it down on your deck with a grease pencil. If you have instruments, note your wind strength and the boat speed at which you are sailing. It is important to write this information down so you don't lose track of your reference point.

Here is the standard operating procedure used by *Defender* and *Courageous* in 1982 and 1983.

Sail Testing and Evaluation

All sail evaluation is based on tests made on the boats sailing in racing condition. Results are based primarily on observations and measurements made during speed tests specially organized to test sail performance, but race results are also taken into account where sail performance is deemed to have been relevant to the result.

Instrumentation is relatively simple, consisting of a compass to measure changes in the bearing between boats, a statometer to measure changes in the distance between boats, and, where appropriate, a calculator to translate the data thus obtained into net gains or losses to windward, or to leeward.

The results of all speed tests and races are recorded in an Apple II computer. As required, the computer can produce detailed printouts of the following:

1. Any or all race results, leg by leg.
2. Any or all speed checks.
3. A list of races in which any particular sail was used.
4. A list of speed tests in which any particular sail was used.
5. The dates on which a particular sail has been used for any purpose, and the number of hours of use it has accumulated.

The lineup between boats is critical.

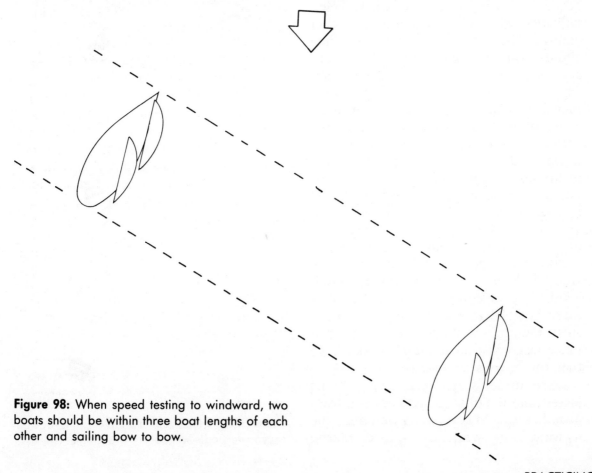

Figure 98: When speed testing to windward, two boats should be within three boat lengths of each other and sailing bow to bow.

The best lineup is bow to bow, one boat windward to the other, and two boat lengths apart (See Figure 98). In shifty winds you will have to spread the lineup to four boat lengths. The wind shadow "snow fence" effect will hurt your partners' performance if the boats are too close.

It is important to test one thing at a time. Testing too many things results in a lot of confusion. Every crew member on the boat should have a clear understanding of the objectives at that time. On *Defender*, Gary repeated the objectives often to remind both crews.

When tuning up against another boat, begin by setting the jib leads, traveler, halyards, vang, Cunningham, and other controls the same on both boats. Then simply sail against each other, constantly trying to make the boat go faster. This will help to improve your helmsmanship and to understand your boat. Top sailors know their boats and how they react in every condition. When tuning for speed, make every attempt to stay in the same wind. Sailing in different air doesn't prove anything. Each boat should be even at the start of a practice maneuver, not blanketing the other boat. One of the best ways to start is a rabbit start, as shown in Figure 99. Boat A dips to the stern of boat B while sailing to windward. Boat B continues on for two or three boat lengths and tacks. The time spent tacking should be equal to the distance lost when boat A dipped boat B, so that the boats start evenly.

Once under way, keep trying to go faster than the other boat. The windward boat has the advantage of watching the leeward boat, while the skipper of the

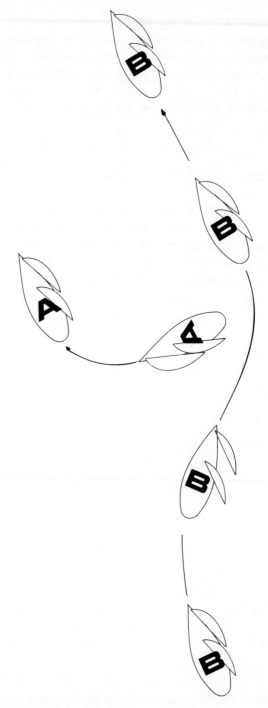

Figure 99: Use the rabbit start to begin a race between two boats without a starting line.

leeward boat must look back over his shoulder to catch a glimpse of the action. Playing your sheets and traveler alone can make the difference in speed, but usually the faster boat is being sailed by a better helmsman.

Once one boat establishes a commanding advantage, start over again. Be honest with the other boat and compare notes about any adjustments you made.

Once you get a reading, it is important to believe your results. If, for example, you test a sail 10 times you might find that one sail proves faster in seven tests, while the other proves faster in three tests. It might be best to accept this ratio, but there probably are reasons for this. Perhaps a trimmer lost concentration, or maybe one sail performs at a higher wind range while another performs better at a lower wind range. On your speed test data sheet (See Figure 101) also make general comments on the test. One way to get accurate results is simply to ask the other team, "If we were to race now, which sail would you use?"

There is no substitute for racing. Each speed test should also be accompanied by either a tacking or a jibing duel. Often boats will perform well in a straight line, but they will be slow maneuvering. Therefore, you must test straight-line speed along with maneuvering speed.

Once your speed tests have been completed, give yourself the final exam by having a series of short-course races. In our 1982–83 12-Meter program we developed a "speed race" where we never tacked on the other boat's wind, but we were racing to the windward mark so we could get an accurate feel for the performance of the boats under racing conditions without tactical considerations.

The most important members of the crew during the speed test are the helmsman, the mainsheet trimmer, the jib trimmer, and the tactician keeping track of the boat's performance.

The wind plays strange tricks even in the steadiest of conditions. We have experienced phenomena where the right side of the course is favored, and the boat to windward on starboard tack or the boat to leeward on port tack always had the advantage because of these "right-side phenomena" (See Figure 100). For this reason it is important to switch positions windward and leeward, port and starboard, often to allow for one side of the course dramatically affecting the results.

On Rhode Island Sound we have found that the favored side of the course changes during the day, and the boats switch positions as soon as the change in the favored side of the course occurs. This completely throws the results out of whack. Concentration and accurate recordkeeping during speed tests help to eliminate this problem.

By practicing with a second boat, a new dimension opens up—namely, a race. A second boat serves as a bench mark, and practicing is equally beneficial to both boats. In this game, both sides win. Setting up a dual practice is easy. Simply contact anyone in your fleet and set a date and time. Unexpected opportunities present themselves often, even before or after a regatta. Not only can two boats tune up against each other, but they can also set up match races and

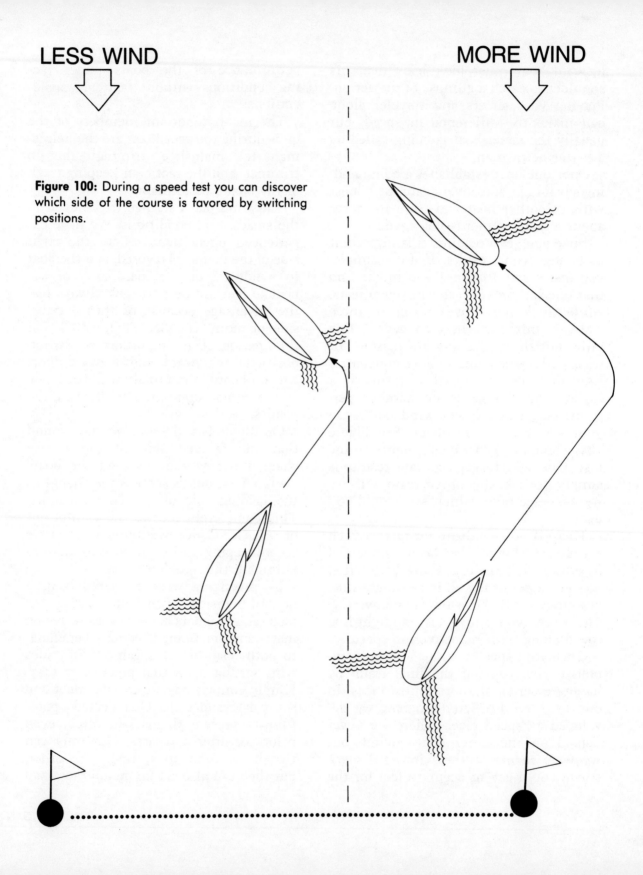

LESS WIND

MORE WIND

Figure 100: During a speed test you can discover which side of the course is favored by switching positions.

an organized series of drills and maneuvers.

You can learn a great deal about a course with two boats. If a big regatta is coming up, try to arrive a day early for the event and get out on the water, tune up, and get a feeling for the wind in that area.

Get together with another boat and start by splitting off on opposite tacks. Sail for a certain length of time (10 minutes), and then tack at the same time, coming back together. You can easily determine the favored side of a course in this manner.

Most sailors spend time tuning up to windward and often forget about tuning for the leeward legs.

Start even and try to beat your partner to a mark. If no available marks or buoys are around, throw out a life jacket with an anchor.

Perhaps the best practice with another boat is to run through several short races and a series of drills. Set up a short starting line with a windward mark. One boat calls the time, and the pair attack, each trying to gain control of the other. The best accepted way to control another boat is by getting behind and driving your competitor away from the line. The famous USYRU Appeal No. 63 allows for offensive tailing. Start a match race at the preparatory signal by approaching from opposite ends of the line and try to gain control of your opponent by getting on his transom. You are in control when you are slightly behind or to leeward because he can't bear off, and if he tacks, you should tack as well, maintaining your control. The trick is to develop the mechanics of your maneu-

vers so you can tack and jibe faster without losing speed.

When tailing another boat, be ready for the skipper's actions. If he slows down, so should you. Be very aggressive and never give in. Plan ahead while maintaining total control of your boat.

The best way to prepare for match-racing starts is to set up a tailing drill where two boats each try to get behind the other. Once one boat gets behind, the skipper should continue tailing until the original leader regains his advantage. Each drill need last only five minutes.

The next drill is a tacking duel. Start with one boat crossing behind the stern of another. The boat in the lead tacks on the opposing boat, while the boat behind tacks to clear. Set up the drill so that no more than 30 seconds elapse between tacks. At best, tacks will become more frequent. Pay attention to every move you make in the boat. When going through a fast series of tacks drive the boat off, picking up speed. Don't let the boat heel and stall.

Tacking duels are physically demanding but are a lot of fun. At the same time you are watching your competitor, be sure you are tacking in clear air and tacking in smooth water. It is worthwhile to hold on a few extra seconds to avoid tacking in sloppy chop.

Throw in some false tacks occasionally to keep him honest. Fake tacks can be very effective in getting rid of a pest who is stealing your wind.

After several sets of tacking duels, switch boats. There is nothing better to even out the competition than to switch boats.

As in any sport, it is better to practice

with opponents who are more experienced than yourself. If you are losing in the practice session, don't give up. Keep a good attitude, knowing that the work you are doing will help you out later against the rest of the fleet, as well as your partner. If you find that you are winning most of the drills, don't get cocky; instead, talk over what you might be doing that is different—as much to keep your partner's interest up as to benefit yourself from a psyched-up partner. To get the most out of each drill, sail as aggressively as you can all the time.

One drill that will develop your 720 turns is to go through a set of five 720's to see who can complete them in the fastest time.

Downwind, try jibing 10 times to see who can complete the jibes in the shorter time. At the same time, try to gain distance through the water on your competitor.

Simulate conditions in which you will be racing. Switch partners often. Trade off information you learn with many sailors, keeping track of what you learned in a logbook as you go along. If possible, try to space your partners out so you can judge your progress when you practice with a former partner. The real test, of course, comes when you put it all together in a regatta. Speed testing is tedious, hard work, but it is essential for success.

Practicing in pairs will improve your racing instantly. Sessions are easy to arrange and provide a variety of excellent drills and practice races.

DRILLS

1. Four sets of tacking duels, two in each boat

2. Two sets of five 720's (who is faster?)

3. Two sets of quick jibes

4. Rabbit start, sail to windward, tune

5. Sail on reach, tune

6. Sail downwind, tune (set chutes; who is faster?)

7. Four sets of tailing (five minutes each)

8. Split tacks on the course (switch sides)

9. Best of seven short races, windward–leeward

10. Race to the dock

Practicing on a 12-Meter

"For every hour of sailing it takes two hours of working on the boat," claim many 12-Meter crew members. The payoffs and rewards are enormous for a successful crew. But the real value of a crew's efforts is happening now, in practice sessions. It is here where sailing techniques and boat speed are fine-tuned before the summer of elimination trials begins.

Practicing and sailing is a relatively new technique favored by many college sailing teams of the past decade, but

```
              DEFENDER  -  COURAGEOUS

                    SPEED TESTS

      DATE OF PRINTOUT: JANUARY 28TH, 1983

          CALIFORNIA SPEED TESTS TO DATE


        SPEED TEST SERIES NUMBER 1 OF DECEMBER 2, 1982  (# 1)
LOCALE: NEWPORT BEACH          WIND ANGLE: UPWIND        OBSERVED FROM: DEFENDER
DEFENDER'S HELMSMAN: BLACKALLER  DEFENDER'S MAINSAIL: 10A    DEFENDER'S HEADSAIL: 2A GEN.
COURAGEOUS' HELMSMAN: KOLIUS    COURAGEOUS' MAINSAIL: 13A   COURAGEOUS' HEADSAIL: 2A GEN.
```

APPARENT WIND SPEED	WINDWARD BOAT	1ST BEARING.	1ST SEPARATION	TIME	2ND BEARING.	2ND SEPARATION	GAINING BOAT
14 KNOTS	COURAGEOUS	NO RECORD	NO RECORD			DEFENDER HIGHER AND FASTER	
14 KNOTS	COURAGEOUS	NO RECORD	NO RECORD			DEFENDER HIGHER AND FASTER	
14 KNOTS	COURAGEOUS	NO RECORD	NO RECORD			RESULTS EVEN	

```
COURAGEOUS SHIFTED TO INBOARD LEAD AFTER THE FIRST TEST.


        SPEED TEST SERIES NUMBER 2 OF DECEMBER 2, 1982  (# 2)
LOCALE: NEWPORT BEACH          WIND ANGLE: UPWIND        OBSERVED FROM: DEFENDER
DEFENDER'S HELMSMAN: BLACKALLER  DEFENDER'S MAINSAIL: 10A    DEFENDER'S HEADSAIL: 2A GEN.
COURAGEOUS' HELMSMAN: KOLIUS    COURAGEOUS' MAINSAIL: 13A   COURAGEOUS' HEADSAIL: 2B GEN.
```

APPARENT WIND SPEED	WINDWARD BOAT	1ST BEARING.	1ST SEPARATION	TIME	2ND BEARING.	2ND SEPARATION	GAINING BOAT
14 KNOTS	COURAGEOUS	NO RECORD	NO RECORD			DEFENDER HIGHER AND FASTER.	
14 KNOTS	COURAGEOUS	NO RECORD	NO RECORD			DEFENDER HIGHER AND FASTER	
14 KNOTS	N.A.	N.A.	N.A.		THIS TEST A TACKING DUEL. WON BY DEFENDER.		

```
THE 2B GENOA SEEMS TO BACKWIND THE MAIN MORE THAN THE 2A DID.  IT IS CLEARLY NOT FASTER.
DEFENDER'S 10A MAINSAIL APPEARS FASTER THAN COURAGEOUS' 13A.


        SPEED TEST SERIES NUMBER 1 OF DECEMBER 3, 1982  (# 3)
LOCALE: NEWPORT BEACH          WIND ANGLE: UPWIND        OBSERVED FROM: DEFENDER
DEFENDER'S HELMSMAN: BLACKALLER  DEFENDER'S MAINSAIL: 13A    DEFENDER'S HEADSAIL: 1A GEN.
COURAGEOUS' HELMSMAN: KOLIUS    COURAGEOUS' MAINSAIL: 13A   COURAGEOUS' HEADSAIL: 1A GEN.
```

APPARENT WIND SPEED	WINDWARD BOAT	1ST BEARING.	1ST SEPARATION	TIME	2ND BEARING.	2ND SEPARATION	GAINING BOAT
8-10 KNOTS	COURAGEOUS	NO RECORD	NO RECORD			COURAGEOUS SLIGHTLY FASTER.	
8-10 KNOTS	COURAGEOUS	NO RECORD	NO RECORD			RESULTS EVEN	
8-10 KNOTS	COURAGEOUS	2.5 L.	EVEN			COURAGEOUS SLIGHTLY FASTER.	

```
CONDITIONS IN THESE THREE TESTS SEEMED TO FAVOR THE WEATHER BOAT.
DEFENDER IS SAILING WITHOUT INSTRUMENTS AND WITH COURAGEOUS' OLD GENTRY MAST.


        SPEED TEST SERIES NUMBER 2 OF DECEMBER 3, 1982  (# 4)
LOCALE: NEWPORT BEACH          WIND ANGLE: UPWIND        OBSERVED FROM: DEFENDER
DEFENDER'S HELMSMAN: BLACKALLER  DEFENDER'S MAINSAIL: 13A    DEFENDER'S HEADSAIL: 1A GEN.
COURAGEOUS' HELMSMAN: KOLIUS    COURAGEOUS' MAINSAIL: 13A   COURAGEOUS' HEADSAIL: 1A GEN.
```

APPARENT WIND SPEED	WINDWARD BOAT	1ST BEARING.	1ST SEPARATION	TIME	2ND BEARING.	2ND SEPARATION	GAINING BOAT
8 KNOTS	DEFENDER	NO RECORD	NO RECORD		RESULTS EVEN. WIND BECOMING UNSTEADY.		
8 KNOTS	DEFENDER	1.5 L.	EVEN		COURAGEOUS FASTER; DEFENDER HIGHER. RESULT ABOUT EVEN		
8 KNOTS	DEFENDER	1.5 L.	EVEN			RESULTS EVEN.	

```
THE RESULTS OF THIS SERIES ARE SUSPECT BECAUSE OF WIND CHANGES BOTH IN DIRECTION AND VELOCITY.
```

Figure 101

RACE NUMBER 1 OF MARCH 8, 1983 (# 36)

LOCALE: NEWPORT BEACH   COURSE: WRRWLW   LENGTH OF FIRST LEG: 4 MI.
WIND DIRECTION (START): 220   TRUE WIND SPEED (START): 9   OBSERVED FROM: CONCORDIA

YACHT	SKIPPER	TACTICIAN	CREW	MAINSAIL	TIME OF START	NOTES ON START
DEFENDER	BLACKALLER	JOBSON	PERMANENT	10A	+2 SEC.	STBD TACK PORT END. TACKED TO PORT SHORTLY AFTER.
COURAGEOUS	KOLIUS	BERTRAND	PERMANENT	10B	+8 SEC.	PORT TACK STARBOARD END.

LEG NUMBER	YACHT	HEADSAIL	TIME AT MARK	NOTES ON THIS LEG
1. (W)	DEFENDER	2D GEN.	LEADER	HAD 10 L. LEAD AT 1ST MEETING.
1.	COURAGEOUS	2C GEN.	+18 SEC.	RECOUPED IN LAST PART OF LEG AS WIND CLOCKED.
2. (R)	DEFENDER	14A SPIN	+13 SEC.	CHANGED IMMEDIATELY TO 13A SPIN
2.	COURAGEOUS	12U SPIN	LEADER	SMALLER SPIN MORE EFFECTIVE. PASSED DEFENDER
3. (R)	DEFENDER	2D GEN.	+20 SEC.	WIND HAD VEERED TO 255 DEG.
3.	COURAGEOUS	2C GEN.	LEADER	ATTEMPTED AND ABANDONED A SPINNAKER
4. (W)	DEFENDER	2D GEN.	LEADER	CHANGED TO 23C. TWS 14-15. 22 TACKS. PASSED COUR.
4.	COURAGEOUS	3A GEN.	+20 SEC.	22 TACKS. MSL. OCCASIONALLY SLIGHTLY OVERPOWERED.
5. (L)	DEFENDER	15B SPIN	LEADER	12 JIBES. GAINING.
5.	COURAGEOUS	15A SPIN	+62 SEC.	12 JIBES
6. (W)	DEFENDER	23C GEN.	LEADER	TWS 15. 16 TACKS. SEA BECOMING ROUGH.
6.	COURAGEOUS	2C GEN.	+135 SEC.	CHANGED TO 3A GEN. 18 TACKS. MSL. LABORING AT TIMES.

REMARKS: DEFENDER WINS 1ST SERIES. OVERALL 10A MSL. OUTPERFORMED 10B IN THIS WIND. 3A GEN INFERIOR TO 23C.

THE WINNER IS: DEFENDER

RACE NUMBER 1 OF MARCH 10, 1983 (# 37)

LOCALE: NEWPORT BEACH   COURSE: WL   LENGTH OF FIRST LEG: 1/2 MI.
WIND DIRECTION (START): 115   TRUE WIND SPEED (START): 7   OBSERVED FROM: CONCORDIA

YACHT	SKIPPER	TACTICIAN	CREW	MAINSAIL	TIME OF START	NOTES ON START
DEFENDER	BLACKALLER	JOBSON	PERMANENT	20A	+2 SEC.	STARBOARD TACK MID-LINE
COURAGEOUS	KOLIUS	BERTRAND	PERMANENT	10B	+3 SEC.	STARBOARD TACK PORT END

LEG NUMBER	YACHT	HEADSAIL	TIME AT MARK	NOTES ON THIS LEG
1. (W)	DEFENDER	2B GEN.	+5 SEC.	BOTH GO RIGHT. TACKED FOR MARK BEFORE COURAGEOUS.
1.	COURAGEOUS	2A GEN.	LEADER	FOLLOWED ON DEFENDER'S HIP TOWARD MARK - GAINING
2. (L)	DEFENDER	12A SPIN	LEADER	3 JIBES. HIGHER SAILING ANGLES THAN COURAGEOUS.
2.	COURAGEOUS	12U SPIN	+23 SEC.	1 JIBE. STAYED RIGHT WHEN DEFENDER WENT LEFT.

REMARKS: WIND VARIABLE AND TENDING TO CLOCK.

THE WINNER IS: DEFENDER

RACE NUMBER 2 OF MARCH 10, 1983 (# 38)

LOCALE: NEWPORT BEACH   COURSE: WL   LENGTH OF FIRST LEG: 1/2 MI.
WIND DIRECTION (START): 120   TRUE WIND SPEED (START): 7   OBSERVED FROM: CONCORDIA

YACHT	SKIPPER	TACTICIAN	CREW	MAINSAIL	TIME OF START	NOTES ON START
DEFENDER	BLACKALLER	JOBSON	PERMANENT	20A	+1 SEC.	PORT TACK STARBOARD END. MOVING FAST.
COURAGEOUS	KOLIUS	BERTRAND	PERMANENT	10B	+12 SEC.	STARBOARD TACK PORT END. MOVING SLOWLY

LEG NUMBER	YACHT	HEADSAIL	TIME AT MARK	NOTES ON THIS LEG
1. (W)	DEFENDER	2B GEN.	LEADER	TOOK STARBOARD SIDE OF COURSE
1.	COURAGEOUS	1B GEN.	+34 SEC.	PORT SIDE OF COURSE
2. (L)	DEFENDER	12A SPIN	LEADER	BACKED SPIN. AND FAILED TO JIBE JIB ON DOUSE
2.	COURAGEOUS	12A SPIN	+14 SEC.	GAINED ON DEFENDER'S DOUSING PROBLEMS

REMARKS: WIND VEERED TO 130 DURING FIRST LEG. COURAGEOUS NOT UP TO SPEED AT THE START.

THE WINNER IS: DEFENDER

Figure 101A

really it is the America's Cup campaigns that have paved the way for practice. In fact, there was a day when practicing seemed to be unfair. Today, one cannot imagine entering a competition without considerable practice first. Perhaps sailing has even lagged behind other sports, but today not only does it take two hours of working on a boat for an hour of sailing, but also for every hour sailed in an actual trial or cup race, there will be close to a full day's sailing backing it up.

A practice day for a 12-Meter crew is intense, fun, demanding, at times, frustrating, but certainly rewarding. The average day starts early in the morning with breakfast followed by the crew's arrival at the boat around eight o'clock. In addition to readying the boat for sailing, letting it off the hoist, wet-sanding the bottom, bending the sails on the boom, and packing the spinnakers, the afterguard will run through a list of items to go over during the day's sailing. New running backstays are installed, winches are maintained, and equipment that has been broken the day before is repaired. By nine-fifteen the boat is ready to go and the crew is summoned on board. The *Defender* crew in 1980 had a strict rule of being on board by nine-thirty each day when the tender pulled away. Those who were late were left behind.

Wind readings are taken the moment the boat leaves the dock. The sails are hoisted upon clearing the moorings in Newport Harbor. On race days, the 12-Meter will be towed all the way out to the racecourse to save time for tuning the rig and reading the wind.

On practice days, the 12 will sail out to the course. The long day goes quickly as the crew changes pace in a variety of functions. The first order of the day is tuning the rig and the sail; the second is speed-testing. Before lunch a race or two is sailed, generally on a windward–leeward course. Lunchtime lasts about 30 minutes.

Afternoons generally consist of more short course races followed by speed testing before the boat returns to the dock at five o'clock. Once again the boat is hauled up on the hoist, the bottom is wet-sanded, and broken equipment is repaired for the next day of sailing. Also at this time sails go back to the loft for recutting. Finally, the crew collects for dinner, and the day's activities are rehashed, looking forward to yet another day of sailing.

21
PRACTICING IN A FLEET

Professional football coach Vince Lombardi once commented, "Practice does not make perfect, only perfect practice makes perfect." Practicing with a fleet of boats takes greater organization than practicing alone or in pairs, but these practice sessions can take several forms. You can use a regatta as a practice or a tune-up for a more important regatta, or you can participate in one of a number of clinics or seminars.

In 1975, Gary helped develop the United States Yacht Racing Union's instructional programs. This included class racing clinics, instructors' seminars, and, later in 1977, the U.S. Olympic Committee training programs. The idea with these programs is to send a qualified instructor to a club or sponsoring fleet and have the instructor lead an intensive instructional program that combines on-the-water drills, demonstrations, racing, individual analysis, and evening lectures. Over 500 of these programs have been sponsored since their inception.

Organized practice sessions help sailors concentrate on specific techniques they might not normally use during a race. Clinics work best if there is a leader or an instructor to set the pace. But the leader can be one of the competitors in your fleet. For example, if there are ten boats in your racing fleet, perhaps one boat can sit out, and each participant can rotate as the leader of the clinic.

The most effective method for teaching people to race at any level is first to discuss exactly what you plan to do, explain theory, give a pep talk to emphasize the importance of what is going on, and then graphically illustrate the technique you are covering. The second method is to give a complete demonstration and then repeat it until the entire class understands. These demonstrations can take the form of anything from sail trim to actual sailing on the water.

The third method is to drill. The class should participate in a specific drill to focus on different techniques. Repetitive drills are the keys to rapid learning.

The fourth teaching technique is to challenge the class by actually racing.

The use of videorecorders is fairly prevalent today and is strongly encouraged when practicing as a fleet.

ONE-DAY ON-THE-WATER CLINIC

Clinic Agenda

0830	Introduction—calisthenics Setting goals, concept of drills, how to train
0900	Rig boats—on board at dock demonstrations
0930	Launch boats—tune-up starts—short course
1000	Sailing—boat-handling drills
1100	Two races
1200	Lunch
1230	Discussion—boat speed and sail trim
1300	Sail trim demonstrations
1330	Mark roundings drills
1500	Three-race series
1700	Secure boats—dinner

1900	Evening lecture
	  1. Racing tactics
	  2. Rules, protests, and appeals

2130	End of Day

TWO-DAY TRAINING CLINIC

Day One

0800	Registration
0830	Introduction—calisthenics Setting goals, concept of drills, how to train
0900	Launch Boats
0930	Tune-up starts—short courses
1000	Boat-handling drills
1100	Two races

1200	Lunch
1230	Discussion—boat speed
1300	Start lecture—big fleet
1330	Short courses' challenges
1500	Formal three-race series
1700	Secure boats—dinner

1900	Evening lecture
	  1. Racing tactics
	  2. Rules, protests, and appeals
	  3. Film

2130	End of day

Day Two

0800	Calisthenics
0830	Sail trim demonstration tuning Introduction to match racing (for speed testing)
0930	On the water—Light-air speed testing Match races—video session
1100	Two fleet races
1200	Lunch
1230	Discussion—sail trim
1300	Mark Roundings—video session
1330	Short courses—mark roundings drills
1500	Three formal races
1700	Secure boats—dinner

1900	Evening lecture—video session
	Review
	  1. Steering
	  2. Trimming sails, balance
	  3. Practice and preparation

2130	End of day

Let regattas be your final examination. While at a practice session, do not be concerned with being first over the line; instead, be more concerned with working on specific techniques, such as starts, boat handling, mark roundings, and boat speed. If someone is watching and helping you from outside your boat, you will probably learn quickly and with greater ease.

The typical training day might include speed testing, boat-handling exercises, and short course races. An entire clinic can be run in just one afternoon or evening. The trick is to concentrate on one thing at a time. All sailors are winners when they participate in training sessions.

The traditional way to train is to put it all together at a regatta, but this really is a hit-or-miss method. With an organized practice session you learn things much sooner and you bring up the overall level of all sailors because everyone at the session is working on a single technique. Collective wisdom speeds the learning process.

You don't necessarily have to make a special day for a training session. This can take place with just a few boats after one race while you are waiting for the next.

Individual drills are fun. They develop comradeship in your fleet. Here are some examples of drills that Gary developed for his clinics.

Starting Drills

Gary once gave his student sailors at the Merchant Marine Academy great incentive on cold practice evenings to get into the dock early. All they had to do was win the start and they were allowed to sail in while the rest of the fleet stayed on the water for the next start. Needless to say, the competition was in-

tense. There are a number of starting drills that can be practiced, including:

Slow Start—From 30 seconds before the start until 10 seconds before it, all sails must be completely luffing. This teaches boat control on crowded lines when you have to get into the "first row" early, hold your position, and accelerate fast.

Speed Start—From 30 seconds until the start, you must sail at full speed on a close-hauled course with sails trimmed optimally. No luffing of sails or bearing away is allowed.

Port Approach Start—From one minute to 30 seconds you must be on port tack—then you are free to go back to starboard whenever you want.

Starting with No Watch—This forces the sailor to concentrate on his technique and keep careful time of his own start. The instructor can give signals at 30-second intervals and eventually expand it to one-minute and finally two-minute intervals and make the sailor start at his own time.

Automatic Recall—On every start two boats are automatically recalled and have to round the ends regardless of whether they were over or not.

Downwind Starts—Race downwind to a leeward mark, which forces crowded leeward mark roundings.

Upwind Drills

Once the fleet has started and is sailing upwind, there are a number of ways

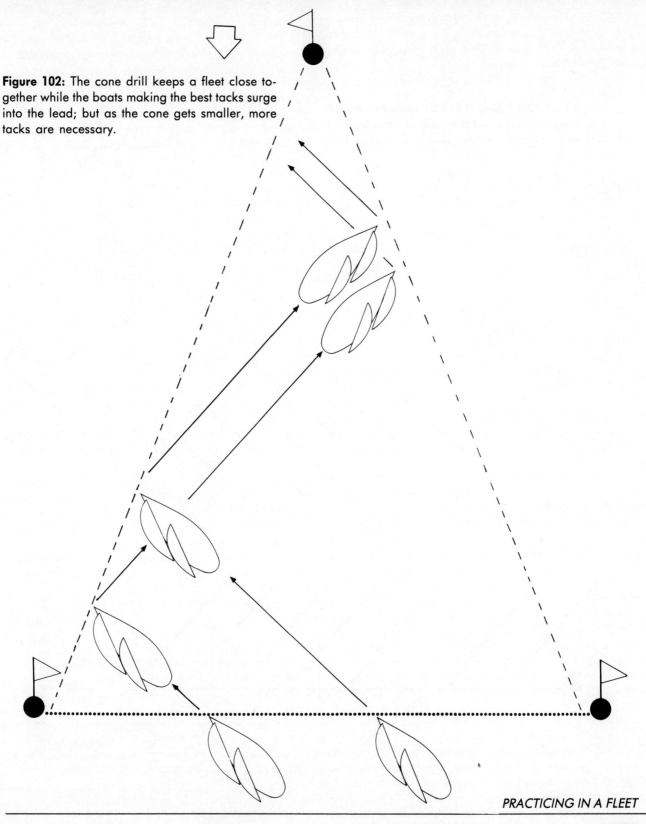

Figure 102: The cone drill keeps a fleet close together while the boats making the best tacks surge into the lead; but as the cone gets smaller, more tacks are necessary.

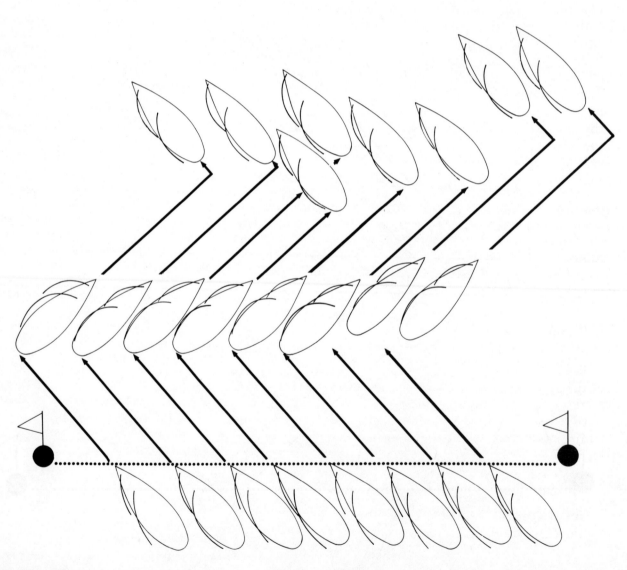

Figure 103: A fleet of boats tacking simultaneously improves one's ability to race in close quarters situations.

to practice boat-handling techniques and tactics on a beat.

Cone Drill—The fleet starts normally, but after the start they are confined to a triangle formed by the two ends of the line and the session leader in a motorboat traveling straight upwind. When a sailboat reaches the imaginary wall of the triangle, it must treat this as an obstruction and tack. The leader tries to hail those boats that go beyond the cone walls. This drill focuses on tacking skills, the mechanics of ducking a starboard tacker, and the use of Rule 43 ("Close-hauled, Hailing for Room to Tack at Obstructions"). The fleet really bunches up as they get farther away from the line and the triangle gets smaller, so the drill must be abandoned before it gets ridiculous (See Figure 102).

Tacking Drill—All boats start normally and remain on starboard tack until a signal (usually preceded by a short countdown for warning) comes from the motorboat upwind of the fleet. At that point, all boats must tack. After several minutes of this drill, it will become obvious which boats are tacking well, and they can be asked to demonstrate their techniques for the fleet (See Figure 103).

Acceleration Drill—This is a variation of the tacking drill where all boats completely luff their sails on starboard tack until they stop. On a signal, all boats trim to accelerate. This is a good way to learn the proper steering, weight placement, and sail control for whenever you're going at less than full speed.

Helm Control—All boats sail on the same tack and make adjustments to their trim (sail, rig, etc.) one at a time on command to determine how each change affects the boat's "helm" and speed.

360 Degrees—Again the boats sail upwind on the same tack, and at the whistle each must do a complete 360-degree turn (or two turns of 720 degrees). This is great for improving execution of turns and 720-degree penalties.

Downwind Drills

After sailing upwind for about three to five minutes, you can use downwind drills to have the fleet end up at the starting line. If the fleet is too scattered, it is time to regroup and start another drill on a line. The trick is to use all the available time concentrating on sailing.

Jibing Drill—All boats bear off to a broad reach (or beam reach or run) on the same tack and jibe on the signal. Spinnaker sets, trim, jibes, and takedowns can be taught and practiced in a similar manner. It's important for the motorboat to remain upwind of the fleet and repeat the instructions before each signal to ensure that everyone understands what is coming next.

Races

Restricted Tacks Race—Only two or four tacks are allowed on the beat. This puts a premium on having clear air at the start and judging layline.

Multiple Tacks Race—In this drill there are a required number of tacks (10, for example), which must be made between the start and the first mark. This rewards good tacking, with very little emphasis on boat speed. Offwind you could require a given number of jibes as well.

Team Racing—This is one of the best ways to practice your racing ability and is great for teaching how to control other boats. It is also fun to be a part of a team effort on the course.

Match Racing—Split the fleet into pairs and give a separate start for each. You can start two races at once by setting the committee boat in the middle of two buoys. This practice is excellent for one-on-one tactical situations and also for straight-line speed development.

Fun Drills—It works well to keep things lively by mixing the more "serious" drills with a few creative and fun ones. If you do it right, these can also help develop specific skills while being fun to do.

Blindfolded Sailing—The skipper is blindfolded on the second beat, when the fleet is spread out, and the crew calls the shots. This promotes the skipper's feel for the boat and encourages him to look around more after the blindfold is off. It also encourages good information flow from crew to skipper. It is not advisable to do this in close quarters.

Backward Sailing—On a signal, all boats must start sailing backward. This is good for developing boat-handling control and sail control but sometimes is not as easy as it seems.

Figure 104: The serpentine is a fun drill that teaches both acceleration and de-acceleration.

No Rudder—Have everyone take out his rudder and try to start sailing on a starboard-tack reach. It is helpful to pull the centerboard up halfway or so to keep the center of lateral resistance aft. This drill is excellent for teaching sailors how to steer using sails and weight. Once the participants have mastered this, have them sail at other angles to the wind and do tacks or jibes.

Crew Race—The crew and skipper trade positions for a race or two. This is a perfect way to emphasize the importance of teamwork and for each person to appreciate the job the other is doing.

Serpentine—This is basic follow-the-leader, and it can lead to some spectacular water ballet with a well-choreographed group. The key is to begin the serpentine with the leader sailing on a beam reach back and forth until all the fleet falls in line. Then the creativity can begin (See Figure 104).

Standing Race—Sailors must stand while skippering their boats; this teaches coordination with weight.

Developing the Scouting Report

You can gain an edge on your competition by collecting valuable information on an area where you might sail. Even if it is several years before you return to a lake or a bay, the information you learn from your first experience will help give you the edge the second time around. If you expect to compete in a major event that you have not sailed in before, it is important to gather local weather information and talk to knowledgeable sailors from the area to start a data base.

Scouting reports can help other sailors. As an example, the ultimate scouting report may have been that of the New York Yacht Club's scout, Graham Hall, who prepared the intelligence data used by *Liberty* after the sixth race of the America's Cup in 1983:

Liberty vs. Australia II— Analysis After Six Races
STARTS

The last several races, *Liberty* has done very well, keeping away from *Australia II*'s strength and making her play our game. This has effectively taken away her tacking and turning advantage and turned the tables strongly in our favor. *Australia II* has been off balance, they have had to make last-minute decisions, they have had to improvise within the last minute of the start, and it has become a disaster for them. We should keep up with our unpredictableness at the start. We can judge the line better; we can estimate the time to get back up to the line better; we can oval out the clockwise circles, taking away their quick tacking—forcing them to jibe on top of us and end up in the dangerous (for them) windward position. We still haven't used the circling of the committee boat, and perhaps we should consider that as our last "unpredictable" start. One thought I have is that they might not attack us as they have in every previous start—they may feel their boat speed is good enough, and their starting ability bad enough, that they would just settle for an even start. If they run from us, I would recommend going after them and trying to entice them out of their game plan, and get them to chase us. Anything we can do to force them to make quick decisions, to change their plan in the last minute will be an advantage for us.

UPWIND

They appear in most all the tapes to be able to point higher and they sail their boat more upright—whether by feathering or being just plain stiffer I don't know. Lots of times, however, they do not go faster, nor do they close up the distance under us or weather out if on our hip. The boats appear very evenly matched in most all wind conditions. Maybe the new configuration (unloading ballast) will mean *Liberty* is superior. The reason, however, for winning or losing in many of the races has been picking wind shifts, as opposed to straight-line boat speed. When we have been good at that we have overcome any boat-speed difference and have won—when we have missed the shifts we have lost by margins that an 18-Meter could not overcome. The recommendation is obvious—super alert, super concentration, use of our experience and intuition and every means at our disposal to be really good at picking the shifts.

OFFWIND

We haven't always showed it, but I continue to believe that with our longer waterline we should be faster off the wind. In the lighter mode we should be even faster. These races aren't being won or lost off the wind —keep going fast, keep believing the numbers, rely on our really good crewwork.

SUMMARY

Obviously we have to want this victory —we have to want to win—we have to know we can win, we should win, we deserve to win. There isn't any problem here—there is plenty of psyche to go around.

We have to handle the mental problem of the statement "What if I lose the Cup?" whirling around in our heads. This is done by replacing that thought with the positive thoughts of the job at hand—"What can I do to help us go faster, smarter, etc?" We can't worry about outcome. The outcome of the race is the sum total of all the little jobs right at hand, right now. The tack, the shift, the numbers, the start, etc. We have to concentrate on the basics. It doesn't take heroics to win a yacht race; it takes basic, solid smooth sailing.

Finally, we have to enjoy Saturday. It's going to be a beautiful day for a yacht race. It's going to be fun. We have to love the entire experience. Only in this way will all of our individual and collective talents come out to the utmost of our ability. And our ability is good enough to win the race and the Cup.

22
WHAT TO DO WHEN YOUR BOAT IS SLOW

By the time you discover you are sailing a slower boat than your competition, it usually is too late because you are in the middle of the racecourse. Certainly all of us have the highest expectations, but until we compete on the water there really is no gauge to tell us how fast we are sailing our boat. Competition, therefore, is the test. Once we have a handle on how our boat is performing against others, we can use this performance as a basis for improvement. The key to improving your performance, particularly when you are slow, is to observe the competition and test changes both on the water and at the dock.

At the dock you have the luxury of time. While on the water you must make instant decisions to test various experiments.

If you sense you are sailing slower than usual (you know this by feel or observing the relative speed of other boats), your first reaction should be to bear off one or two degrees to gain more speed. Sailboats increase speed when the sails are eased out (See Figure 105). If you are sailing on a leeward leg, try sailing a little closer to the wind to gain speed.

Sometimes reduced speed is simply a result of sailing in a bad patch of water. Waves might be more intense, shorter, and steeper where you are. Wave conditions can vary within 100 yards, so we suggest tacking away to a new piece of water. If you are slow on one tack, try the other tack. It might be better.

Look around. How are other boats performing? Is their angle of heel greater or less than yours? Try to copy what the faster boats are doing. If you feel you are losing distance every time you maneuver by either tacking or jibing, plan your race so you tack less than your competition.

In the 1983 America's Cup competition, *Liberty* used this tactic very successfully to win three of the seven races in a series that perhaps should have been a four to zero rout by the Australians. Knowing that *Liberty* lost considerable distance on every maneuver, helmsman Dennis Conner simply chose to maneuver as little as possible.

During a race, line up in clear wind alongside a competitor and test your speed. Continually ask yourself these questions: Am I gaining? Am I losing? Who is pointing higher? Which boat is

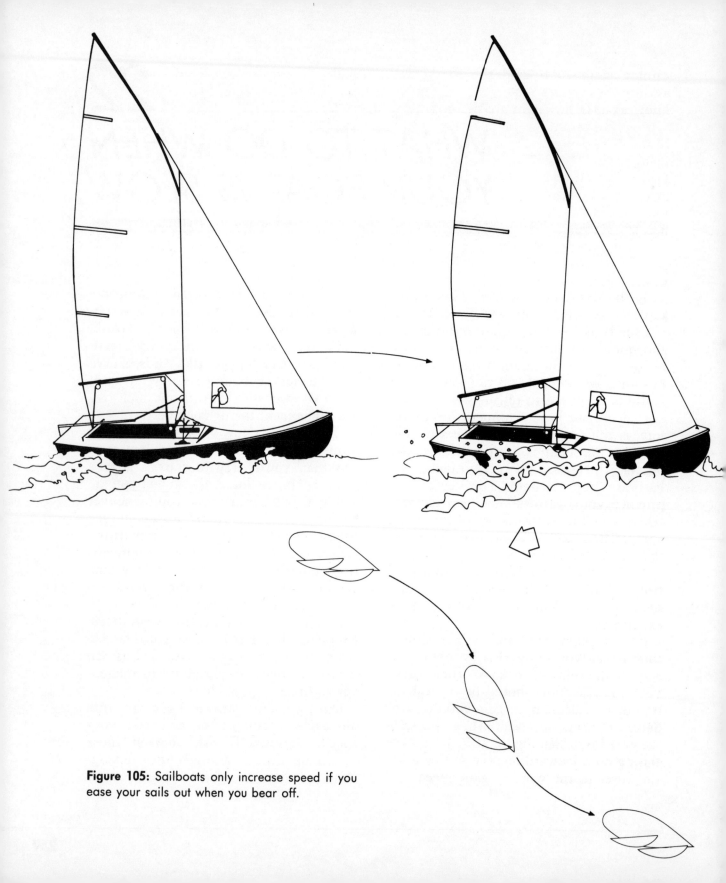

Figure 105: Sailboats only increase speed if you ease your sails out when you bear off.

gaining distance toward the mark? By asking these questions you will soon know exactly how you are performing.

It is important to be clear of other boats. Remember, there is a "snow fence" effect caused by other boats (See Figure 78). Be particularly sure to stay away from larger boats because the wind-shadow effect normally slows down your boat.

You can be satisfied sailing at the same speed as your competitors, although this is against human nature. But if you are equal in speed, tactics and boat handling will make the difference.

Test your speed against other competitors. Don't continually key up against the same one. You might find it helpful to speed-test alongside the favorite in the regatta while coming off the starting line.

During the race you should be making changes in boat handling with the changes in the wind and wave patterns. The best sailors continually adjust their trim, angle of heel, weight position, and steering technique to allow for shorter chop or stronger wind shifts. By staying in phase with the changes in the sailing conditions, you will automatically gain an edge over two thirds of your competitors. Few sailors react adequately to changes in sailing conditions. As you practice shifting gears, you will soon find yourself making small adjustments for the slightest changes in the conditions.

At the 1982 Yacht Racing/Cruising Hall of Fame regatta, Gary port-tacked the fleet of 15 of the world's top sailors. His ace crewman, Jud Smith, immediately calmed Gary down by asking for several small but significant adjust-ments. "Ease the backstay a quarter inch?" was Smith's first request. Instantly Gary knew that he had a competent crew that could be trusted throughout the regatta. Smith never let up calling sail trim in microscopic proportions, and it was enough to give the team a victory in the regatta.

If you are not steering well, or if a crew member is not trimming well, you can keep your crew fresh by rotating position. Fatigue forces crews to lose concentration.

Perhaps you are sailing slow due to external forces. We have been in regattas where we are sailing in relatively shallow water and the bottom of the keel is dragging in a slim layer of silt. Or perhaps seaweed is stuck on the keel or rudder. If you are slow and you believe you are sailing well, go through your checklist on all pieces of equipment, sails, and rig. Check for kelp on the bottom. But avoid making too many changes at one time because you will never get a handle on which change is faster and which is slower.

We find it is most helpful to return to the basics and to sail strictly by the numbers. It is unsettling to be sailing slowly. So it is important to give yourself a fresh start. When things are not going well, say to yourself, "O.K., from this point on we have a new race, just for fun. Let's see how well we can do." Start by setting every adjustment to its normal position.

Small adjustments can make big differences in speed. During one speed-testing session in 1976 on *Independence*, *Courageous* was continually sailing closer to the wind than *Independence*.

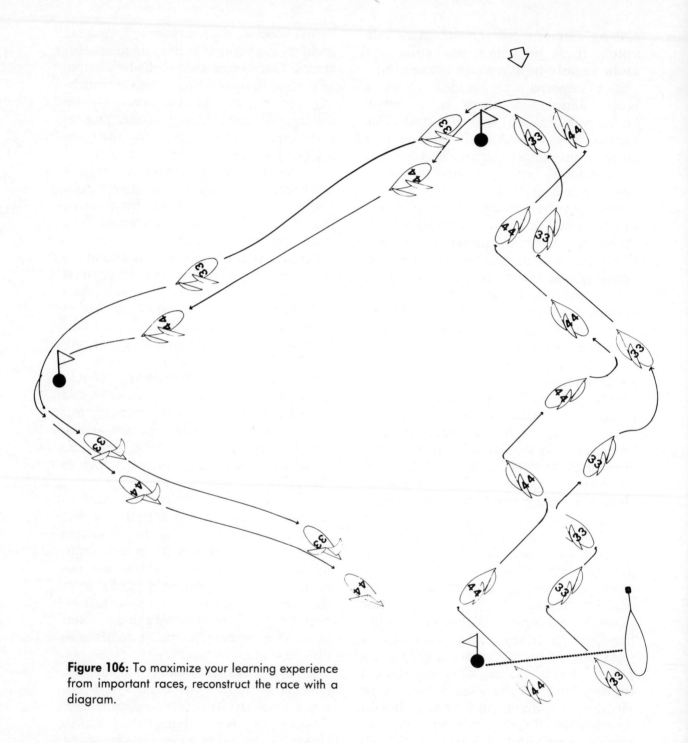

Figure 106: To maximize your learning experience from important races, reconstruct the race with a diagram.

No matter how the trimmers adjusted the sails, or the helmsman steered, there was no way to get *Independence* pointing as high as *Courageous*. Finally, an adjustment was made to the mast, raking it aft one inch. Immediately *Independence* started pointing almost a degree higher than *Courageous*.

If you are sailing more than one race in a day, use the time between races to tune up against your competitors. This keeps you in good sailing form and also gives you some idea of why you may not be performing well. Be bold and ask specific questions. Sailors like to be stroked and congratulated and can become talkative after a race.

When the day is over, rehash the events of the race and find out what you can do to improve. Remember, this is only a sailboat race, and the worst thing that can happen is to lose. Do not let yourself be disappointed. Going slow is not the end of the world, but you do want to improve, and a step-by-step approach is the best method.

First, reconstruct the race by drawing a diagram and making notes in the margin of what went right and what went wrong. (See Figure 106).

Many sailing events are now filmed on videotape. We find these tapes to be extremely useful in reviewing a race. The key points can be repeated as often as possible to see things on video that can't be seen on the racecourse. If your racing is going particularly badly, it might be best to spend a day in a powerboat observing your competitors race. You can learn very quickly by watching others.

Coaching in any sport helps to improve performance quickly. The key is to trust your coach. A coach can take many forms. Some of the best collegiate sailing coaches in the country with consistently top-ranked teams are not actually sailors themselves, but they get their own team members discussing with each other what is happening on the water. Ask your coach to keep an eye on specific things. How many tacks am I making on windward leg vs. two or three other top competitors? How much angle of heel do I have? What is the average crew weight in the fleet? Are our sails trimmed any differently? How much mast rake do we have compared with our competitors?

Coaching is relatively new to sailing, yet coaching has become the lifeblood of sports. After all, some professional football coaches are better known than many players. In fact, some of these coaches call every play. Coaches participating at this level would detract from sailing, but observers on nonracing boats or on the shore can be considerably helpful. Coaches are most effective when they spend time training with sailors before a big event.

The United States Olympic Yachting Committee regularly sends a team manager to act as a coach at major world championships. The manager helps to make logistics easier, gives encouragement, takes notes on performance, and may also give instruction.

Many top sailors use a coach successfully. Finn and Laser champion John Bertrand uses a former high-school teacher to help with his psyche. Tom Blackaller has used Bob Keefe as a manager and coach for his championship wins in the Australian/American 6-Meter Challenge cups. Marty O'Meara served as our coach for the *Courageous* team in 1977. He took endless and detailed notes on our tactics, boat handling, and relative boat speed. Because O'Meara was familiar with every job on a 12-Meter, he was helpful to everyone on the crew. It is difficult to criticize yourself objectively, but a coach can be both accurate and helpful. O'Meara, for example, served as a settling influence, particularly on days when *Courageous* lost. It really helps to have a coach rooting enthusiastically for you whether you win, lose, or draw.

Recently, it seems the top sailors are getting younger, thanks in part to the international competition being provided for our teams. Young sailors are more apt to accept coaching because they have seen it work in other sports. The coach should enjoy talking with other people to gather ideas and detailed notes for review.

After winning numerous ocean racing championships and the America's Cup, Ted Turner decided to jump into Hobie cat racing. He and his young son, Rhett, went to their first Hobie 18 regatta in South Carolina. In the first race, Turner got hammered by the competition. During the lunch break, while reporters and TV cameras recorded Turner's every move, Ted went about the task of finding out why he was slow. His first stop was with the guys who won the race. He studied how their mast was raked. He next found out where he should put his weight and the proper way to trim the sails. By the time the lunch period had ended, Turner had a newspaper reporter help him rerig his boat, and he and Rhett were soon off to the racecourse. The

Turners placed a respectable second that afternoon.

Some sailors won't talk about why they win, believing that it is in their best interest to keep quiet. But usually the most successful ones are happy to discuss why they won and lost after a regatta is over. After all, the exchange of ideas makes our sport better.

Keep a checklist of items that can potentially improve your speed. Some examples of what to put on your checklist follow:

1. **Weight of Boat**—If possible, weigh your boat and your competitors' boats to be sure you are not sailing with a handicap. Gary once went through a weight-testing program with 20 interclub dinghies at the Merchant Marine Academy to understand why some boats were faster than others. He found that the range in weight was as much as 100 pounds. The lighter the boat, the faster the boat. Even one-design boats are manufactured with considerable differences in weight. It is important when purchasing a boat to get the lightest available.

2. **Weight of Crew**—In 1983 the International Yacht Racing Union established a crew limitation rule to discourage yachts from sailing with more people than necessary to sail the boat. Some skippers have recruited extra sailors for their boats to give them added weight and more stability. Many collegiate teams travel to regattas with light-air crews and heavy-air crews. For overall performance, have a combined crew weight in the middle of the average of your competitors (See Figure 107).

Some classes have a weight rule to

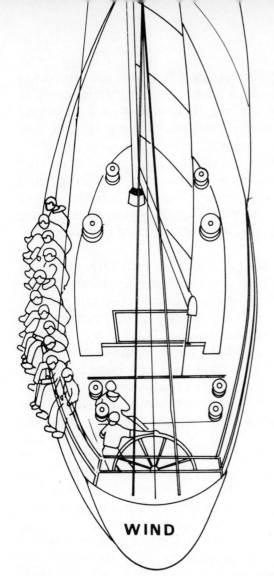

WIND

Figure 107: Keep your crew in the optimum position so you sail with the optimum angle of heel.

promote fair competition. The Penguin class, for example, insists on 275 pounds as a minimum for skipper and crew. Other classes have an unwritten weight limit. To be competitive in a Snipe, for example, the combined weight should be approximately 280 to 300 pounds. A Star, by contrast, requires at least 400 pounds for skipper and crew.

3. Mast Rake—The best way to mea-sure the rake of your mast is to haul a tape measure to the top of the mast and measure the distance to the transom. This number will give you a quick refer-ence on where you stand relative to your competition. If you find that your mast rake is considerably different, make a change so your rake is close to the aver-age of other boats.

Also check to see that your mast is in the middle of the boat athwartships. Hang a weight on your halyard and mea-sure the distance from the top of the mast to the deck of the boat on either side. Some spars are perfectly tuned ex-cept that the top is canted to one side. This will produce drastically different re-sults on either tack.

4. Sails—Over the years it has become apparent that the fastest sails are gener-ally the newest sails. The shelf life of a sail can be increased by taking good care of it. Rolling a sail as opposed to folding it keeps sails from cracking. Wash your sails in fresh water periodically to get the salt and dirt off. Salt and dirt are heavy and will hurt your sails' perform-ance, particularly spinnakers. Avoid sail-ing with sails over their wind range. If you find your sails are aging, the first step is to recut the sail, normally moving the draft farther forward. A good test of whether your sails are aging is to speed-test with another boat and then swap sails to see if there is a difference in per-formance.

5. Sailing Adjustments—You should be able to make adjustments in the greatest range you can. We like to have the longest traveler or the greatest dis-tance between inboard and outboard jibe leads to give us the most flexibility in making adjustments. The greater the range you have, the more possibilities you have for making the correct adjustment.

6. Your Equipment—Check to see that every piece of gear is working properly. Make sure the springs in your cam cleats are working. Soak every line in fresh water to get the salt and dirt out so they run easier. Clean and lubricate all your winches, tracks, and blocks to keep them at peak proficiency. Even with large work crews, three races during the 1983 America's Cup competition were decided on the basis of equipment failures—two by *Australia II* and one by *Liberty*. *Australia II* broke her steering gear on the fifth leg of the first race and lost her main halyard prior to the start of the second race. The two handicaps hurt the Australians just enough so they had no chance in either race. In the fifth race, *Liberty* started with a commanding lead but lost her advantage when a jumper strut broke, causing the mainsail to be untrimmable for most of the race.

7. Reduce Extra Equipment—In the final race of the 1983 America's Cup competition, *Liberty* improved her performance dramatically in light wind by lightening the boat as much as possible. She sailed the race with just three sails, no tools, and no foul-weather gear. Every extra piece of equipment you add to your boat potentially slows it down.

8. Condition of Bottom—It is important to have a fair and smooth bottom. We like to soap the bottom of a boat before every race so the boat has this protection at least through the harbor, where there is the greatest chance of getting oil on the bottom, which will slow

the boat down. Check for the fairness of your hull when the rig is under tension.

9. Sailing Techniques—By observing your competitors you might find that your sailing techniques need improvement. Are you hiking out as far as your competitors? Are you adjusting your sails as often? Are your telltales in the correct place, or are you getting false readings because they are misplaced?

Look at yourself critically and honestly to discover your mistakes. Others will help you speed up the process, but the real truth comes in your performance on the racecourse. There is no magic to winning but lots of reasons for losing. It might be time for a new boat, but this is the most radical adjustment you could make. Many successful sailors have won regatta after regatta with the same old reliable boat. Al Van Metre has been racing *Running Tide* successfully for more than a decade, and she continues to win her fair share of silver. *Windward Passage*, built in 1969, is still one of the hottest boats on the maxi circuit. The Nye family has raced *Carina* for over a decade and most recently won the 1982 Bermuda race.

The advantage all these winning sailors obtain is by updating their equipment and sails and just plain sailing their boat hard. Victory usually results from your best efforts plus the mistakes of your competitors.

Keep your eyes open for new opportunities, and always seek an edge if it's presented, but it is usually the basics of applying what you know and concentration on technique that bring the most consistent results.

Tips on Sail Trim

Gauge your boat speed compared to that of the competition and note proper sail trim according to the following points:

Leech Distance off Spreaders—Trim the leech a consistent distance off the spreader tips; this is especially useful when tacking.

Position of Draft—Note the position of the draft in relation to speed, pointing, and how the boat is moving through the water. Remember, draft goes aft if you need to point higher. Draft goes forward if you need to drive (Figure 108).

Amount of Helm—By determining the amount of helm, you can easily tell if the boat is being overpowered; the remedy is to reduce the amount of draft or shorten sail.

Angle of Heel—An inclinometer is a good reference in determining the angle of heel for a particular wind speed, sea state, or sail; if the angle of heel is too great, leeway and loss of speed will result.

Apparent-Wind-Speed Indicator—This can become an important reference when deciding which sail to use, or for halyard settings and lead positions.

Masthead Fly—The wind will often change first at the top of the mast, so by

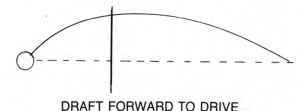

DRAFT FORWARD TO DRIVE

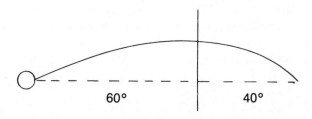

60°   40°

MAXIMUM DRAFT AFT TO POINT HIGHER

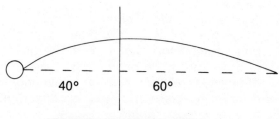

40°   60°

MODERATE DRAFT FOR
AVERAGE WIND CONDITIONS

Figure 108

observing the masthead fly you can get a good feel for what is about to happen.

Yachtmeter—Know the optimum set at top speed.

Genoa Sheet Markings—The best way to attain optimum trim tack after tack is with a Magic Marker.

Gauge your boat speed and note proper sail trim according to the following points:

Striping—You can observe the position of the draft by having horizontal stripes placed on the sail. I find a mark in the middle of the boom angled toward the head of the mast helpful in finding the draft's optimum position.

Mast Bend Marks—Mast bend marks are drawn on the sail with a Magic Marker and are spaced three inches apart along the luff near the spreaders. By sighting from the bottom of the mast through one of the mast bend marks to the head of the sail, you can observe how much mast bend you have in inches.

Telltales—Sew a red yarn telltale onto each batten pocket. Also, space three telltales four to six inches apart on the luff of the sail 40 percent of the way up. One of these telltales will be in the correct place in all conditions and on all points of sail.

Angle of Heel—Determining the amount of draft required is largely a question of whether the boat is sailing on its lines.

Backwind in the Main—If over 20 percent of the sail is backwinded, you are either sheeted too closely with the jib or you have too much draft.

Mainsheet Marks—Noting how much the sail has been trimmed or eased is one way to fast sailing.

Gauge boat speed compared to the competition and note proper spinnaker trim according to the following points:

Telltales—Use three telltales on both the leech and the luff. The telltales will break before the sail curls. Use a telltale on the spinnaker pole; this will indicate when the pole is set optimally, perpendicular to the apparent wind.

Masthead Fly—The wind should also be perpendicular to the masthead fly for most offwind conditions. Also, the masthead fly will signal changes in the wind before the changes reach deck level.

Sheet Tension—The amount of tension on a sheet indicates if the sail is drawing properly. Obviously, the more tension, the more power being generated.

Boat Speed—Comparing speed to boats around you is an obvious reference. In chutework it should tell you if you're sailing too high or too low.

Angle of Heel—When the boat is overpowered and heeling too much, it's time to go to a smaller chute.

Anemometer—Using a wind-speed in-

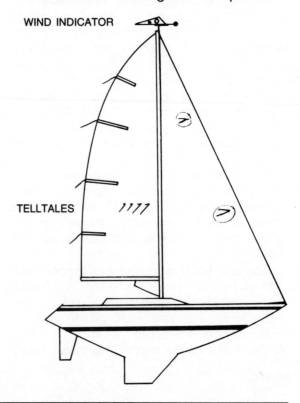

WIND INDICATOR

TELLTALES

dicator is more effective than a knot-meter in sustaining boat speed. If you get a puff, simply bear off several degrees. As the wind diminishes, head up a few degrees.

MAINSAIL TRIMMING

It would at first appear that the adjustments one can make with a mainsail—unlike headsails and chutes—are limited. But there are many ways to attain a fast shape in mainsail trim, based on references that can indicate when to shift from the kind of even-sail curves that light air and smooth water demand, to a depowered configuration when the wind and chop start to build.

There are important elements to consider. Foremost is the idea that the trivial wrinkles in the luff of the sail that always bedevil sailors should be ignored. The leech is the most effective part of the sail, not the luff. Backwinding from the headsail, and airflow disrupted by the spar conspire to diminish the effect the luff has on sail power.

Next, keep in mind that while going to windward, mainsail trim is a question of power vs. pointing. The more draft, or power, you put in the sail, the faster (and lower) the boat will sail until the leech stalls out and you have to slack sheets. And the position of the draft can be ultra-critical. If you need power to get through waves, for instance, you can move the draft forward by easing the mainsheet out, tightening the Cunningham, straightening the mast, and in some cases tightening the boom vang. Conversely, to point higher in smooth water, move the draft aft by trimming the mainsail in, bending the mast to flatten the luff and raking the mast aft.

Through all these gyrations, the main-sheet is contributing the most to mainsail shape by tightening or loosening the leech and helping to steer the boat. This kind of "trimming" is, of course, an essential part of driving the boat. But trimming can also mean maintaining optimum angle of heel by controlling the main. For instance, a quick test to judge whether you're overpowered is to ease the mainsheet out significantly and determine whether you are going faster or not. If speed increases, then you should reduce, or at least flatten, the sail.

If you find that the boat has a weather helm, you can reduce it by easing the main, easing the traveler down, or reducing rake. If you find that the boat has a lee helm, you can trim the sail or rake the mast aft.

OTHER ADJUSTMENTS YOU CAN MAKE

The traveler positions the mainsail. As a rule, the mainsail leech should never be hauled above the center line of the boat. The position of the traveler, though, may change dramatically in various wind conditions. For instance, the traveler may be pulled all the way to windward, leaving the boom on the center line in light air when a looser leech may be called for. The traveler should be dropped down considerably in heavy air to help alleviate weather helm. Generally, however, if the traveler has to go a long way to leeward it means the sail should be reefed or the mainsheet should be eased to spill some of the wind out of the top part of the sail.

The outhaul controls the amount of draft, which will vary depending on the amount of power required.

The Cunningham is used to flatten the sail and draw draft forward.

The boom vang tensions the leech, keeping the top batten parallel with the

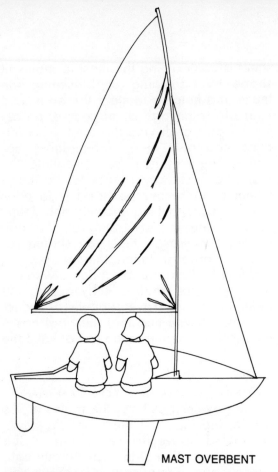

MAST OVERBENT

Figure 109: Long wrinkles will appear from the mainsail clew to the middle of the mast when the mast is overbent.

boom in most cases. In heavy-air sailing, one quick way to depower is to ease the boom vang, spilling the top of the sail.

Mast bend is one of the best ways to move the draft aft for higher pointing. You can either tighten the backstay, or trim the mainsheet tighter, which places an even tension along the luff of the sail (Figure 109).

Leech lines prevent flapping that can completely destroy the airflow, especially in the hardworking aft 25 percent of the sail.

The foot inhaul adjusts the forward half of the foot of the sail, like a horizontal Cunningham.

The battens support the leech. In light winds, flexible battens are used to help shape the sail. In heavy air, use stiffer battens.

Reef lines should be organized so they cut windage.

Zippers on the foot and luff admit more cloth when offwind.

With a Fractional rig trim the mainsail so the second batten from the top is parallel to the boom.

HEADSAIL TRIMMING

The same principles apply to trimming all sails—mains, spinnakers, staysails, and jibs or genoas. The key is proper use of a combination of trimming references and constant experimentation with adjustments to achieve the optimum.

The most important point when trimming any sail is to observe your competition. How are you doing and how are you trimmed compared to the rest of the fleet? In particular, how are you doing compared to the boats that appear to be sailing at nearly the same speed as you are? By observing competitors, you'll know in a short time what kind of adjustments are needed either to create or to maintain a fast sail shape.

It seems that each year sailmakers come up with a new shape for sails; yet year after year, the same principles apply to headsail trim. Generally, the position of the draft is just as important as the amount of draft. The position (forward and aft) determines your pointing ability, while the amount of draft determines the power in the sails.

As a rule, keep the maximum amount of draft in the middle of the sail as you look toward the head. To have an accurate reference, always observe the draft from the same point. If you sit by the clew and look up, the draft looks too far aft; looking up from the tack, the draft will appear to be too far forward. Standardize the point from which you make the observations somewhere near the middle of the sail. While the standard draft position is near the middle, to point the boat closer to the wind, move the draft aft. Place the draft farther forward in the sail when you encounter choppy seas, light air, or any other condition where you think more power is needed. While the amount of draft affects the amount of power the boat can generate, it also affects heeling moment, which can affect the amount of leeway the boat makes. As wind velocity increases, the boat can become overpowered, which increases heel and weather helm, so flatten or change the sails. Open leech opens the slot.

Other Adjustments You Can Make

Halyard Tension—Easing the halyard off helps move draft aft and will cause it to break first at the top and also creates draft. Tightening the halyard will cause the sail to break first at the bottom and will move draft forward and flatten the sail. In choppy seas, for instance, the trick is to get power forward in the sail by easing the halyard, although the obvious trade-off is sacrificing pointing ability. A jib Cunningham helps to take draft out of the sail and at the same time move the draft forward.

Barber Hauler—A barber hauler is used to pull the clew of the genoa inboard. Theoretically, the boat will point higher, although you often run the risk of stalling the sail by trimming it too far to windward, which forces the air to exhaust improperly off the leech of the jib creating backwind in the mainsail.

Jib Leads—If the sail breaks at the top first, as you move the boat closer to the wind, move the leads forward. If the sail

luffs at the bottom first, the lead should be moved aft. Sails should always luff evenly along the leading edge.

The Backstay—Eliminate headstay sag, which hurts pointing ability, by increasing backstay tension, which tightens the forestay.

The Jib Sheet—The jib sheet involves the most effective adjustment. As the helmsman rounds the boat into the wind, trim the genoas in. When the boat is lifted, the sail should be eased to generate speed. If you find that the boat is being overpowered for a considerable amount of time and a sail change is taking too long, ease the jib sheet out until the jib luffs to depower. This is preferred over sailing too high or heeling too much.

Trimming genoas is not the mystery many people make it out to be. It is a question of coordinating your adjustments by keeping your senses attuned to the wind to achieve the desired sail shape.

SPINNAKER TRIMMING

Spinnakers work in much the same way as mainsails and genoas. The wind strikes the leading edge first and bends around both sides of the sail, which acts like the foil of an airplane wing. The energy this produces is transferred to the boat, causing it to go forward. But unlike the main and the genoa—where shape is considerably more important than area—spinnaker shape and area are both elemental to fast-spinnaker trim, requiring continuous adjustment by both the trimmer and the helmsman.

Sailing the fastest course downwind is the obvious goal, and that's a function of trim and intelligent helmsmanship. For instance, in heavier winds, you can sail directly with the wind along a rhumb line, marking the shortest distance between two points. However, as the wind lightens, the faster course may be a course closer to the wind. As a rule, if you are going slower, simply reach a couple of degrees closer to the wind until you attain greater boat speed. In a short time you will discover your optimum sailing angle. If the wind is very light (five knots of true wind or less) you will have to reach, keeping the apparent wind at an 85-degree angle. In 22 knots of true breeze, you may discover that your boat will sail with the apparent wind at 170 (just about dead astern). As the wind lightens to, say, eight knots, your optimum apparent wind will have to go forward to 120. By reaching closer to the wind, you will be sailing a greater distance but will be going faster.

For the person handling the sheet, trimming the chute requires special concentration. The trimmer must keep a continuous dialogue with the helmsman. When a puff hits, for example, the trimmer should feel extra tension on the sheet and should pass the word to the helmsman so he can begin to bear off. If the wind lightens, the trimmer should tell the helmsman to come back up, drawing the apparent wind farther forward. One crew member should look aft to see puffs approaching.

Be sure to keep as few turns on the winch as possible and constantly test trim by easing the sheet. It may be helpful to keep a curl of from six inches to a foot in the luff of the sail, usually the signal for optimum sheeting.

The trimmer should also note that like the main and genoa, the fastest spinnaker shape is with the draft at 50 percent aft of the luff. But the trimmer should also keep in mind that the chute has a lifting force up high in the sail, which helps the bow ride over the waves. As a rule, the luff of the spinnaker should break at a point 40 percent below the head. This gives you the best balance between optimum draft and lift. A spinnaker can be flattened out effectively by trimming both the sheet and the guy simultaneously.

Other Adjustments You Can Make

Spinnaker Sheet—Keep the sheet eased, with as few turns on the winch drum as possible.

Spinnaker Guy—The spinnaker guy positions the pole fore and aft. The pole should be perpendicular to the wind, for the most part, and the guy should be led to the center of the boat.

Pole Height on the Mast—Keep the inboard end of the spinnaker pole at a perpendicular angle to the mast.

Topping Lift—This controls the outboard height of the spinnaker pole. To move the draft forward in the sail, lower the pole; to move the draft of the sail aft, raise the pole.

Foreguy—Keep the foreguy tight at all times to help stabilize the chute.

Spinnaker Halyard—Ease the halyard off when running downwind and reaching, which keeps the chute away from the boat.

Your spinnaker will have a long life if you take care of it. Do not dry the chute by hauling it up a halyard and letting it flap. The chute will dry just as quickly if you lay it out on a lawn. But that doesn't mean you should let it bake. Sunlight destroys the sail's finish. Keep salt water off the sail, and rinse it with fresh water if it gets dunked.

When packing a sail, use rubber bands or yarn to gather the sail every two feet starting from the head down to the middle of the sail, then stop each clew.

Always carry insignia cloth on your boat, and repair the chute any time there's a tear.

Setups for New Boats

FLYING JUNIOR

MINIMUM WEIGHT: 209 pounds.
OPTIMUM CREW WEIGHT: 270 pounds.
MAST RAKE: 19 feet, 3 inches, jib tight.
MAST BUTT: 8 feet, 9 inches from the transom

Spreader Length
TRAVELER: Boom is 15 inches off center line until the breeze comes up.

JIB LEADS: Leads are set 15½ inches from center line. Lead settings vary. Even break is suggested.

BOARD SETTINGS: The centerboard jibes at 2½ degrees of the boat's center line.

Skipper/Crew Weight Settings
MODERATE AIR UPWIND: Slight heel 3 degrees.

VERY LIGHT AIR UPWIND: Skipper and crew move forward to shrouds and heel to leeward to reduce wetted surface.

WIND INCREASE: Skipper and crew move aft.

IN HEAVY AIR: Skipper sits next to mainsheet lead, with crew right next to him.

OVERPOWERED: Ease jib 2 inches and ease main in and out to promote planing upwind.

FLYING JUNIOR

MAST RAMS: Use a prebent strut on the mast and deck. Also put a 2:1 purchase on the mast end of the strut.

COMET

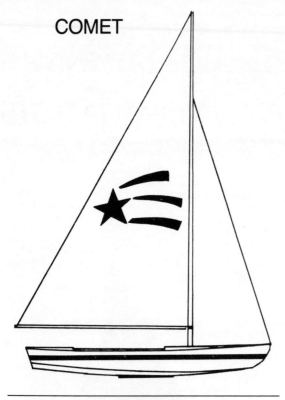

OPTIMUM CREW WEIGHT: 500 to 550 pounds.

MAST RAKE: 31 feet, 1 inch, rig set very tight.

J-MEASUREMENT: minimum 67 inches.

RIG TENSION: Very tight; a good way to gauge this is when all three crew members are on the high side beginning to hike just when the leeward shroud begins to go slack.

DIAMOND TENSION: Very tight; when you squeeze the diamonds to touch the mast it should be no farther away than four inches from the attachment points on the mast.

TRAVELER: The bridle traveler is used with the bridle height measured to the top of the block at 28½ inches. Ease traveler in the puffs.

MAST BUTT: Place a shim ⅛ foot to ³⁄₁₆

HIGHLANDER

COMET

MINIMUM WEIGHT: 295 pounds.

OPTIMUM CREW WEIGHT: 260 to 285 pounds.

	Light	Medium	Heavy
Rate	22'5"	22'4"	22'1"
Traveler	centered	centered	6" to leeward
Rig tension	tight	tight	tight
Vang tension	none	snug	tight
Jib leads off centerline	12½"	13"	13"–13½"
Jib leads aft	70"	70"	71"
Spreader length	19¼"		
Mast butt	19½" forward of centerboard pin		

HIGHLANDER

MINIMUM WEIGHT: 830 pounds.

INTERLAKE

foot under the back of the mast butt. This will reduce reverse bend in light air and induce bend in heavy air.

JIB LEADS: Best lead angle is ten degrees. This is for the standard clew jib. Lead is inside seat 1 inch and 9 feet, 5 inches aft of the jib luff wire on the stern plate.

INTERLAKE

MINIMUM WEIGHT: 650 pounds.
OPTIMUM CREW WEIGHT: 390 pounds.
MAST RATE: 25 feet, 2 inches.
MAST BUTT: Place as far forward as 6 feet, 4 inches from the stern to the front of the mast.
RIG TENSION: Very tight. Leeward shroud should just start to go slack at 10 knots.

JIB LEADS: Light air, 8 feet, 4 inches from stern; medium air, 8 feet, 6 inches from stern; heavy air, 8 feet, 8 inches from stern.
BARBER HAULERS: In puffy conditions, barber haulers should be pulled 1 inch out, and 2 inches out in heavy air. When reaching, barber haulers should be out all the way.
TRAVELER: Bridle height 24 inches from deck level.
BOARD SETTINGS: When lowered, the board should be perpendicular to the hull.

FLYING SCOT

MINIMUM WEIGHT: 850 pounds.

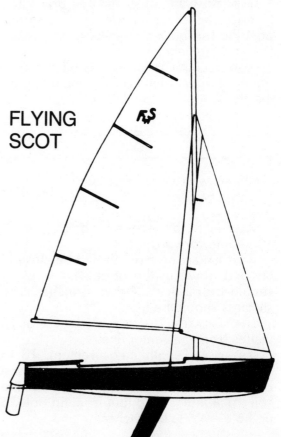

FLYING SCOT

APPENDIX B: SETUPS FOR NEW BOATS

OPTIMUM CREW WEIGHT: 380 to 420 pounds.

MAST RAKE: Jib up and jib the toggle horizontal 28 feet 6 inches. Light air rake the mast aft until the toggle is 28 feet, 4 inches. Push the mast forward until the shrouds are snug. The play should be 3 to 5 inches. The sloppy rig should be adjusted to keep the toggle horizontal in all winds. In very light air ease the jib halyard off until the forestay takes the load.

JIB LEADS: Always far forward.

JIB TRIM: The center of the leech should be pulled to the center line of the boat.

WINDWARD SHEETING: Pull the clew to windward 2 inches maximum. Pull the windward sheet until the curl in the foot disappears.

MAIN TRIM: In heavy air it is advisable to ease the sheet as far as 20 degrees past the top batten parallel to the boom (to ease the helm).

CENTERBOARD TRIM: Board all the way down upwind; 1 inch behind the hump on the trunk.

WINDMILL

MINIMUM WEIGHT: 198 pounds.

OPTIMUM CREW WEIGHT: 260 to 280 pounds.

MAST BUTT: 59 inches aft of station O. Maximum forward.

MAST RAKE: The mast should be straight up and down in the boat. The forestay should be at least 14 feet, 4 inches. The shrouds should be tight.

CHAIN PLATES: They should be set at 18 inches from the center line.

SPREADER: Length measurement, 13 to 14 inches; tip-to-tip measurement is done by holding a cord directly in back of the sail track that is held taut from tip hole to tip hole—4½ to 5½ inches.

WINDMILL

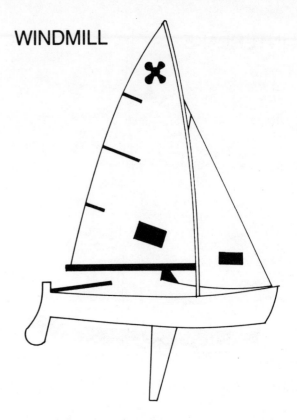

DAGGERBOARD SETTINGS: Angle the board forward slightly in all but heavy air. A good gauge is just having a slight weather helm.

FAIRLEADS: 83 inches from the forestay and 17 inches from the center line. In light air, move the lead forward 1 inch. In heavy air, move the lead back 2 to 3 inches.

BARBER HAULERS: Move the lead out 1 to 2 inches in light, choppy conditions and 2 to 3 inches in heavy air.

REBEL

MINIMUM WEIGHT: 700 pounds.

OPTIMUM CREW WEIGHT: 280 to 330 pounds.

MAST BUTT: Maximum forward 4 feet, 2 inches, stem to center of mast.

MAST RAKE: Without the jib up and with the rig hanging on at the forestay, 26 feet, 6 inches. Then pull the rig forward at the forestay until the shrouds are tight. This should be 26 feet, 7 inches (the boom should be parallel to the deck in 8 knots of breeze).

RIG TENSION: Very tight. Pull the jib up and the jib halyard measurement up to 26 feet, 8 inches. This pulls tension into the rig. In heavy winds pull the jib halyard even tighter, up to 26 feet, 9 inches. In light air, pull the halyard up to only 26 feet, 7 inches (use a 10-foot Magic Box and mark the dimensions on the Magic Box).

DIAMOND TENSION: Very tight.

JIB LEADS: The leads should be set fore

Y-FLYER

REBEL

and aft until you have balance in the jib, telltales breaking evenly.

CENTERBOARD ANGLE AND TAPER: Sailing upwind, the rollers on the head of the centerboard should be set at the base of the trunk incline. The taper on the trailing edge of the centerboard should be 1/16 inch squared off edge. The leading edge should be of parabolic shape. The angle of the rudder should always be set at 180 degrees up and down to the hull.

TRAVELER: Use the bridle system, with the top of the bridle 2 inches from the end block on the boom.

Y-FLYER

MINIMUM WEIGHT: 500 pounds.

OPTIMUM CREW WEIGHT: 280 to 330 pounds.

MAST RAKE: With the jib down and shrouds snug, the rake should be 24 feet, 5 inches. Now put the jib up and with the jib halyard pull the rake up to 24 feet, 6 inches, which pulls 1 inch of tension into the rig.

MAST BUTT: Maximum aft position, 16 inches forward of the centerboard pin.

FORESTAY: 100 inches forward from the centerboard pin.

RIG TENSION: Tight. The leeward shroud should start to slacken in 6 to 8 knots of wind, sailing upwind.

LOWER STAYS: Should be set up so the mast does not bend sideways when sailing upwind.

SPREADERS—STIFF MAST: Free-swinging spreaders 9 feet, 1 inch above the deck, 21 inches long.

SPREADERS—BENDY MAST: Fixed spreaders 10 feet above the deck, 17½ inches long.

JIB LEADS: 14 inches from the center line and 5 inches aft of the mast; 90 inches from the forestay in medium air; in light winds, 1 inch forward, and in heavy air, 1 to 2 inches aft.

CENTERBOARD ANGLE: Should be lowered to its maximum, with as little of board as possible showing in the trunk.

THISTLE

MINIMUM WEIGHT: 515 pounds.

OPTIMUM CREW WEIGHT: 455-470 pounds.

MAST RAKE: 26 feet, 11 inches to 27 feet measured to top of tiller hole. Tension in flat water, extra tight.

MAST STEP: Grind off the mast step ³⁄₃₂ inch to ⁵⁄₃₂ inch. Grind till it is just flush. This eliminates reverse bend from the extra-tight rig.

THISTLE

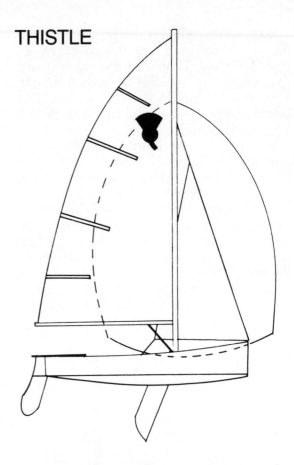

DIAMOND TENSION: Very tight. Squeeze them so you touch the mast 2 inches from the attachment points from the mast. Wooden spars should be 4 inches.

JIB LEADS: Set up 16 inches off center line; 106 inches from forestay for medium air; 106 inches for light air; 108 inches for heavy air; 1½ inches of barber hauler for heavy air.

Note: The mainsheet tie on the end of the boom should be tied on the bail of the block. This will allow tighter mainsheet tension when desirable.

505

MINIMUM WEIGHT: 280 pounds.

OPTIMUM CREW WEIGHT: 300 pounds.

MAST RAKE: 25 feet, 8 inches from the top of tiller hole to the top of the mast using the main halyard.

MAST BUTT: 10 feet, 1½ inches from transom to front side of mast step.

RIG TENSION: Using a tension gauge on ⅛-inch wire, 500 pounds on shrouds, and 350 pounds on headstay (jib wire).

SPREADER: 10 feet, 3½ inches above-deck, ¼ inch long, and a 4-inch deflection.

CENTERBOARD POSITION: Pivot position 8 feet, 7 inches from transom. The front of the centerboard should always be vertical to the hull.

CREW WEIGHT: Crew should just let bow curve touch the waves.

5-0-5

FINN

FINN

MINIMUM WEIGHT: 319 pounds.

OPTIMUM SKIPPER WEIGHT: 185 to 210 pounds.

MAST RAKE: Light air, 22 feet, 3½ inches; heavy air, 22 feet, 2 inches.

CENTERBOARD: Kept all the way down upwind regardless of conditions. Downwind only pull it up slightly. Reaching pull up just before you start to sideslip.

CUNNINGHAM: Never use any until it is blowing 15 knots.

OUTHAUL: 1½ to 2 inches off black band from 5 to 12 knots in flat water, and 1 to 1½ inches off the band in choppy water of 1 to 18 knots.

INHAUL: Should be tightened up from 1½ inches off the band in light air to ½ inch off in 12 to 18 knots of wind. In heavy air the Cunningham, outhaul, and inhaul should be at maximum tightness at all times.

GP-14

MINIMUM WEIGHT: 293 pounds.

MAST STEP: Butt should be all the way aft in step.

RAKE: 20 feet, 11 inches to 21 feet, 2 inches.

SPREADER: Length, 15 inches; tip to tip, 24 inches.

TRAVELER: Bridle on rails at transom; bridle is spliced into mainsheet.

BOOM VANG: 8 to 1 and led to both sides to control leech tension.

JIB LEADS: Mount on inboard edge of deck.

GP-14

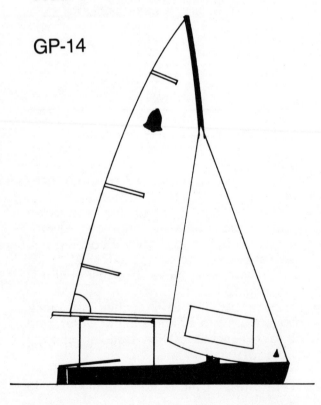

SNIPE

SNIPE

MINIMUM HULL WEIGHT: 381 pounds.

OPTIMUM CREW WEIGHT: 300 pounds.

MAST RAKE: Forward puller on with snug shrouds, jib down, 21 feet; forward puller off with jib up and tight, 21 feet, 4 inches to 21 feet, 5 inches; heavy air, 21 feet, 6 inches.

SPREADER LENGTH: 16 to 16½ inches; length from 25 to 27 inches for tip-to-tip measurement.

TRAVELER: Bridle arrangement off transom with bridle lines spliced into mainsheet. Mainsheet purchase, 1 to 1. To build a bridle mainsheet, use 26 feet of ⁵⁄₁₆-inch prestretch and 15 feet of ⁵⁄₃₂-inch prestretch.

JIB LEADS: To start with, set leads straight across from the trailing edge of the centerboard. Most boats set leads from 15½ inches to the center line of boat. Move 1 inch forward in light air and chop. Move 1 inch back in heavy air.

SKIPPER AND CREW WEIGHT PLACEMENT: Upwind in flat water, the skipper is sitting forward next to the crew. Upwind in chop, the crew angles back toward the skipper. In light air downwind, the skipper is far forward with the crew. Downwind in moderate air, the skipper and the crew remain aft to keep the bow from driving. The harder it blows off the wind, the farther back for surfing and planing.

SHARKS

MAST RAKE: 30 feet from the top of the

SHARK 24

mast to the deck and the topsides intersection.

Tension on outer shrouds should be tight enough so the leeward shroud is still tight in upwind in 12 to 15 knots.

JUMPERS: Set very tight.

SPREADER LENGTH: 26 inches long.

BACKSTAY TENSION: 1 inch on in light air; 4 inches on in 10 to 12 knots; 7 to 8 inches on in 20 knots.

JIB LEADS: Telltales should break evenly. In 0 to 18 knots the inboard leads should be used with the leech of the jib; 3½ to 6 inches off the spreader tip.

SPINNAKER: Keep pole high except in light air.

J-24 AND FRACTIONAL RIGS

MINIMUM WEIGHT: 3,300 pounds.

OPTIMUM CREW: 4 to 5.

MAST RAKE: Mast should be cut to a minimum length to achieve more rake and to help decrease leeward helm. The aft edge of the mast should be ¾ inch from the back of the deck. The rig should be set up very tight. Do this by setting the lowers until the rig is centered and then putting the backstay on close to all the way. Tighten the uppers until they are extra tight. Release the backstay and tighten the lowers equally until you have 2 inches of prebend. For the headstay, use the maximum legal length; this will give you the optimum rake.

CREW POSITIONING: Always centered in the boat and close together. Helmsman even with the traveler. The aft crew member should straddle the stanchion at the forward edge of the cockpit, and the other crew members should be right next to him. In heavy air, move aft downwind.

SAIL TRIM: In light air and choppy water, jib leads are set for even break; in heavy

J 24

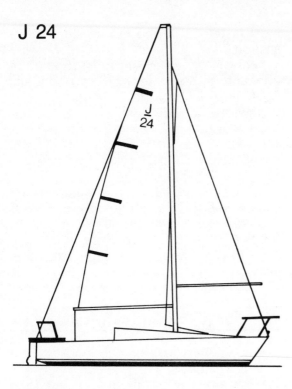

RUDDER: Should be set down at all times.

TRAPEZE PLACEMENT: The skipper should be next to the backside of the traveler, and the crew should be trapezing next to him.

SPINNAKER: Pole should be set high except in light air.

MAIN TRIM: Should set the main so as to have the top batten parallel with the boom. The mast should have mast blocks in front unless it is very light air (blocks in back). In heavy air, fewer blocks in front.

air, depower by vang sheeting and playing the backstay. More backstay flattens the main and tightens the headstay. Barber-haul the jib once the boom is farther than 1 foot from the center line.

INTERNATIONAL 420

INTERNATIONAL 420

OPTIMUM CREW WEIGHT: 230 to 250 pounds.

RAKE: Jib up 20 feet, 1 inch to 20 feet, 2 inches. The rig should have 300 to 350 pounds of tension on loose-tension gauge.

JIB TRIM: In snug with 2 inches of weather sheet in all conditions of 8 knots and up.

CENTERBOARD SETTINGS: Flush with the centerboard cap in all airs upwind.

S 2 9.1

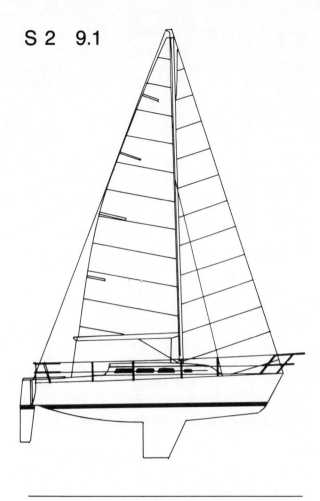

S 2 9.1

ANGLE OF HEEL:

UPWIND—7 to 10 degrees is optimum. In heavy air, you can go as far as 15 to 20 degrees as a maximum, but 7 to 10 degrees is better if possible.

REACHING—more heel is allowable on a reach, but adjust main to control weather helm.

MASK RAKE: 8 to 10 inches of rake. The 9.1 needs helm in light air. Add rake to increase helm. Forestay extended approximately three quarters of the way.

MAST BEND: After setting forestay length, move mast butt aft approximately 1½ to 2 inches to induce 2- to 3-inch prebend. Maximum bend should be 8 to 10 inches with backstay on hard (no babystay). Leeward upper should not go slack with maximum backstay, full main, heavy #1, six to seven people on high side. Tighten lowers and intermediates to remove any sag. Don't overtighten. Backstay bridle blocks should go all the way up backstay when tensioner is released. If not, tighten backstay turnbuckles.

WEIGHT POSITION:

LIGHT AIR UPWIND—Skipper and two sail trimmers in cockpit with other four crew forward of cockpit, but aft of standing rigging. Put enough weight to leeward to induce 7- to 10-degree heel.

MODERATE AIR UPWIND—Everyone to windward to maintain 7- to 10-degree heel. As breeze increases, crew moves slowly aft.

HEAVY AIR UPWIND—Put one crew aft of helmsman to help keep rudder in water.

DOWNWIND—Crew moves slowly aft as wind increases to keep bow from burying, but not too far aft to submerge transom.

OPTIMUM CREW: Six to seven are a must.

SAIL TRIM:

GENOA: Flat water—trim leach 2 to 4 inches from spreader. As waves increase, genoa will have to be eased 5 to 6 inches from spreader to keep boat moving. Set lead for an even break on luff. In flat water, #1 genoa can be barber hauled inboard about 3 inches to increase pointing ability. In rough water or heavy air, move lead aft slightly to increase twist. Genoa halyard tension should always be as light as possible to narrow entry angle of genoa and help pointing ability. If groove is too narrow, and helmsman is experiencing problems steering, then tighten slightly.

MAINSAIL: Flat water—boom on center line, top batten parallel to boom or slightly cocked to weather. Top batten tell-tale should fly 50 percent to 75 percent of time. Rough water—boom on center line with top batten twisted off enough to keep tell-tale flying 100 percent of time. Lower boom off center line as weather helm becomes a problem.

OPTIMUM SAIL COMBINATION: The 9.1 is a stiff boat which carries the #1 genoa into about 18 to 20 knots apparent windspeed. Continue to change down in head sail size, carrying a full main as long as possible by blading it out and adding twist. The main should be reefed with the #3 jib before going to a #4 and no reef.

S 2 7.9

S 2 7.9

ANGLE OF HEEL:

UPWIND—7 to 10 degrees is optimum. In heavy air, you can go as far at 15 to 20 degrees as a maximum, but 7 to 10 degrees is better if possible.

REACHING—more heel is allowable on a reach, but adjust main to control weather helm.

MASK RAKE: Use forestay length of 31 feet, 7 inches to 31 feet, 8 inches, which is approximately 18 to 20 inches of rake. Boat needs the helm in light air.

MAST BEND: Set uppers tight. Backstay should be on hard release. Tighten backstay tensioner. Adjust lower shrouds, removing all but 1- to 2-inch pre-bend. Be careful not to over tighten uppers, so that headstay can sag in light to moderate air.

WEIGHT POSITION:

LIGHT AIR UPWIND—Skipper and sail trimmer in cockpit with other three crew forward of cockpit, but aft of standing rigging. Put enough weight to leeward to induce 7- to 10-degree heel.

MODERATE AIR UPWIND—Everyone to windward to maintain 7- to 10-degree heel. As breeze increases, crew moves slowly aft.

HEAVY AIR UPWIND—Put one crew aft of helmsman to help keep rudder in water.

DOWNWIND—Crew moves slowly

aft as wind increases to keep bow from burying, but not too far aft to submerge transom.

OPTIMUM CREW: Five people are a must (900 to 1000 pounds).

BOARD POSITION:

FLAT WATER, LIGHT AIR—From beam reach to downwind, board up at least halfway.

FLAT WATER, HEAVY AIR—Board can come all the way up.

ROUGH WATER—Board down to control rocking and add control.

SAIL TRIM:

GENOA: Flat water—trim leach 2 to 3 inches from spreader. As waves increase, genoa will have to be eased 5 to 6 inches from spreader to keep boat moving. Set lead for an even break on luff. In rough water or heavy air, move lead aft slightly to increase twist. Genoa halyard tension should always be as light as possible to narrow entry angle of genoa and help pointing ability. If groove is too narrow, and helmsman is experiencing problems steering, then tighten slightly.

MAINSAIL: Flat Water—boom on center line, top batten parallel to boom or slightly cocked to weather. Top batten tell-tale should fly 50 percent to 75 percent of time. Rough Water—boom on center line with top batten twisted off enough to keep tell-tale flying 100 percent of time. Lower boom off center line as weather helm becomes a problem.

OPTIMUM SAIL COMBINATION: Carry full main and genoa up to 15 to 18 knots true. When changing to #3, power main all the way back up by releasing backstay. Carry full main as long as possible by blading out with backstay and adding twist. Boat is much faster if you hang onto full main before reefing by sailing it on the leech and living with a lot of backwind.

INDEX

Farr, Bruce, 29
Floatation, 15

Genoas, 103–13, 136–38
  for cruising, 136–38
  inventory recommendations,
    136–38
  See also Headsails
Go-fast techniques. *See* Maneuver-
    ing; Rounding marks;
    Steering
Grinders, 69–72
  duties of, 69–72
  tailer and, 69–72

"Half jibe" maneuver, 218–19
"Half tack" maneuver, 218–22
Hall, Graham, 212
Hand-bearing compass, 186–89
Handicapping systems. *See* Rating
    formulas
Headsail changes, 49–51
  crew positions and, 49–51
Headsails, 49–51, 103–13
  cloth selection for, 104
  draft location and, 106–7
  easing out, 111–13
  headstay tension, 107–9
  pictorial record of, 111
  the reacher and, 113
  Sailscope and, 111
  sheet tension, 109–10
  staysail and, 113
  trimming, 105–13
  twist and, 105–6
Helmsman, 66–68
  tactician and, 66–68
H. Irving Pratt Race Handicapping
    Project, 31
Holland, Ron, 157
Hull speed, 16–17

International Offshore Rule (IOR),
    24, 25–31
  correction factors of ORC, 27–29
  loopholes in, 26
  measurements included in, 25
  Ocean Racing Club (ORC) and,
    26
  older boats and, 30
  responsibilities while racing, 31
  yacht designers and, 29

Jibing, 56–58, 167–70
  crew positions and, 56–58
  in a dinghy, 167–68
  roll, 170
  with the spinnaker, 168

Keefe, Bob, 261
Keefe, Ken, 62

Kevlar sails, 31

Leech line, 93
Lee helm, 23
Leeward mark, 183–85
Logbooks, 202, 236–37
Lombardi, Vince, 248
Loran interface, 143–44
Luff curve, 91

Mainsail controls, 89–95
  broadseaming, 90–91
  flattening reef and, 92
  leech line and, 93
  luff curve, 91
  mainsheet traveler, 93–94
  mast bend and, 91
  measurements for sailmaker, 91
  outhaul and, 92
  stretching to shape, 91
  vang sheeting, 93, 94–95
Mainsail in downwind use, 102–3
  twist and, 102
Mainsails for cruising, 135–36
  reefing, 135
  shape, 135
  weight, 135
Mainsail trimming, 95–102
  babystays and, 99
  backwind and, 98
  draft stripes, 95
  Frisbee-cut sail, 98
  increasing power, 97
  leech controls, tightness of, 96
  racing upwind and, 96–97
  reefing, 100–102
  running backstays, 99–100
  tension and, 95–96
Mainsheet traveler, 93–94
Maneuvering, 162–70
  jibing, 167–70
  heeling and, 163
  movement and, 162–63
  speed and, 162, 163
  tacking, 164–67
Marine electronics. *See* Electronics
Marks. *See* Rounding marks
Marshall, John, 89
Mastman, 72–74
  bowman and, 72–74
  duties of, 72–74
Masts, 77–83
  centering, 81
  defined, 77
  hydraulic jumper system and, 80
  lateral bend and, 79–81
  shrouds, tightening of, 81–83
  small, with multiple spreaders,
    77
  tuning, 79–83
  unnecessary items, removal of,
    78–79

unstayed, 77
  weight and, 78–79
  windage and, 78–79
Measurement Handicap System
    (MHS), 24, 31–33
  nonspinnaker racing and, 33
  objectives of, 31
  regional conditions and, 33
  Standard Hull Program and,
    32–33
  Velocity Prediction Program
    (VPP) and, 31–32
  wind-condition ratings, 32
Melges, Buddy, 198, 228
Midget Ocean Racing Club
    (MORC), 24, 36–38
  corrections based on model,
    37–38
  objectives of, 36
  rating criteria of, 36–37
Monohulls, 20

National Hurricane Center, 193
National Weather Service, 193
Navigator, 66–67
  tactician and, 66–67
Night sailing, 140, 212–16
  apparent-wind-angle instrument,
    213–14
  common sense and, 216
  flashlights, use of, 212–13
  physical senses and, 212
  practice with entire crew,
    215–16
  safety and, 214
  spotlight use, 212
  instrumentation and, 213
  VMG and, 213
  watch systems, 214–15
No-wind sailing, 207–11
  "anchoring in light air," 211
  anticipating new breeze, 211
  crew moved forward, 209
  dehydration and, 211
  flattening sails during, 209
  heeling and, 207–9
  pacing and, 207
  sitting still during, 209–11

Ocean Racing Club (ORC), 26
Ocean Sailing Yacht, The (Street),
    18
Offshore Racing Council, 25
O'Meara, Marty, 261–62

Parker, Tony, 106
Passing, 217–18
  bearings and, 222
  "bizarre" moves and, 228
  double tack forced on com-
    petitor, 219
  extra speed for, 217–18